ELEMENTS OF
CONTRACT INTERPRETATION

ELEMENTS OF
CONTRACT INTERPRETATION

STEVEN J. BURTON

OXFORD
UNIVERSITY PRESS

OXFORD
UNIVERSITY PRESS

Oxford University Press, Inc., publishes works that further Oxford University's objective of excellence in research, scholarship, and education.

Oxford New York
Auckland Cape Town Dar es Salaam Hong Kong Karachi Kuala Lumpur Madrid Melbourne Mexico City Nairobi New Delhi Shanghai Taipei Toronto

With offices in
Argentina Austria Brazil Chile Czech Republic France Greece Guatemala Hungary Italy Japan Poland Portugal Singapore South Korea Switzerland Thailand Turkey Ukraine Vietnam

Published by Oxford University Press, Inc.,
198 Madison Avenue, New York, New York 10016

Library of Congress Cataloging-in-Publication Data

Burton, Steven J.
Elements of contract interpretation / Steven J. Burton.
p. cm.
Includes bibliographical references and index.
ISBN 978-0-19-533749-5 ((hardback) : alk. paper)
1. Contracts—United States—Interpretation and construction. I. Title.
KF801.B875 2009
346.7302—dc22

2008032375

Note to Readers

This publication is designed to provide accurate and authoritative information in regard to the subject matter covered. It is based upon sources believed to be accurate and reliable and is intended to be current as of the time it was written. It is sold with the understanding that the publisher is not engaged in rendering legal, accounting, or other professional services. If legal advice or other expert assistance is required, the services of a competent professional person should be sought. Also, to confirm that the information has not been affected or changed by recent developments, traditional legal research techniques should be used, including checking primary sources where appropriate.

(Based on the Declaration of Principles jointly adopted by a Committee of the American Bar Association and a Committee of Publishers and Associations.)

For Zachary Pan, Julio Stier, Noah Stier, and Kestrel Stier

CONTENTS

PREFACE

Contract law in the United States empowers people to make their own legal relations by promising, subject to certain constraints on seriously unfair contracts. It pursues four main goals. First, it seeks to ascertain and implement the parties' intention when they have concluded an enforceable agreement. This goal permits parties to exercise their freedom to contract as they wish (freedom of contract) and not to have contractual duties imposed upon them unjustifiably (freedom from contract). Second, contract law seeks to protect and enhance the security of contractual transactions. That is, it seeks to protect a promisee's reasonable expectations arising from, and reasonable reliance on, a promise. When fair, contract law seeks to hold promisors responsible for their expressions of intention. Third, like the law generally, contract law seeks to settle disputes non-arbitrarily. This is to say that contract law implements Rule of Law values, such as the values of consistency in the application of the law, predictability of legal results, and results that are justified in law. Fourth, again as in other areas of the law, contract law seeks to achieve the administrability of its rules and principles: A rule or principle is of little utility if interpreters, including parties, their attorneys, judges, and juries, cannot implement it at reasonable cost. Together, these goals pursue an overarching goal—to allow a contract to serve as an authoritative guide to the parties' proper conduct in contract performance.

Contract interpretation pursues these same goals. It does so through the performance of three practical tasks. First, an interpreter identifies the terms to be interpreted. Second, an interpreter determines whether the terms are ambiguous and encompass the rival interpretations favored by the parties. Third, if the terms are ambiguous in a contested respect, an interpreter resolves that ambiguity by choosing between the rival interpretations.

To elaborate, identifying the terms to be interpreted is primarily the province of the parol evidence rule. It can be stated in several ways. We will state only part of it for the moment—as a first approximation—as follows: When a written contract is the final and complete expression of the parties' agreement, prior agreements do not establish contract terms if the terms of the prior agreement contradict or add to the terms of the written contract.[1] When applied, the rule renders many prior agreements legally inoperative. As a consequence, it precludes the admission of evidence of the prior agreement for the purpose of establishing the contract's terms. When the parties conclude a final and complete written agreement, they normally intend it to supersede any prior agreements reached in the course of negotiations. The writing then becomes the sole container of the contract's terms.

Determining whether the terms are ambiguous usually is the province of the plain meaning rule. A few jurisdictions (and many contracts scholars) shun this rule. We will suggest that, despite significant criticism, the rule—properly understood—is a persistent and reasonable one as practiced by most courts. Even in litigation, written contract terms often are clear for the practical purpose at hand. Even though the governing term is ambiguous in the abstract, it may permit only one of the rival interpretations advanced by the parties. If this is the case, a judge should hold that the language is unambiguous and that the unambiguous meaning (the plain meaning) is the legal meaning. The key question concerns how much context a judge needs in order to answer the question of ambiguity while pursuing the goals of contract interpretation. That is, the question concerns which elements of contract interpretation a judge should take into account when considering whether there is an ambiguity.

Resolving an ambiguity, if any is found, often is the province of a jury, acting under the court's supervision. Because juries operate in secret and have such wide discretion, we will focus on cases in which judges acted as the finders of fact. Again, the problem will be to understand which elements of contract interpretation a judge or a jury are or should be allowed to take into account. Under the prevailing law, the fact-finder generally is allowed to consider more elements when resolving an ambiguity, such as relevant parol evidence, than a judge may consider when identifying contract terms or deciding whether there is an ambiguity.

---

[1] For a full statement of the parol evidence rule, see § 3.1.1.

To perform these three tasks, the courts draw on various resources for interpretation, which we shall call the *elements of contract interpretation*. The elements include the governing contract term, if any, and such features of its context as the law may allow the interpreter to take into account when performing a task. The features of the context may include dictionaries, the document as a whole, the circumstances when the contract was made, the contract's purpose(s), trade usages, courses of dealing, practical constructions, statements of intention made during negotiations, and a party's testimony in court as to its own past intent. The law may allow interpreters to take into account different sets of elements when performing the different tasks.

Three theories of contract interpretation are supposed to guide interpreters to perform the three tasks to further the four goals. The first is *literalism*. In a strict form, it restricts the elements that interpreters may rely on to the governing words and the dictionary. The second is *objectivism*. It broadens the set of elements to include the document as a whole, the objective circumstances at formation, trade usages, the document's evident purpose(s), and any practical construction. The third is *subjectivism*, which further broadens the set of relevant elements to include all relevant evidence, including evidence of the parties' course of dealing and the course of negotiations, and testimony by a party about its own past intention.

The law of contract interpretation (as distinct from theory) has been the subject of remarkably few scholarly works. The obstacle is that the scholarly works, including the great treatises, generally address the extremes of contract interpretation. That is, they focus on a tense dualism between objective and subjective theories of interpretation, ostensibly as advanced by Professors Samuel Williston and Arthur L. Corbin, respectively. Corbin's subjectivism is said to have increasing influence, though there are signs of a revival of some form of objectivism. This book suggests that, conceptually and practically, there are *three* theories that should be considered—literalism, objectivism, and subjectivism. Many subjectivist critiques of objectivism really target literalism, leaving objectivism (and Williston) untouched and misunderstood. In the final chapter, we will suggest that a moderate version of objectivism, to be called *objective contextual interpretation*, should be the preferred theory of contract interpretation. Objective contextual interpretation allows an interpreter to consider enough context to avoid Corbin's and others' criticisms of literalism. It best guides an interpreter to perform the tasks in a way that furthers the goals.

A note on scope: We will make three key assumptions that define the scope of this study. First, we will assume that there is a domain of free contracting within which contract law governs promissory transactions. People may differ over whether this domain is or should be large or small. That is a question mainly for legislation, such as the minimum wage laws. Few societies have no domain of free contracting. There surely is a large one in the United States. Contract law operates in the domain of free contracting whether it is small or large. Second, we will assume that, in any event, a court or other interpreter has decided that the parties have made an enforceable contract. A question of interpretation, as the term is used here, arises after this decision. We will not consider the interpretation of purported offers and acceptances. Put another way, interpretation is necessary to guide the parties' conduct in contract performance. Once we have decided to enforce a contract, we should do what we decided to do. Questions of unconscionability, mistake, duress, and other invalidating causes then drop out of the analysis, with an exception to be indicated below. Interpretation concerns the three tasks identified above, which together determine the parties' rights, duties, and powers under a contract. Third, we will not consider the law of negotiable instruments, which contains some specialized rules for interpreting notes, checks, and drafts, and gives holders in due course special rights against obligors.

I wish to thank several people for their help and advice in conceiving, researching, and writing this book. Foremost are Serena Stier, Paige Nelson, Eric G. Andersen, and Andrew Banducci. Lawrence W. Newman suggested that I write a book on this topic. Dean Carolyn Jones of the University of Iowa College of Law provided me with a research leave in 2006 and an extraordinary semester free of teaching responsibilities in 2008. I also thank participants in the University of Iowa College of Law Faculty Seminar held on February 1, 2008.

Steven J. Burton
May 10, 2008

CHAPTER 1

Goals, Tasks, and Theories

Issues of contract interpretation are important in American law. They probably are the most frequently litigated issues on the civil side of the judicial docket. They are central to the settlement of a larger number of contract disputes and to the predispute conduct of contract parties. Yet the law of contract interpretation is sometimes difficult to understand and apply as a practical matter. This book describes, analyzes, and evaluates this law in an effort to clarify it for the benefit of lawyers (as drafters, counselors, negotiators, or litigators), judges, and legal scholars. This chapter begins the venture with an introductory, general explanation of the goals, tasks, and theories of contract interpretation. The remainder of the book elaborates within this framework, refining the ideas considerably as we go along.

§ 1.1. Goals of Contract Interpretation

American courts universally say that the primary goal of contract interpretation is to ascertain the parties' intention at the time they made their contract.[1] To do this, contract interpretation generally proceeds lexically

---

[1] 5 Margaret N. Kniffin, Corbin on Contracts § 24.5 (Joseph M. Perillo ed., rev. ed. 1998).

to perform three tasks. First, courts identify the terms to be given meaning. Second, courts determine whether those terms are relevantly ambiguous in any of four ways—term ambiguity, sentence ambiguity, structural ambiguity, or vagueness.[2] If there is ambiguity, the third task is for a fact-finder to resolve the ambiguity.

For each of these tasks, three alternative theories of contract interpretation can be employed. The first is *literalism*, which holds that the literal meaning of the contract's governing word or phrase, as found in a dictionary, determines the parties' rights, duties, and powers. The second is *objectivism*, which looks for the parties' intention as expressed (manifested) in the contract document as a whole and its objective context, but not the parties' mental intentions. The third is *subjectivism*, which looks for the mental intentions or knowledge of the parties when they manifested their intentions, taking into account all relevant evidence. It is not that a jurisdiction will employ only one of these theories at all three steps in contract interpretation; the law is too complex and confused for that. As will be seen, we can clarify the law if we view the resolution of an issue as resting on one or another of these theories.

As the term is used in this book, a *theory* tells an interpreter how to perform the three tasks to further the goals of contract interpretation. In brief, there are four main goals. The first is to implement the contractual freedoms—freedom of and freedom from contract. We do this by ascertaining and implementing the parties' intention when they concluded their contract. The second is to protect and enhance the security of transactions. This goal requires the protection of reasonable expectations arising from, and reasonable reliance on, enforceable promises. It also requires holding parties responsible for their manifestations of intention when it is fair to do so. The third goal is to settle contractual disputes non-arbitrarily, in accordance with the Rule of Law. This goal requires, among other things, that the law of contract interpretation be predictable and coherent with the law of contracts generally. The fourth goal requires that the law of contract interpretation be reasonably administrable by parties and courts. When these goals are reasonably realized, the parties' contract serves as the authoritative guide to their conduct under the contract.

---

[2] *See* § 1.2.2.

§ 1.1.1. *The Contractual Freedoms*

The parties' intention can be thought of as jointly constituting an imaginary world that we may call "the world of the contract."[3] By making a contract, the parties commit themselves to making this world into the actual world through their actions. Thus, *A*, who has a book, and *B*, who has $25.00, may imagine a world in which *A* has the money and *B* has the book. *A*, by promising to deliver the book to *B* in exchange for $25.00, commits herself to perform her promise by doing her part to make that imaginary world into the actual world. *B*, by promising to pay, commits himself to reciprocate as promised. When both parties perform their promises, the world of the contract comes into existence: The parties' intention is realized. It is not significantly different for an architect to imagine and describe a bridge and to undertake to build it, for a business person to imagine a better way for a market to register its cash flow and to commit to making that happen, or for someone to imagine torn clothing repaired and to secure a tailor's or seamstress's promise to make it right, all in return for a price. The parties' promises, when interpreted according to their intentions, create and describe the imaginary world and manifest a commitment to make it real.

When the parties perform according to their intentions at the time of formation, and their agreement was a valid and enforceable contract, they exercise the contractual freedoms. When a court enforces their agreement, the court respects the contractual freedoms. Thus, the parties exercise freedom of contract by making their own legal relations. That is, after contracting, they have legal rights, duties, and powers as between each other when they did not have those rights, duties, and powers before contracting. To continue the above example, *A* now has a right to the money and a duty to deliver her book. *B* has a right to *A*'s book and a duty to pay the price. The parties also enjoy freedom from contract. Neither imposes a duty on the other without a justification (*i.e.*, their agreement), and an enforcing court does not do so either.

The parties' intention when making the contract, however, is contested in a great many reported contract cases. That is, the parties disagree over what the world of the contract looks like and/or what they intended for each of them to do to make that world happen. Let us modify

---

3 Steven J. Burton & Eric G. Andersen, *The World of a Contract*, 75 Iowa L. Rev. 861 (1990).

the example above. *A* had two books, one a rare, leather-bound volume of Homer's *Iliad* and the other a common paperback edition. The parties agreed that they would exchange *A*'s *Iliad* for B's twenty-five dollars. When *A* tenders the cheap paperback, *B* objects that they had intended for *A* to deliver the rare volume. *A* denies this.

There may be a contest here because the parties gave different meanings to *A*'s *Iliad* when the contract was made, and each sticks to its interpretation. Alternatively, both parties gave the same meaning to *A*'s *Iliad*, but one of them regrets having made the deal and makes false claims about their original intentions. When intentions are contested for either reason, each party may act in accordance with its view. A contract dispute then may ensue.

It might be tempting to think that there is no way to settle this dispute by ascertaining and implementing the parties' intention. Their express agreement called for the delivery of *A*'s *Iliad* without specifying which one. What was in their minds cannot be discovered. And the parties did not supply any criteria for choosing between the two interpretations. How can a court decide the dispute without disrespecting the contractual freedoms? Failing to implement the parties' undertakings would be at odds with the primary conventional justification for contract law generally, which is to implement the parties' autonomous undertakings, subject to appropriate constraints (*i.e.*, the requirements for validating an agreement as a contract, such as an absence of unconscionability).

The parties' intention might be ascertained using one or another of the three theories introduced briefly above. First, as an approximation to be elaborated on further below, literalism suggests that their intentions are fixed by the literal meanings of the specifically applicable words they used when making the contract, regardless of the context of those words. Under this approach, *A* may have tendered her *Iliad*, thereby performing her promise, even though both parties had the rare volume in mind (and *B* can prove it). A paperback *Iliad* literally is an *Iliad*, and so it may be held that *A* has performed her promise.[4] Alternatively, the contract may be incomplete because the literal meaning of *A*'s *Iliad* is ambiguous. The contract does not resolve the dispute because there is no literal meaning. In such a case, some observers have suggested, a court should dismiss any

[4] *Cf.* Dennison v. Harden, 186 P.2d 908 (Wash. 1947) (obligation to provide "fruit trees" held satisfied by the provision of scrub-variety fruit trees, though excluded extrinsic evidence showed that the parties intended the trees to be of a fruit bearing variety).

resulting lawsuit, leaving the contract parties and others to draft more completely next time, if they wish.[5]

Second, objectivism suggests that the parties intended what a reasonable person would expect or understand from their manifestations of intention, taking into account some of the governing term's context, such as the contract as a whole, its evident purpose(s), the objective circumstances when it was made, and other objective elements. The contract stems from the parties' manifestations of intention, understood according to the relevant conventions of language use, even when this objective intention differs from their subjective intentions. On this approach, *A* may have satisfied her obligation by tendering her *Iliad* in accordance with the parties' objective intentions. Focusing on the contract as a whole and the objective circumstances, an interpreter might notice that the price term, twenty-five dollars, is more in line with the market price of a paperback book than a rare, leather-bound volume. It reasonably may be inferred from this that *A*'s *Iliad* refers to the paperback book in this context.[6] If so, *B* probably regrets having made the deal and is trying to get out of it. *A* should win.

Third, judges and juries could base a solution on all available evidence of the parties' subjective intentions—what they had in mind as the meaning of their manifestations when manifesting them. On the facts given above, the only contextual feature is the price. As with the second approach, an interpreter could infer from the price alone that both parties intended for *A* to tender the paperback version. But additional evidence may suggest that the parties had the rare volume in mind. During negotiations, for example, *A* may have shown *B* the rare book but not the cheap one. *B* may testify that, on this basis, he formed an intention to buy the rare one. *A*, however, may deny that she showed *B* the rare book. Or she may claim that she showed *B* the rare book to show off part of her coveted rare book collection, not to show the book over which they were bargaining. In the latter case, we might accept that the parties intended different books, but that one party knew or should have known of the

---

[5] Alan Schwartz & Robert E. Scott, *Contract Theory and the Limits of Contract Law*, 113 Yale L.J. 541, 572, 609 (2003). *See also* Robert E. Scott, *The Rise and Fall of Article 2*, 62 La. L. Rev. 1009, 1021 (2002). *See* Richard A. Posner, *The Law and Economics of Contract Interpretation*, 83 Texas L. Rev. 1581, 1606 (2005); Robert E. Scott, *The Case for Formalism in Relational Contract*, 94 Nw. U. L. Rev. 847 (2000).

[6] *Cf. Frigaliment Import. Co. v. B.N.S. Int'l Sales Corp.*, 190 F. Supp. 116, 120–21 (S.D.N.Y. 1960) (drawing inference from prices when interpreting an ambiguous term).

other's intention. We might disfavor the meaning advanced by the party at fault for the misunderstanding. Thus, if *B* knew or should have known that *A* showed him the rare book only to show off her collection, and *A* did not know and had no reason to know of the misunderstanding, *B* would be at fault.[7]

In light of the three theories, there is an important ambiguity in the idea of *the parties' intention*. Literalism regards the literal meaning of the contract's words to be the sole indicator of the parties' intention.[8] Objectivism often regards their intention solely as their manifested intention, as a reasonable person familiar with the objective circumstances would understand the manifestations.[9] Subjectivism regards the parties' intentions preferably as what both had in mind as the meaning of their manifestations.[10] When we speak of *the parties' intention* in this book, the term is meant to be deliberately ambiguous in this way unless otherwise specified; that is, our use of the word generally will encompass all three approaches in the alternative.

Under any of the three theories, there is reason for concern that an interpretation might not respect the parties' contractual freedom in some cases. The literal meanings of their words can easily fail to track their objective or subjective intentions, most clearly when the parties use technical meanings rooted in trade usages, but also in other cases. The objective meanings of their expressions, taking into account the objective context, also can come apart from their subjective intentions, as when more evidence of the context would bring the interpreter closer to an accurate picture of their minds when the contract was formed.[11] Inquiring directly into subjective intentions, however, runs into a critical and well-known problem: We simply cannot get inside of the parties' heads to see what was there in the past, when the contract was made. Testimony by a party of its own past state of mind, moreover, is apt to be consciously or unconsciously self-serving. Under any of these models, then, admissible evidence

---

7 RESTATEMENT (SECOND) OF CONTRACTS § 201(2) (1981).

8 *See* Rose v. M/V "Gulf Stream Falcon," 186 F.3d 1345, 1350 (11th Cir. 1999) (contract provisions given "plain meaning" without reference to context).

9 KNIFFIN, *supra* note 1, at § 24.6; 2 SAMUEL WILLISTON, WILLISTON ON CONTRACTS § 31:1 (4th ed. 2006) [hereinafter WILLISTON 4th ed.].

10 KNIFFIN, *supra* note 1, at § 24.6; WILLISTON 4th ed., *supra* note 9.

11 *See* Castellano v. State, 374 N.E.2d 618, 620 (N.Y. 1978) (in interpreting a contract, a court may consider whether the parties intended to use "Lessee" rather than "Lessor" in the particular clause).

of party intent may be too narrow, scant, or unreliable to get at their subjective intentions in the past.

§ 1.1.2. *Other Goals*

There are other goals that may need to be weighed along with the contractual freedoms. They may not have as much weight as the parties' intention. Contractual freedom surely is a weighty value. The other goals, however, are significant and may outweigh the contractual freedoms in some circumstances.

One important accompanying goal is to foster the security of transactions. This goal also draws support from the Rule of Law value of predictability. The contract, as well as the law, ideally should leave parties clear about their rights, duties, and powers. As above, predictability encourages performance, discourages disputes, and fosters settlement. It also makes it easier for a party to assign its contract rights or for third parties to rely on the contract. The security of transactions requires that we protect reasonable expectations arising from, and reasonable reliance on, promises. Security in this respect is a goal of contract law generally. It is important with respect to interpretation, especially when a contract is in writing. A promise may be ambiguous. Expectations arising from, and reliance on, one of several meanings of a contract may be more reasonable. If so, that expectation and reliance should be protected, all else being equal.

A part of the goal of fostering the security of transactions is that of holding people responsible for their manifestations of intention when it is fair to do so. As indicated, it is difficult to discover what was in a party's mind when the contract was made. The contract document and other objective evidence, by contrast, can evidence a party's manifestations of intention more reliably. The rules of offer, acceptance, and consideration focus on manifestations of intention, not mental intentions.[12] According to the primary versions of subjectivism, however, key aspects of contract interpretation do not so focus.

A further goal is to foster the peaceful settlement of disputes nonarbitrarily, in accordance with the Rule of Law. This goal is a primary function of the courts generally. It calls upon Rule of Law values, such as those of giving reasons for a judgment, treating cases consistently, employing

---

[12] Restatement (Second) of Contracts § 200, cmt. b (1981).

fair procedures, and fostering predictability in the law. It favors a high degree of coherence among contract doctrines. The dispute settlement goal calls into question literalism's propensity to dismiss a case whenever there is no single, literal meaning of a contract's governing language.

A fourth goal is that of formulating legal rules that are administrable by the courts and by the parties. This goal may weigh in the balance in favor of rules that draw relatively clear lines and require objective proof. The most administrable rule, of course, is one that requires a court always to dismiss the plaintiff's action or to dismiss it when the contract language is unclear. The law's dispute settlement function may outweigh that alternative.

Far less important in contract interpretation is a group of possible goals involving general fairness, equality, and justice, apart from the goals outlined above. These goals sometimes override the contractual freedoms. In particular, they are important when a court decides whether an agreement is enforceable under invalidating doctrines, such as duress, mistake, unconscionability, public policy, and the like. These doctrines, however, are applied *before* a court reaches a question of contract interpretation, as the term is used in this book. Once a court has decided that an agreement is an enforceable contract, we should do what we decided to do—enforce it.[13] Consequently, the force of these goals largely is spent at an earlier step of the analysis. They play a very small role in contract interpretation.

§ 1.2. Tasks in Contract Interpretation

What is it we interpret? We interpret the *terms* of a contract. (Rather than introduce the complicated parol evidence rule here, we will put aside the task of identifying the terms until Chapter 3.) The terms are linguistic formulations that form the basis of the parties' legal relations—their contractual rights, duties, and powers. It is important to recognize that all three theories focus interpretation centrally on the contract's terms. This focus is obviously true of literalism, which targets the parties' intention as revealed by the governing word(s). It also is true of objectivism, which focuses on the parties' words, the whole contract, the objective circumstances, and other contextual elements. Further, in an opinion essentially

---

[13] *E.g.*, Rory v. Continental Ins. Co., 703 N.W.2d 23, 30–31 (Mich. 2005).

endorsing the subjective theory on the question of ambiguity, Justice Roger Traynor wrote that

> the intention of the parties *as expressed in the contract* is the source of contractual rights and duties. A court must ascertain and give effect to this intention by determining what the parties meant *by the words they used.*[14]

Accordingly, to interpret a contract using any of the three theories, an interpreter should ascertain the meaning of the contract's terms.

§ 1.2.1. Unambiguous Terms

The parties state contract terms in language or, if implied, the terms are statable in language. When used in a contract, language generally *refers* to classes of ideas, actions, events, states of affairs, persons, and other things in the imaginary world of the contract.[15] This is what we shall mean when we speak of a contract term's *meaning*—its referents in the world of the contract. Once a contract has been concluded and the terms identified, the language is supposed to describe the world that the contract envisioned at formation. The language also is supposed to refer to the actions that the contract prohibits, permits, or requires of the parties in performance of their contract. And it may refer to a state of affairs, as when it describes circumstances that would constitute the occurrence or nonoccurrence of a condition to a party's obligation. Once interpretation has given shape to the world of a contract, we can compare it with the real world and determine whether the imaginary world became the real world as envisioned. If it did not, we can determine whether the reason is that a party breached by failing to perform its promise when due, without excuse or justification.

There should be no interpretive dispute when the contract language refers clearly to an action prohibited, permitted, or required under the contract under the relevant circumstances. In practice, many, many reported cases involve purported interpretive disputes when the language is clear as between the meanings advanced by the parties. When there are

---

[14] Pacific. Gas & Elec. Co. v. G.W. Thomas Drayage & Rigging Co., 69 Cal.Rptr. 561, 564 (Cal. 1968) (emphasis added).

[15] Steven J. Burton, Principles of Contract Law 383–84 (3d ed. 2006).

two contested meanings, a third or fourth possible meaning is irrelevant. To find a relevant ambiguity, the applicable contract language or the contract as a whole must be ambiguous in the contested respect.[16]

In *Roman v. Roman*,[17] for example, a married couple had contracted with an agency for the agency to freeze and store the couple's embryos. A dispute arose when the couple was divorced, and one of them wanted to keep the embryos. The contract between them said:

> If we are divorced or either of us files for divorce while any of our frozen embryos are still in the program, we hereby authorize and direct, jointly and individually, that one of the following actions be taken: The frozen embryo(s) shall be . . . [d]iscarded.[18]

The appellate court found that this language was clear. The embryos could be destroyed.[19] The applicable term was "discarded." Whatever else it might mean, it does not mean that one of the spouses could keep the embryos. Consequently, the contract was unambiguous in the contested respect.

Professor Arthur L. Corbin, a severe skeptic about finding actual party intentions from the face of a contract document, saw, too, that many reported cases involved clear contract language:

> [A]n interpretation is not to be scorned merely because it seems obvious; words are, indeed, not to be condemned because they seem plain and clear and unambiguous. . . . There are cases in which the words of the writing are ambiguous to nobody; the contracting parties may themselves not even assert different interpretations. . . . [T]heir attorneys may argue with eloquent and wearisome repetition for an interpretation favorable to their clients, without producing any relevant or credible evidence in support. . . . [20]

Again,

> [w]ithout a doubt, in supporting the interests of their clients, counsel often urge upon the court interpretations of language that are

---

[16] Eternity Global Master Fund Ltd. v. Morgan Guar. Trust Co. of N.Y., 375 F.3d 168, 177 (2d Cir. 2004); Donoghue v. IBC USA (Publications), Inc., 70 F.3d 206, 215–16 (1st Cir. 1995); Bank of the West v. Superior Court, 833 P.2d 545, 552 (Cal. 1992).

[17] 193 S.W.3d 40 (Tex.App. 2006).

[18] *Id.* at 44.

[19] *Id.* at 52.

[20] Arthur L. Corbin, *The Interpretation of Words and the Parol Evidence Rule*, 50 CORNELL L.Q. 161, 171 (1965).

> far removed from common and ordinary usage, without producing any substantial evidence that the other party to the transaction gave the unusual meaning to the language or had any reason to suppose that the first party did so. In such cases, the harassed judge is justified in saying that the words are too plain and clear to justify such an interpretation.[21]

For another example, in *Namad v. Salomon, Inc.*,[22] an employee sued his employer claiming that he was entitled to a bonus of $170,000, an amount equal to his previous annual salary. His written contract's compensation clause provided:

> The amounts of other compensation and entitlements, if any, including regular bonuses, special bonuses and stock awards, shall be at the discretion of the management.... Such bonuses as are awarded will be consistent with the customary policy of the company.[23]

The New York Court of Appeals held that summary judgment was properly awarded to the employer because this clause was unambiguous. The first sentence clearly gave the employer discretion to give any bonus or no bonus at all ("if any"). The employee argued that the customary policy of the company was to give bonuses approximately equal to his annual salary, and that the second sentence therefore supported his claim. The court, however, considered the compensation clause as a whole. It pointed out that interpreting the second sentence as the employee wanted would render the first sentence a nullity. Consequently, the contract on its face was reasonably susceptible to only one meaning. It may be added that the second sentence itself applies only to "[s]uch bonuses as are awarded," confirming that the employer was free to refrain from awarding a bonus. The second sentence was not rendered a nullity, however, because it might apply when the employer did award a bonus.

In cases like *Roman* and *Namad*, one party is advancing an implausible meaning on the off-chance that a court will find the contract to be ambiguous. If the court does so, the case goes to a jury or a judge as finder of fact. For this reason and others, hopeful counsel may advance an implausible interpretation without any basis. Courts sometimes endorse such interpretations due to noncontractual considerations or simple error.

---

21 3 Arthur L. Corbin, Corbin on Contracts § 542 (1960).

22 543 N.E.2d 722 (N.Y. 1989).

23 *Id.* at 752–53. *See also* SAS Institute, Inc. v. Breitenfeld, 167 S.W.3d 849 (Tex. 2005).

From an advocacy standpoint, advancing an unlikely interpretation is not a bad strategy when the stakes are high; one wants to and might get to a jury; one is litigating the case anyhow on formation or remedies issues; as an obfuscating tactic; or when non-legal considerations might be weighty. But, from a more neutral standpoint, these are not reasonable interpretive disputes. They do not show that the contract language was not clear enough to settle the dispute before the court as a matter of law.

We should not, moreover, gauge the extent of clear cases by confining our attention to the many reported cases in which the applicable terms were rightly held to be unambiguous. In many reported cases involving ambiguous terms, the evidence of party intent cuts only or predominantly in one way.[24] As a practical matter, one supposes, the parties' intention is being implemented when the interpreter follows the predominant evidence. Many cases in litigation, moreover, involve uncontroversial contract terms and only a factual controversy or a real dispute over formation, breach, remedies, or other issues. Further, few contract disputes ever see the light of day: Many disputes do not come to court, but are settled quickly—with and without the aid of lawyers—because the contract is clear. And, in light of the millions of contracts concluded each day, interpretive disputes must be rare; by far, most contracts are performed without a hitch. In clear cases, the goals converge to support the single relevant meaning.

§ 1.2.2. Kinds of Ambiguous Terms

Contract interpretation often focuses on the finding of relevant ambiguity—the failure of contract terms to refer singularly to states of affairs or actions that are relevant to deciding what the contract prohibits, permits, or requires of a party. Terms may allow an array of plausible referents for three main reasons. First, all language is general and in itself indeterminate. That is, each meaningful term refers to at least one class of things in the world, not to one and only one particular thing, and it does not provide dispositive criteria for the classification of a particular case. Language would be useless for communication if it were so fine-grained as to have a separate word for each bit of sand on each beach in the world. Even two neighbors would be unlikely to share much of a vocabulary. Second, the

[24] *See* In re Soper's Estate, 264 N.W. 427 (Minn. 1935).

parties' knowledge, foresight, and attention spans are limited.[25] They (and their lawyers) tend to communicate in detail only about the most salient parts of their contract. As possibilities seem more remote, as when drafting a *force majeure* clause, the parties tend to express themselves, if at all, with less clarity and completeness. Third, the stakes in many transactions do not justify lengthy and therefore costly negotiation and drafting exercises. Here, it is bluster to say, "if you write at all, write it all." The parties may leave the details to interpretation, if it should become necessary. The law of contract interpretation (and implication) facilitates less expensive, truncated contracts.

Contract language may fail in at least four ways. Following Professor E. Allan Farnsworth, we will call these ways term ambiguity, sentence ambiguity, structural ambiguity, and vagueness.[26] Distinguishing them should help when looking for terms that permit an array of reasonable and relevant meanings.

Term ambiguity is the most familiar kind of ambiguity. Technically, unlike vagueness, a word or phrase is ambiguous when it has two or more distinct meanings. It then can refer to two or more distinct classes of ideas, actions, events, states of affairs, or persons. When it does, the contract parties may each favor a different referent from within the array of meanings, producing an interpretive dispute. For example, the word *bank* refers to distinct things when it is used in descriptions of rivers and financial institutions. In an example above,[27] the parties agreed on the sale and purchase of *A*'s *Iliad*. When a commercial contract calls for the purchase and sale of *chicken*, can the seller fulfill its obligation by delivering stewing chicken rather than the younger, more marketable, and more expensive broilers and fryers?[28]

Usage also allows *ambiguity* to be used in a broader sense to refer to any failure of language. (*Ambiguity* is ambiguous.) In this book, we will usually use the word in its broader sense, following judicial practice.

Problems of sentence ambiguity plague the contract drafter. Consider: "The house had a gazebo in the yard which was white." Is it the house or the gazebo or the yard that was white? In a land sale contract, the seller may commit to "put in gas and electricity lines at no cost to the buyer; property

---

[25] *See generally* James W. Bowers, *Murphy's Law and the Elementary Theory of Contract Interpretation: A Response to Schwartz and Scott*, 57 Rutgers L. Rev. 587, *passim* (2005).

[26] E. Allan Farnsworth, *"Meaning" in the Law of Contracts*, 76 Yale L.J. 939, 952–57 (1967).

[27] *See* § 1.1.1.

[28] *Frigaliment Importing Co.*, 190 F.Supp. at 116.

also to be surveyed at once." Must the seller put in the gas and electricity "at once?"

There is a structural ambiguity when a contract document as a whole is ambiguous because two provisions have incompatible implications, both of which are relevant to the dispute.[29] Assume that the termination clause of a contract provides that either party may terminate at any time but only with one year's notice. The *force majeure* clause, however, says that the buyer may terminate upon the occurrence of a *force majeure* event. When a *force majeure* event occurs, may the buyer terminate without notice?

A word or phrase is vague when it has no distinct boundaries between its range of referents and the range of neighboring words. For example, the referents of *orange* shade into those for *yellow* and *red* with no lines of demarcation. Rather, there is a band in which reasonable people may differ over the proper use of the term; indeed, there is no proper use within the band. A contract that calls for a delivery of goods of "fair and average quality" or "reasonable quality" may lead to a dispute due to vagueness.

§ 1.2.3. Resolving Ambiguities

The elements of contract interpretation are relevant evidentiary considerations to be taken into account and if necessary weighed to reach a decision when an interpreter identifies contract terms, determines whether a term or a contract is ambiguous, or resolves an ambiguity. Insofar as the question of ambiguity is concerned, under literalism, only the dictionary and the governing contract words in the document may be taken into account. Under objectivism, the whole document, objective circumstances at the time of formation, the contract's purpose(s), usages and customs, and other objective factors, may be taken into account. Under subjectivism, all evidence that is relevant to ascertaining the parties' mental intentions when the contract was formed may be considered, including the parties' prior dealings and a party's statement of its own intention during negotiations or in court.

Under the prevailing law, all of the elements are available after a court has determined that a contract is ambiguous. When extrinsic evidence is

---

[29] *E.g.*, Commander Oil Corp. v. Advance Food Serv. Equip., 991 F.2d 49, 53–55 (2d Cir. 1993).

admitted, resolution of the ambiguity generally is the province of the finder of fact, whether jury or judge.[30] Consequently, in addition to the elements objectivism allows, extrinsic evidence of subjective intentions may be introduced and considered as relevant to resolving the ambiguity.[31] How finders of fact consider and weigh the factual elements is something of a mystery. The jury, in particular, is a black box. Nonetheless, in Chapter 5, we will examine cases in which judges resolved an ambiguity.

§ 1.2.4. The Limits of Parties' Intention

A cautionary note: Interpretation will not suffice in every case to determine the parties' contractual rights, duties, and powers. In some contract disputes, interpretive resources are exhausted before a resolution can be found. This may happen when no express term addresses the point at all, even ambiguously. For example, many contracts do not address a party's right to cancel should the other materially breach. The law adds constructive conditions of exchange to most contracts. These conditions allow one party to cancel if the other materially breaches.[32] Constructive conditions of exchange are not based on an interpretation of the parties' intention. When concluding a contract, the parties typically are optimistic and do not think about material breaches and cancellation for breach. Hence, they may have no ascertainable intention on the point. These constructive conditions are implied as a matter of fairness and policy to enhance a non-breaching party's security with respect to further performances due from the party in breach.[33]

When interpretation is indeterminate or no applicable express terms are available, a court must settle the dispute with noninterpretive tools, such as a default rule like *contra proferentem* (interpretation against the drafter). Such a tool is available when, after interpretation is exhausted, there is a gap on the disputed point.

---

[30] 2 E. Allan Farnsworth, Farnsworth on Contracts § 8.9 (3rd ed. 2004).

[31] Pepcol Mfg. Co. v. Denver Union Corp., 687 P.2d 1310, 1314 (Colo. 1984); Eagle Indus., Inc. v. DeVilbiss Health Care, Inc., 702 A.2d 1228, 1233 (Del,Super. (1997); *see* Regency Commercial Assocs. v. Lopax, Inc. 869 N.E.2d 310, 317 (Ill.App. 2007).

[32] Bruner v. Hines, 324 So. 2d 265 (Ala. 1975); Joseph M. Perillo, Calamari and Perillo on Contracts §§ 11.16, 11.18(a) (5th ed. 2003).

[33] Restatement (Second) of Contracts § 231, cmt. a (1981); Steven J. Burton & Eric G. Andersen, Contractual Good Faith § 6.2 (1995).

Some authorities support a court's power to "supply" an omitted term to settle a dispute in the absence of any applicable term or default rule. This alternative does not purport to give meaning to contract terms or otherwise to implement the parties' intention. Rather, as the Restatement (Second) of Contracts [Restatement (Second)] puts it, "where there is in fact no agreement, the court should supply a term which comports with community standards of fairness and policy."[34] Some courts have openly done this, but not many.[35] Some skeptical observers suspect that the courts sometimes are supplying terms in disguise, rather than giving meaning to contract language or implying terms to implement the parties' intention.[36]

In addition, a very few judges follow Judge Richard A. Posner in pursuing the goal of economic efficiency when there is no dispositive literal meaning. Judge Posner would decide what the parties, as rational economic actors, would have agreed to had they bargained on the point.[37] This alternative, however, lacks sufficient support in judicial practice to earn further treatment in the descriptive and analytical portion of this book (Chapters 2 to 5). Several academic legal analysts offer a number of other formulae geared to pursuing economic efficiency in contract interpretation.[38] As of yet, however, the courts have not endorsed any of them. Some comments on economic analysis are included in Chapter 6.[39]

Still, there will be cases in which the parties' intention runs out and there is no available default rule. In *Raffles v. Wichelhaus*,[40] a buyer agreed to buy goods to be shipped on a ship called the *Peerless*. There turned out to be two ships named the *Peerless*, sailing at different times. On which

---

[34] RESTATEMENT (SECOND) OF CONTRACTS § 204, cmt. d (1981).

[35] Haines v. City of New York, 364 N.E.2d 820, 822 (N.Y. 1977) (supplying a "reasonable time" term); S. Bell Tel. & Tel. Co. v. Fla. E. Coast Ry. Co., 399 F.2d 854, 858–59 (5th Cir. 1968) (supplying a "terminable upon reasonable notice" term); Toch v. Eric Schuster Corp., 490 S.W.2d 618, 621–22 (Tex.App. 1972) (holding that trial court may designate a reasonable time and area for a noncompetition clause in an employment contract).

[36] For a case where this may be suspected, *see* Spaulding v. Morse, 76 N.E.2d 137 (Mass. 1947).

[37] Beanstalk Group, Inc. v. AM Gen. Corp., 283 F.3d 856, 860 (7th Cir. 2002) (Posner, J.); Posner, *supra* note 5, at 1590–91, 1605–06; *see* Baldwin Piano, Inc. v. Deutsche Wurlitzer GmbH, 392 F.3d 881, 883–85 (7th Cir. 2004).

[38] *See, e.g.*, Ian Ayres & Robert Gertner, *Filling Gaps in Incomplete Contracts: An Economic Theory of Default Rules*, 99 YALE L.J. 87, 91–92 (1989); Charles J. Goetz & Robert E. Scott, *The Limits of Expanded Choice: An Analysis of the Interactions Between Express and Implied Contract Terms*, 73 CAL. L. REV. 261, 308–09 (1985); Avery Wiener Katz, *The Economics of Form and Substance in Contract Interpretation*, 104 COLUM. L. REV. 496 (2004); Eric A. Posner, *The Parol Evidence Rule, the Plain Meaning Rule, and the Principles of Contractual Interpretation*, 146 U. PA. L. REV. 533, 573 (1998).

[39] *See* § 6.2.2.

[40] 159 Eng. Rep. 375 (Ex. 1864).

one must the seller ship the goods? There was no way to resolve the dispute. The court held that there was no contract.[41]

§ 1.3. Theories of Contract Interpretation

From the foregoing, it may be apparent that the three theories of contract interpretation are of practical importance. They capture much of what is involved when various interpreters identify terms, determine whether the contract is ambiguous, and then resolve any ambiguity. The theories seek to guide interpreters on how to perform these tasks to further the goals, as best we can. In particular, they are the bases for determining what elements of contract interpretation the parties, their lawyers, a judge, or a jury may take into account when making an interpretive judgment. Different jurisdictions tend to follow one or another theory on one or another of these issues, at least for a time, though some mix them up. Of course, the theories simplify the reality. Some courts will depart from what is required under the bulk of its precedents in hard cases: They may take into account more or fewer elements to justify what they regard as a just result.[42] Other courts stick rigidly to their precedents even when the result may not be justified by the parties' evident or subjective intentions.[43] Nonetheless, it is best to view the practical legal issues through the trifocal lens of the theories. Because the theories play a substantial role in the detailed analysis in subsequent chapters, it may be helpful to elaborate further on them here.

§ 1.3.1. Literalism

Literalism requires interpretation according to the literal meaning of the directly applicable words used in a contract, without taking into account

---

41 *Id.* at 908, 376; *see* Oswald v. Allen, 417 F.2d 43 (2d Cir. 1969); RESTATEMENT (SECOND) OF CONTRACTS § 201(3) (1981).

42 *Compare* Gilmor v. Macey, 121 P.3d 57, 70 (Utah Ct.App. 2005) (rejecting strict application of the four corners rule even where a contract appears to be unambiguous) *with* Oakwood Village LLC v. Albertsons, Inc., 104 P.3d 1226, 1232 (Utah 2004) (strictly applying the four corners rule) *and* Bakowski v. Mountain States Steel, Inc., 52 P.3d 1179, 1184 (Utah 2002) (stating the four corners rule as controlling law) *and* Cent. Fla. Invs., Inc. v. Parkwest Assocs., 40 P.3d 599, 605 (Utah 2002) ("If the language within the four corners of the contract is unambiguous, the parties' intention are determined from the plain meaning of the contractual language").

43 *See, e.g.*, W.W.W. Associates, Inc. v. Giancontieri, 566 N.E.2d 639 (N.Y. 1990).

their context. According to this theory, the targets of interpretation are single words, and maybe a phrase, in the governing contract term. The interpreter may consult a dictionary. A word is ambiguous only if it bears more than one meaning or grammatical function (as do most words in dictionaries). That is, ambiguity is determined without resorting to any context, such as the document as a whole or the circumstances when the contract was formed. In this respect, the literal meaning of a contract's words should be, though it sometimes is not, distinguished from the plain meaning of a contract.[44] The latter concept may state a conclusion, whether or not reached on the basis of contextual evidence, that a term is unambiguous in the contested respect. Logically speaking, if there is an ambiguity on the key point in controversy, literalism requires that the case be dismissed. This is because a word cannot have a literal meaning—one true meaning apart from its context—and be ambiguous at the same time. Hence, literalism offers no resources for resolving an ambiguity.

Literalism is far from popular in the courts. Nonetheless, commercial arbitrators apparently choose literalism frequently.[45] A few courts also purport to do so.[46] For example,

> Delaware follows the plain meaning rule of contract construction which instructs courts to rely solely on the clear, literal meaning of the words if a contract is clear on its face.[47]

Such a statement of the law, however, may be in tension with other authority in the same jurisdiction. The court that characterized Delaware law as above, for example, went on in the same case to quote the following statement from the same Delaware case:

> An unambiguous integrated written contract should be construed in the way that an objective, reasonable third party would understand it.[48]

---

[44] Lipson v. Anesthesia Services, P.A., 790 A.2d 1261 (Del.Super. 2001).

[45] Lisa Bernstein, *Private Commercial Law in the Cotton Industry: Creating Cooperation Through Rules, Norms, and Institutions*, 99 MICH. L. REV. 1724, 1735 (2001); Lisa Bernstein, *Merchant Law in a Merchant Court: Rethinking the Code's Search for Immanent Business Norms*, 144 U. PA. L. REV. 765, 1769–70 (1996).

[46] *E.g.*, O'Donnell v. Twin City Fire Ins. Co., 40 F.Supp.2d 68, 72 (D.R.I. 1999); Elkhart Lake's Road America, Inc. v. Chicago Historic Races, Ltd., 158 F.3d 970, 972 (7th Cir. 1998); State Highway Admin. v. Greiner Engineering Sciences, Inc., 577 A.2d 363, 370–72 (Md.App. 1990). *See also* Posner, *supra* note 5, at 1605–06.

[47] Swiss Bank Corp. v. Dresser Industries, Inc., 942 F.Supp. 398 (N.D. Ill. 1996) ((citing Myers v. Myers, 408 A.2d 279, 281 (Del. 1979)).

[48] *Id.*

This statement opens the door to more than the "literal meaning of the words." It is objectivist because an objective, reasonable third party would not follow literalism. It seems more plausible to suppose that such a party inevitably would consider at least the whole document, the document's purpose(s), and some other elements in the document's context. No one but a pedant reads woodenly, word-by-word, with a dictionary at hand, without attending to some context. As Judge Learned Hand wrote, "it is one of the surest indexes of a mature and developed jurisprudence not to make a fortress out of the dictionary."[49]

Moreover, no court interprets contract language to reach a literal result when it is unreasonable or absurd upon a reading of the contract as a whole.[50] This rule is a check on literalism's propensity for reaching a result that simply is not apt. Thus, at least in New York, *lessor* in a written contract can mean lessee when *lessor* is grammatically inconsistent with the rest of the document.[51] As Judge Hand, a staunch objectivist, wrote, "[t]here is no surer way to misread any document than to read it literally."[52]

Literal interpretation can come apart from the parties' subjective and objective intentions, impairing the contractual freedoms. Literalist courts are not bothered by this. Their mantra is that:

> [w]hen the language of a contract is plain and unambiguous, the court must afford it its literal meaning, despite a party's contention that he understood the contract to mean something else.[53]

Courts often recite this or a similar mantra. Such mantras, however, can be misleading. They assume that the unambiguous language of a contract represents its "literal" meaning. If there were another meaning, of course, the language would be ambiguous, and there would be no literal meaning. The statement, up to the comma, consequently is a tautology. It amounts to saying, "If the language has only one meaning, the court must afford it that meaning." Surely!

Dennison v. Harden[54] is an example of literalism. A contract for the sale of real estate containing a commercial orchard indicated that the

---

49 Cabell v. Markham, 148 F.2d 737, 739 (2d Cir. 1945).

50 *Beanstalk Group*, 283 F.3d at 860.

51 *Castellano*, 374 N.E.2d at 620.

52 Guiseppi v. Walling, 144 F.2d 608, 624 (2d Cir. 1944).

53 Sofran Peachtree City, LLC v. Peachtree Holdings, LLC, 550 S.E.2d 429, 432 (Ga.App. 2001).

54 186 P.2d 908 (Wash. 1947). It is doubtful that the Washington Supreme Court would reach the same result today. *See* Hearst Communications, Inc. v. Seattle Times Co., 115 P.3d 262, 267 (Wash. 2005); Berg v. Hudesman, 801 P.2d 222, 226–27 (Wash. 1990).

purchase price included "fruit trees." Apparently, the buyer refused to close. In court, it argued that there was a warranty that there were 276 Pacific Gold peach trees in the orchard and that the seller breached this warranty when the land turned out to have only worthless scrub peach trees. The buyer offered evidence of a parol agreement consisting of the seller's representations during negotiations and the seller's agreement to furnish documents from the nursery company that supplied the trees. The seller furnished the documents, and they substantiated the buyer's allegation. The trial court excluded this evidence pursuant to the parol evidence rule—even though the buyer offered it to clarify and properly identify the subject matter of the contract—because "fruit trees" was unambiguous. The Supreme Court of Washington rejected the buyer's appeal because "the contract called for fruit trees, and he got fruit trees."[55]

Many would criticize the *Dennison* court's apparent view that words in a contract may have a single meaning apart from their context. Corbin famously insisted on the crucial role of context in interpretation:[56]

> [I]t is men who give meanings to words and . . . words in themselves have no meaning; . . . when a judge refuses to consider relevant extrinsic evidence on the ground that the meaning of written words is to him plain and clear, his decision is formed by and wholly based upon the completely extrinsic evidence of his own personal education and experience. . . . A word has no meaning apart from [its context]; much less does it have an objective meaning, one true meaning.[57]

It is certainly true that words *in themselves* have no "objective meaning, one true meaning" apart from a context, such as the conventional usages at a time and place. Words in themselves are mere sounds or ink on paper. In addition, in the legal context, a court need only choose between the meanings advanced by the parties. Third and fourth meanings are irrelevant. (Ironically, Corbin ignored this important context!) As any dictionary suggests, moreover, words typically bear an array of possible meanings and grammatical functions in a sentence. Context and purpose are required to select the relevant meaning and function from the array.

---

[55] *Dennison*, 186 P.2d at 910.
[56] Corbin, *supra* note 21, at § 535.
[57] Corbin, *supra* note 20, at 164.

The interpreter, at the least, must know the parties' language, which may include trade usages or dialects, and which may be the minimum necessary context for ascertaining the parties' intention. The key questions for the law of contract interpretation are: How much context is needed and appropriate in light of the law's goals here? More concretely, what elements of contract interpretation should be considered when identifying the terms, determining whether there is an ambiguity in those terms, and, if the terms are ambiguous, resolving the ambiguity?

Corbin used literalism as a foil to dramatize the advantages of his subjective theory of contract interpretation, as he saw them. He clearly rejected objective meanings because, he asserted, there is no "objective meaning, one true meaning"—an apt criticism of literalism. Corbin was not, it should be noted, opposing these views to Professor Samuel Williston's, as often is thought. Williston believed that there are four "primary rules of interpretation," applicable to written contracts, which rules apply whether or not a contract is ambiguous.[58] His statement of the four rules makes it clear that he would take into account, in interpreting any written contract, the circumstances at the time and place it was made, "context" (undefined), local usage, the whole document, and the document's general purpose.[59] The goal for him was to find "the meaning of the writing at the time and place when the contract was made."[60] That meaning was not constituted by the parties' subjective intentions as to the meaning of the words they used, nor from the meaning of a word as stated in dictionaries. Instead, meaning for him flowed from local usage—usage in its context—thus taking into account trade usages, dialects, purposes, and circumstances. Accordingly, Williston did not believe that words have "an objective meaning, one true meaning." He was an objectivist, not a literalist.[61] He was sensitive to the way in which the meaning of language varies with the context.

§ 1.3.2. Objectivism

Objectivism neither assumes nor holds that words have "an objective meaning, one true meaning" apart from a context. That is a feature of literalism. By contrast with subjectivism, however, objectivism takes into

---

58 2 Samuel Williston, The Law of Contracts § 617 (1926).

59 *Id.* at § 618.

60 *Id.*

61 *See id.* at § 608. *See also* Restatement (First) of Contracts §§ 230, 235 (1932).

account a limited context to find the conventional meanings of the parties' expressions as used in the context. Depending on the specific interpretive issue, that context may include several elements of contract interpretation—at least the document as a whole, ordinary meanings, the document's purpose(s), and the objective circumstances when the contract was made. Unlike literalism, as will be seen, objectivism has a modern justification for limiting the relevant context, excluding parol agreements (when a written contract is integrated), statements of intention during negotiations, the parties' prior dealings, and a party's testimony in court about its own past intention.[62]

Several versions of objectivism are widely employed by American courts for determining whether there is a relevant ambiguity.[63] In a departure from its generally subjective approach, the Restatement (Second) includes, as a key consideration, an objective standard: "Unless a different intention is manifested, . . . where language has a generally prevailing meaning, it is interpreted in accordance with that meaning."[64] Contradictory manifestations of intention probably are rare, leaving objectivism in place for the lion's share of contracts.

New York has had a well-deserved reputation for taking a strong objectivist stance on the question of ambiguity. In *W.W.W. Associates, Inc. v. Giancontieri*,[65] for example, the parties entered into a contract for the sale of real property. At the time, litigation was pending in relation to the property. The contract included, on a printed form, two relevant provisions. One said:

> In the event the closing of title is delayed by reason of such litigation it is agreed that closing of title will in a like manner be adjourned until after the conclusion of such litigation provided, *in the event such litigation is not concluded, by or before 6-1-87 either party shall have the right to cancel this contract. . . .*[66]

Second, the printed form contained a standard merger clause providing that "[a]ll prior understandings between *seller* and *purchaser* are merged in this contract [and it] completely expresses their full agreement."[67]

---

[62] *See* § 6.

[63] *See* Farnsworth, *supra* note 30, at § 7.12; Kniffin, *supra* note 1, at § 24.7; Perillo, *supra* note 32, at § 3.10; Williston, *supra* note 9, at § 31.1.

[64] Restatement (Second) of Contracts § 202(3)(a) (1981).

[65] 566 N.E. 2d 639 (N.Y. 1990).

[66] *Id.* at 640 (emphasis in original).

[67] *Id.* at 640–41 (emphasis in original).

The parties, however, had added to the form several paragraphs providing that the purchaser alone could cancel. Apparently, due to a rise in the value of the land above the contract price, the seller delayed the litigation past the June 1 deadline and canceled.

The New York Court of Appeals held that the additional paragraphs could not add to nor vary the terms on the form. It reasoned that, "before looking to evidence of what was in the parties' minds, a court must give due weight to what was in their contract."[68] Further,

> [a] familiar and eminently sensible proposition of law is that, when parties set down their agreement in a clear, complete document, their writing should as a rule be enforced according to its terms. Evidence outside the four corners of the document as to what was really intended but unstated or misstated is generally inadmissible to add to or vary the writing.[69]

The result can be criticized. If the added terms were part of the contract, they would be protected by the merger clause and would create a structural ambiguity. If they were added later, they might have been beyond the scope of that clause.

Giancontieri nonetheless illustrates that objectivism, like literalism, allows the legal effect of a contract to come apart from the parties' subjective intentions. It appeared in that case—from the added paragraphs—that the parties did intend for the buyer alone to have a right to cancel. Williston, a champion of objectivism, clearly recognized that it may result in interpreting an agreement such that it fails to conform to the parties' subjective intentions.[70] It might do so less often than literalism because it takes into account some context. Nonetheless, objectivism is willing to depart from the parties' shared subjective intentions.

When objectivism fails to implement the parties' subjective agreement, it is usually in pursuit of the security of transactions.[71] The main judicial rationale for New York's strong objectivist stance is that the rule imparts

---

[68] *Id.* at 642.

[69] *Id.*

[70] 4 Samuel L. Williston, Williston on Contracts §§ 607-607A (3rd ed. 1961). *See also* Eustis Mining Co. v. Beer, Sondheimer & Co., 239 F. 976, 984 (S.D.N.Y. 1917) (Hand, L., J.); New York Trust Co. v. Island Oil & Transport Corp., 34 F.2d 655, 656 (2d Cir. 1929) (Hand, L., J.); Oliver Wendell Holmes, Jr., *The Theory of Legal Interpretation*, 12 Harv. L. Rev. 417, 417 (1899).

[71] 2 Farnsworth, *supra* note 30, at § 7.12.

> stability to commercial transactions by safeguarding against fraudulent claims, perjury, death of witnesses . . . infirmity of memory . . . [and] the fear that the jury will improperly evaluate the extrinsic evidence.[72]

This rationale has been harshly criticized, especially by Corbin and Professors John D. Calamari and Joseph M. Perillo.[73] The thrust of the criticism is that the rationale proves too much because the law generally is capable of detecting fraudulent claims, perjury, *etc.*, in other contexts to an acceptable degree. It generally trusts a jury to evaluate evidence properly. What, then, distinguishes contract interpretation such that the substantive law should not tolerate the risk of these problems here? A better criticism is that New York's strong approach allows the contract to come apart from the parties' shared subjective intentions. Ideally, the parties' actual agreement should be implemented, and they should not be imposed on unjustifiably. Yet, in the end, this may not be a convincing criticism of objectivism for four main reasons.

First, the goal of respecting the contractual freedoms, even if taken to involve only subjective intentions, need not be absolute. Like any goal when there are multiple goals, it may need to be weighed against the other goals. Weighing goals implies a possible compromise of a goal in some situations. Holding parties responsible for their expressions of intention when fair, for example, is part of a competing goal—furthering the security of transactions. The parties are being held responsible when a court treats a document's objective meaning as its legal meaning, whether or not this is what the parties had in mind. Objectivism poses an incentive to contract parties to express themselves clearly, which enhances the security of transactions and makes the law more administrable.

Second, as we shall see, the more plausible alternative to objectivism, subjectivism, also carries substantial risks that the contract that gets enforced will not implement the parties' subjective intentions. Proof of subjective intention is well known to be hazardous, even when one considers all relevant evidence. A party's testimony as to its own intention may be credible to the fact-finder yet false because it is self-serving or based on unconscious, self-deceiving memories. The available evidence typically will be fragmentary, and inferences from fragmentary evidence

[72] *Giancontieri*, 566 N.E.2d at 642. *See also* WILLISTON, *supra* note 70 at § 611.
[73] CORBIN, *supra* note 21, at § 573; PERILLO, *supra* note 32, at § 3.2(b).

may be biased heuristically. The parties may not have had any subjective intentions on the disputed point. When decisions under the subjective theory are inaccurate, the law will fail to implement their intentions or will impose on the parties unjustifiably. From this standpoint, subjectivism may be unattractive in terms of its own primary goal. We may be faced with a choice between alternatives, all of which sometimes impair the contractual freedoms.

Third, some third parties form reasonable expectations and reasonably rely on written contracts without investigating the contracts' negotiating histories or the parties' minds when the contract was formed.[74] Lenders, some assignees, third party beneficiaries, auditors, investors, executors, and trustees in bankruptcy, all may fall into this category under some circumstances, whether or not they have rights under the contract in question. Such reliance may be reasonable due to the costs to a third party of investigating both parties' subjective intentions or knowledge, if such investigations are even possible without rights to discovery like those in litigation, and even if then. Protecting the security of transactions for third parties, together with other considerations, may outweigh the goal of respecting the contractual freedoms. It may be fair, moreover, to hold parties to their manifestations of intention because they are in the best position to speak their subjective intentions clearly and thus to secure the contract for both parties. Consequently, it may be justified to ascertain and implement the parties' objective intention—those that are evident from their manifestations of intention in their objective contexts—even when that intention does not track their subjectivities.

Fourth, contracts perform a number of functions that they did not perform when they were mainly between individuals or individuals and small, local businesses. Today, contracts frequently are with or between large commercial entities. Many are international and with parties whose legal traditions are strongly tied to the written agreement. Adhesion contracts, which allow for no bargaining over pre-printed, standardized terms, are common. There are reasons for these developments.

As Professor Todd D. Rakoff suggested in a discussion of adhesion contracts,[75] modern firms are internally segmented. Form contracts promote

---

[74] *E.g.*, Shelby County State Bank v. Van Diest Supply Co., 303 F.3d 832, 838 (7th Cir. 2002).

[75] Todd D. Rakoff, *Contracts of Adhesion: An Essay in Reconstruction*, 96 HARV. L. REV. 1173 (1983).

efficiency and reliance within a segmented and complex organization for two main reasons he identified:

> First, the standardization of terms . . . facilitates coordination among departments. The costs of communicating special understandings rise rapidly when one department makes the sale, another delivers the goods, a third handles collections, and a fourth fields complaints. Standard terms make it possible to process transactions as a matter of routine; standard forms, with standard blank spaces, make it possible to locate rapidly whatever deal has been struck on the few customized items. Second, standardization makes possible the efficient use of expensive managerial and legal talent. Standard forms facilitate the diffusion to underlings of management's decisions regarding the risks the organization is prepared to bear, or make it unnecessary to explain these matters to subordinates at all.[76]

In addition, form contracts promote a similar kind of efficiency and reliance between allied firms on one side of a contract when parts of the process are subcontracted or outsourced, especially when outsourced to several firms, some of them overseas. They also are reliable evidence of a contract after the contract's negotiators have left their employment with a party.

Objective interpretation operates similarly to foster reasonable expectations and reasonable reliance on written contracts within and between firms on one side of a contract. None of the functions of standardized terms would work as well if the various departments in party firms or allied firms had to investigate the subjective intentions or knowledge behind a contract before relying on it. The goals of securing transactions, protecting expectations and reliance, holding parties responsible when fair, and ensuring administrability, consequently, may qualify the goal of implementing the parties' subjective intentions.

The original Restatement of Contracts offered yet another rationale for objective interpretation:

> Where a contract has been integrated the parties have assented to the written words as the definite expression of their agreement. In ordinary oral negotiations and in many contracts made by correspondence the minds of the parties are not primarily addressed to

[76] *Id.* at 1222–23.

> the symbols which they are using, but merely to the things for which the symbols stand. Where, however, they integrate their agreement they have attempted more than to assent by means of symbols to certain things. They have assented to the writing as the expression of the things to which they agree, therefore the terms of the writing are conclusive, and a contract may have a meaning different from that which either party supposed it to have.[77]

This rationale bases the objective theory on the parties' intention. It is true that they assent to the writing as the sole expression of their agreement *when they integrate their contract.* (An integration, as we will see in Chapter 3, is a final, or a final and complete, written expression of the agreement.) As the quotation suggests, however, *whether* the parties have integrated their contract turns on their intentions. Consequently, the argument begs the question.

New York may be loosening its commitment to strong objectivism, at least to a degree.[78] In *Kass v. Kass*,[79] which was decided after *Giancontieri*, the Court of Appeals wrote:

> And in deciding whether an agreement is ambiguous courts 'should examine the entire contract and consider the relation of the parties and the circumstances under which it was executed. Particular words should be considered, not as if isolated from the context, but in the light of the obligation as a whole and the intention of the parties as manifested thereby. Form should not prevail over substance and a sensible meaning of words should be sought. Where the document makes clear the parties' over-all intention, courts examining isolated provisions "should then choose that construction which will carry out the plain purpose and object of the [agreement]."[80]

This broadens the relevant context to include the entire contract, the relations between the parties, the circumstances under which it was made,

---

[77] RESTATEMENT (FIRST) OF CONTRACTS § 230, cmt. b (1932). *See also* Air Safety, Inc. v. Teachers Realty Corp., 706 N.E.2d 882, 885–86 (Ill. 1999).

[78] *See, e.g.*, Madison Ave. Leasehold, LLC v. Madison Bentley Associates, LLC, 861 N.E.2d 69 (N.Y. 2006); Westmoreland Coal Co. v. Entech, Inc., 794 N.E.2d 667, 670 (N.Y. 2003); Matter of Riconda, 688 N.E.2d 248, 252 (N.Y. 1997); Aron v. Gillman, 128 N.E.2d 284, 288–89 (N.Y. 1955).

[79] 696 N.E.2d 174 (N.Y. 1998).

[80] *Id.* at 180–81 (internal citations omitted) ((quoting Atwater & Co. v. Panama R.R. Co., 159 N.E. 418, 419 (N.Y. 1927)).

and the purpose of the agreement—not only the ordinary meanings of the words. Also in the opinion, the court took into account the parties' practical construction of the contract.[81] *Kass* still represents objectivism because, by comparison with subjectivism, it is limited to objective elements. It does not allow, for example, extrinsic evidence of statements of intention during the negotiations, or testimony by a party about its own past intentions. Notably, by comparison with literalism, it adds context to literalism's scant elements of interpretation. Consequently, unlike under literalism, the meaning of language will vary with the context.

§ 1.3.3. Subjectivism

Some courts employ subjectivism at all stages of contract interpretation, but especially when resolving an ambiguity. In its strongest form, subjectivism is the theory that prefers to interpret a contract according to the shared meaning the parties attached to the contract's language. Like objectivism, it does not recognize unexpressed intentions.[82] Subjectivism calls on an interpreter to draw inferences as to a party's mental state from its manifestations of intention on the basis of all relevant evidence. Corbin, for example, believed that an interpreter presumptively should give an agreement's *words* the meaning the parties gave *them*.[83] In accord, the Restatement (Second) gives the following dramatic illustration involving an agreed private code:

> A and B are engaged in buying and selling shares of stock from each other, and agree orally to conceal the nature of their dealings by using the word "sell" to mean "buy" and using the word "buy" to mean "sell." A sends a written offer to B to "sell" certain shares, and B accepts. The parties are bound in accordance with the oral agreement.[84]

The result would be different under objectivism. Objectivism does not look to what the parties had in mind as the source of the meaning of language, so an agreed private code cannot constitute the meaning of the

---

[81] *Id.* at 181.

[82] Goddard v. S. Bay Union High Sch. Dist., 144 Cal. Rptr. 701, 706–07 (Cal.App. 1978).

[83] Corbin, *supra* note 21, at § 538.

[84] Restatement (Second) of Contracts § 212, cmt. b., illus. 4 (1981); *see id.* § 201(1); Corbin, *supra* note 21, at § 544.

words they use.[85] Rather, objectivism looks to the meaning of the contract's language as a matter of convention in the relevant context of use. Oliver Wendell Holmes, Jr. stated a strong form of objectivism as follows:

> You cannot prove a mere private convention between two parties to give language a different meaning from its common one. It would open too great risks, if evidence were admissible to show that when they said five hundred feet they agreed it should mean one hundred inches, or that Bunker Hill Monument should signify the Old South Church.[86]

Williston, however, did not agree in principle because, for written contracts, he rejected the use of "common" meanings in favor of "local usages"—"the natural meaning of the writing to parties of the kind who contracted at the time and place where the contract was made, and [under] such circumstances as surrounded its making."[87] Accordingly, he wrote, "local or technical usage, if different from ordinary or normal usage, may be competent to [change the meaning of Bunker Hill Monument to Old South Church]."[88] The parties' subjective intentions, however, may not.

The parties' subjective intentions, of course, do not always coincide. In such a case, subjectivist courts may follow Corbin's fault principle, as elaborated in the Restatement (Second):[89]

> (2) Where the parties have attached different meanings to a promise or agreement or a term thereof, it is interpreted in accordance with the meaning attached by one of them if at the time the agreement was made
>
> (a) that party did not know of any different meaning attached by the other, and the other knew the meaning attached by the first party; or

---

85 *See* Hershon v. Gibraltar Bldg. & Loan Ass'n, Inc., 864 F.2d 848, 851, 857 (D.C. Cir. 1989).

86 Goode v. Riley, 28 N.E. 228, 228 (Mass. 1891).

87 WILLISTON, *supra* note 70, at § 607.

88 *Id.* at § 611. *See also* RESTATEMENT (FIRST) OF CONTRACTS § 230, cmt. a (1932).

89 CORBIN, *supra* note 21, at § 537. *See* Found. Intern., Inc. v. E.T. Ige Const., Inc., 78 P.3d 23, 33–34 (Haw. 2003); Centron DPL Co., Inc. v. Tilden Financial Corp., 965 F.2d 673, 675 (8th Cir. 1992); Fashion Fabrics of Iowa, Inc. v. Retail Investors Corp., 266 N.W.2d 22, 27 (Iowa 1978).

> (b) that party had no reason to know of any different meaning attached by the other, and the other had reason to know the meaning attached by the first party.[90]

If the requirements of neither (a) nor (b) are satisfied, a court may supply a term or declare a failure of mutual assent.[91] Requirement (2)(a) is subjective because the "attaching" of meaning, and knowledge of an attached meaning, are subjective. In (2)(b), attention shifts to whether one party should have known of the meaning subjectively attached by the other. At least one party must "attach" an eligible meaning. In other words, (2)(a) and (2)(b) are subjective because they require the interpreter to give the contract language a meaning that one party attached to it when the other party is at fault for a misunderstanding. This approach is not a strong subjective theory, which would require that both parties attach the same meaning in any case. It does treat only the strong subjective case as an instance of an *agreement*.

Sprucewood Investment Corp. v. Alaska Housing Finance Corp.[92] illustrates the kind of evidence that some courts will consider when determining the parties' subjective intentions. A housing finance company (AHFC) decided to revitalize a low-income area in Fairbanks, Alaska. To do so, it had to remove or demolish several existing buildings. It contracted with a construction company to do the work. The construction company then decided to remove the buildings from the site and salvage them. It contracted to sell them to a third party. AHFC then brought an action against the construction company for breach of contract, claiming that the contract required the complete demolition of the buildings, not their removal and sale. The court, relying on extrinsic evidence, affirmed the trial court's grant of summary judgment for AHFC.

The invitation to bid set the terms of the contract. It provided, among other things, that the scope of the work would be "the removal and satisfactory disposal of all buildings," and that "the buildings and foundations will be completely razed."[93] Another provision, the salvage provision, said that the removed items would become the contractor's property, and an addendum to the bid packet said, "[t]he disposal of the building materials

---

[90] RESTATEMENT (SECOND) OF CONTRACTS § 201(2) (1981).

[91] *Id.* at §§ 201(3), 204.

[92] 33 P.3d 1156 (Alaska 2001).

[93] *Id.* at 1158.

is at the contractor's discretion."[94] When the contractor contracted to sell the salvaged buildings to the third party, both relied on the salvage provision.[95]

The dispute involved one party relying on the "completely razed" contract language and the other relying on the salvage provision. The court did not, however, determine that the written contract was ambiguous in the contested respect, nor did it require the ultimate interpretation to coincide with one prong of an ambiguity.[96] Instead, it went directly to indications of the parties' subjective intentions at the time of contracting. In particular, it relied on evidence showing that, before the award of the contract, the construction company's president (Timmons) agreed to "demolish" the buildings;[97] that upon his inquiry whether the contract allowed the removal and sale of the buildings, he was told that his company was required to completely demolish the buildings and could not sell them;[98] and that Timmons did not form an intention to remove and sell the building until after the contract was formed.[99] Based on these uncontroverted facts, the court reasoned as follows:

> Because AHFC and [the construction company] attached the same meaning to the contract's terms and knew or had reason to know (through the discussion between AHFC's representatives and Timmons) of the other's intended meaning, the contract is enforceable in accordance with that meaning.[100]

The court gave no weight to the written salvage provision, even though the construction company and a third party had relied on it. By contrast, objectivism probably would find a structural ambiguity in the written contract, as between the "completely razed" language and the salvage provision. It would allow a different result when resolving this ambiguity. (Ironically, if not in bad faith, following the construction company's breach, AHFC removed and sold the buildings.)[101]

The chief virtue of subjectivism is its strong insistence on freedom of and freedom from contract. In *Sprucewood*, it was fairly clear that the

---

[94] *Id.*
[95] *Id.* at 1159.
[96] *Id.* at 1162.
[97] *Id.* at 1163.
[98] *Id.*
[99] *Id.*
[100] *Id.*; *see* Restatement (Second) of Contracts § 201 (1981).
[101] *Sprucewood*, 33 P.3d, at 1160.

parties both attached the same meaning to the contract as a whole at the time it was made. To give it any other meaning might fail to enforce the agreement they had in mind or to impose on them an agreement that neither (subjectively) intended. No policy goal other than respecting the contractual freedoms seems to have played a role in the court's opinion, even though the construction company and a third party had relied on the written salvage clause. The court hinted that it would reach the same result had the contract not contained the "completely razed" language, but all else remained the same.[102] If so, the case is somewhat like the Restatement (Second) illustration involving an agreed private code by which *buy* shall mean sell.[103]

Few subjectivist courts would go quite so far. In the famous *Pacific Gas and Electric Co.* case,[104] for example, Chief Justice Roger Traynor required that, to be an eligible meaning that can render a contract term ambiguous, a proffered meaning must be one to which the contract language is "reasonably susceptible."[105] Such susceptibility is the same as a requirement that the language be ambiguous—that it reasonably bear more than one meaning. This requirement imposes a constraint on subjectivity. The "completely razed" language in *Sprucewood* probably would satisfy this constraint. But *buy* means sell would not.

A second virtue, in the eyes of some, is that the subjective theory moves the locus of interpretation from judges to juries and so particularizes the decision. For example, in *Masterson v. Sine*,[106] a grant deed reserved to the grantors an option to repurchase the property for the selling price. The grantees were the grantor's sister and brother-in-law. The grantor went bankrupt, and the trustee in bankruptcy sought to exercise the option. Based on extrinsic evidence, the grantor argued that the parties had made a parol agreement to keep the property in the grantor's family; therefore, the option was personal to the grantor and could not be exercised by the trustee in bankruptcy. Over a strong dissent, the court held that the trial court erred by applying the parol evidence rule to keep extrinsic evidence of the parol agreement from the jury. The court appeared to eviscerate the parol evidence rule by turning it from a rule of

---

[102] *Id.* at 1162 ("a party will thus be bound not by the outer limits of an ambiguous document, but by the terms agreed upon by the parties").

[103] *See* § 1.3.3.

[104] *Pacific Gas & Elec. Co*, 69 Cal.Rptr. at 561.

[105] *Id.* at 564. *See also* RESTATEMENT (SECOND) OF CONTRACTS § 212, cmt. c (1981).

[106] 65 Cal.Rptr. 545 (Cal. 1968).

substantive law into a rule of evidence aimed at finding "the true intent of the parties."[107] Accordingly, the court wrote, "[e]vidence of oral collateral agreements should be excluded only when the fact finder is likely to be misled."[108]

Criticisms of the subjective theory largely are the converse of the virtues of the objective theory. First, respecting the parties' contractual sovereignty over their contract's meaning should not be the only goal. The security of transactions, including holding parties responsible for their expressions when fair, and predictability, also may qualify the search for subjective intentions by giving effect to their intentions as manifested and conventionally understood. Second, due in part to the problems of proving subjectivities, the contract as interpreted under subjectivism easily can come apart from the parties' subjective intentions or knowledge. Third, as indicated above, some third parties form reasonable expectations arising from, and reasonably rely on, written contracts without investigating their negotiating histories or other evidence of the parties' subjective intentions when the contract was made.[109] Fourth, coordination among the divisions of a modern firm, and between firms on one side of a contract, similarly is facilitated by keeping to the objective meanings of the contract. In addition, parties may rely on the document in its objective context after the employee(s) who negotiated and drafted the document have left their employment with the party.[110]

One criticism may be added. The key question is: How much context is needed for appropriate interpretation? Subjectivism admits all evidence relevant to the parties' mental intentions when using the language in question. It presupposes that more context will get an interpreter closer to these intentions, even though the evidence remains fragmentary, and that there were relevant intentions. Or, in its more sophisticated form, in the case of an interpretive dispute, subjectivism requires inquiries into whether a party knew or should have known of the other's subjectively held meaning. The link between context and subjective intention or knowledge, however, is tenuous. Consider, for example, unilateral statements of intent made in negotiations before the contract is concluded. Some such statements will not have been accepted by the other party and,

---

107 *Id.* at 548.

108 *Id.*

109 *See* Shelby County State Bank v. Van Diest Supply Co., 303 F.3d 832, 838–40 (7th Cir. 2002).

110 *See, e.g.*, Nanakuli Paving & Rock Co. v. Shell Oil Co., Inc., 664 F.2d 772, 785 (9th Cir. 1981).

therefore, will not represent the parties' joint intentions, rendering them of no legal effect. Even agreements may be way-station agreements that were dropped as the negotiations evolved. Parol agreements on one term may be traded off later for another term; even well-evidenced parol agreements may have been superseded. Reconstructing the evolution of negotiations can be difficult and misleading. Consequently, statements in negotiations may not indicate the parties' subjective intentions when they signed the contract, which intentions are the only authoritative intentions. Testimony in court of a party's own intentions when the contract was made can be self-serving, especially when that party has convinced itself of the truth of its erroneous testimony. Ironically, the written contract, interpreted objectively based on something like the limited context approved by *Kass v. Kass*, might come closer to subjective intentions in the probably unusual cases in which these two theories would lead to different results.

CHAPTER 2

The Elements

As indicated in Chapter 1, theories of contract interpretation tell us how to perform the interpretive tasks—identifying the terms to be interpreted, deciding whether the terms are ambiguous, and resolving any ambiguity that appears—to achieve the goals of contract interpretation—respecting the contractual freedoms, enhancing the security of transactions, settling disputes non-arbitrarily, and achieving reasonable administrability. More specifically, the theories tell us how to perform the tasks by licensing the use of different sets of interpretive elements in the interpretive process.

The elements are the raw materials or resources for interpretation, categories of evidence that judges and juries may take into account when performing the interpretive tasks. All of them should be considered as they bear on ascertaining the parties' intention, the "polestar" of contract interpretation, as well as the other goals.[1] The elements can be grouped usefully in terms of the three theories. Thus, literalism licenses the use only of the contract's words and the dictionary. Objectivism licenses, in addition, the contract as a whole, the circumstances at formation bearing on the parties' objective intentions, the document's purpose(s), ordinary meanings, trade usages and customs, legal precedents and practical constructions (courses of performance). Subjectivism licenses, in addition

[1] Kearny PBA Local No. 21 v. Town of Kearny, 405 A.2d 393, 400 (N.J. 1979).

again, all relevant evidence, including any prior course of dealing between the parties, the course of negotiations, testimony by a party about its own intentions, and circumstances bearing on the parties' subjective intentions.

This chapter will explain and illustrate these elements generally. It will conclude by looking at some additional general considerations that are not elements, which are factual, but guides for interpretation, which are legally normative. Throughout this chapter, the assumption, unless otherwise specified, is that the relevant task is that of resolving an ambiguity. Most courts will admit all relevant evidence in connection with this task, as we will see in Chapter 5. When courts identify terms or determine whether there is an ambiguity, by contrast, the set of allowable elements often is more restricted, as we will see in the next two chapters.

2.1. Literalist Elements

Literalism allows an interpreter to take into account only the words of contracts and the dictionary. Professors Alan Schwartz and Robert E. Scott, leading economic analysts of contract law, advocate literalism when interpreting firm-to-firm contracts. They would license the use only of the following elements:

> the parties' contract, a narrative concerning whether the parties performed the obligations that the contract appears to require, a standard English language dictionary, and the interpreter's experience and understanding of the world.[2]

There is some confusion here. The narrative to which Schwartz and Scott refer is mistakenly included. We cannot determine whether a party performed its contract obligations until *after* we have identified and interpreted the contract's terms, which ground the parties' rights, duties, and powers. The last element also is problematic because it is not an interpretive element, part of what Schwartz and Scott call the *evidentiary base*, at all. It is not a category of provable facts that judges and juries may take into account when interpreting. Different interpreters, moreover, will come to an interpretive problem with different experiences and understandings.

---

[2] Alan Schwartz & Robert E. Scott, *Contract Theory and the Limits of Contract Law*, 113 Yale L.J. 541, 572 (2003). *See also* Richard A. Posner, *The Law and Economics of Contract Interpretation*, 83 Texas L. Rev. 1581, 1606 (2005).

Schwartz and Scott understand the world through the lens of economics; others see the world through such lenses as common sense, religion, philosophy, and social science. For the sake of predictability and equal treatment, a key function of the law and the evidence is to leaven these differences by providing an obligation to follow the law, common legal standards, and evidence made relevant by the legal standards. It is hard to believe that contracting parties would want the resolution of their disputes to turn on whether the interpreter is an economist, a philosopher, or a common sense lawyer. The interpreter's experience and understanding of the world consequently should be excluded in principle, though it inevitably will have some effect. We are left (by the best interpretation of the passage) with literalism—the contract's words and the dictionary.

§ 2.1.1. The Words of the Contract

Contract interpretation normally involves identifying a contract's terms and giving meaning(s) to those terms. Interpretive issues frequently (but surely not always) focus on a single word. An issue then can be stated in the following way: Is a tomato a *vegetable* within the meaning of the contract? Interpretive questions in contract cases do not arise in the abstract, as though the issue could be stated as, What is a tomato? Rather, they arise when interpreting a particular contract as a step preliminary to applying its terms to the facts of a case to determine whether or not a party breached. Literalism focuses interpretation on a single word as defined in the dictionary. The dictionary, of course, provides general definitions of words. Literal interpretation does not take into account even the document as a whole, much less sentence or structural ambiguities. The holistic idea of a document contemplates meaning(s) that may be different from the sum of a whole document's individual words, taken one by one according to a dictionary (if summing words makes sense). When the courts speak of a contract as a whole, they suppose that the relevant meaning(s) may be of a word, a sentence, a paragraph, or even the whole document, and that one part of a document may shed light on the meaning or intention of another.[3] Practically speaking, focusing on a single word might be unobjectionable in some cases, as when one party

---

[3] *See* § 5.2.2.

offers an absurd meaning for a key word and the other offers a reasonable meaning.[4] There are, however, many other kinds of interpretive disputes and better ways to ascertain the meaning(s) of terms.

§ 2.1.2. Dictionaries

Dictionaries provide lists of a word's definitions along with the grammatical functions of the word (noun, verb, adjective, *etc.*) on the list. Courts and other interpreters under all theories use dictionaries, sometimes including legal dictionaries,[5] at least to identify candidates for an apt interpretation. Literalism tells them to use *only* the dictionary. The dictionary, however, often does not suffice for giving apt meaning(s) to contract terms. A dictionary typically gives several definitions and grammatical functions for each word. Different dictionaries may give different definitions. Their definitions may not make the fine distinctions needed to resolve an interpretive dispute.[6] They do not provide criteria for choosing among the multiple meanings and grammatical functions. The meanings, moreover, are cast in words. Conceptually, the user of a dictionary must define the words in the definition, define the words in the definition of the definition, and so forth *ad infinitum*. As we will see in the next section, choosing from among the dictionary meanings and grammatical functions, when there are more than one of each, requires an interpreter to employ contextual elements, at least implicitly. Yet literalism eschews all context.

§ 2.1.3. Literalism and Context

In truth, a literalist or any other interpreter considers context at least implicitly when using a dictionary. As Professor Arthur L. Corbin insisted, context is essential to finding the meaning of language.[7] Thus, an interpreter considers the sentence or phrase in which a key word appears, which sentence or phrase is the smallest part of the key term's context,

---

4 USA Life One Ins. Co. of Indiana v. Nuckolls, 682 N.E.2d 534, 538–40 (Ind. 1997).

5 *E.g.*, Williams v. Metzler, 132 F.3d 937, 947 (1st Cir. 1997).

6 Teg-Paradigm Environmental, Inc. v. United States, 465 F.3d 1329, 1340 (Fed. Cir. 2006).

7 *See* 3 A. CORBIN, CORBIN ON CONTRACTS § 542 (1961).

though in many cases even a sentence may be inadequate. She also considers the rules of grammar and punctuation, not only the functions of words.[8] The dictionary identifies the part of speech that goes with each definition. If it does not list two noun meanings, or two verb meanings, *etc.* (as is often the case), an interpreter might infer the meaning that the word has in the contract's key sentence or phrase from the definition and the word's grammatical function in a sentence. This is the closest even a literalist can come to literalism unless the dictionary gives one and only one grammatical function and one and only one meaning (which is unusual), and the meaning is precise enough to settle the dispute and the problem of defining the words in the definition is put aside.

It seems probable that an interpreter, supposing herself to be a literalist, implicitly and perhaps unconsciously but inevitably, uses more context than just a sentence or phrase. In *Steuart v. McChesney*,[9] for example, a potential buyer of real property held a right of first refusal entitling it to buy the property if the seller received a third party's good faith offer,

> at a value equivalent to the market value of the premises according to the assessment rolls as maintained by the County of Warren and Commonwealth of Pennsylvania for the levying and assessing of real estate taxes.[10]

In the event, the seller received good faith offers to buy for $35,000 and $30,000. The buyer tendered $7820, representing twice the assessed value of the property as listed on the tax rolls maintained in Warren County. The seller refused to tender a deed, and the potential buyer brought a suit for specific performance. The trial court found that the parties intended the assessed value to serve as "a mutual protective minimum price for the premises rather than be the controlling price without regard to a third party offer."[11] It construed the contract as granting the potential buyer a right to purchase the property for $35,000, the amount of the first offer. The Supreme Court of Pennsylvania, in a well-known opinion, reversed, holding that the contract was unambiguous. It wrote that the writing

---

8 *See* New Castle County, Del. v. National Union Fire Ins. Co. of Pittsburgh, Pa., 174 F.3d 338, 347–49 (3d Cir. 1999).

9 444 A.2d 659, 660 (Pa. 1982).

10 *Id.* at 660.

11 *Id.* at 661 (quoting the Court of Common Pleas).

"speaks for itself,"[12] although it also wrote that "the language of the Right of First Refusal, *viewed in context*, is express and clear. . . ."[13] The court did not describe what constituted the relevant context.

It is improbable that the court found the key phrase unambiguous after consulting only a dictionary for the meaning of each word and its function in the sentence as a part of speech. Because it sought the parties' intention as expressed in the document, viewed in context, it is more likely that the court implicitly imagined a context that would make sense of the document as an expression of intention. Thus, it might have imagined that, at the time of contracting, the property had not been sold in some considerable time. No appraisal was commissioned, so its market value was unknown. No offers from other buyers were on the table. The parties did not know whether the market value would go up or down before the seller received a good faith offer from a third party. The parties did not know whether a good faith offer would reflect the market value. They assumed that the assessed value would be the market value. Though this imagined context includes a critical erroneous assumption, it or something like it might well have been the context of contracting in *Steuart*. If so, the result arguably would reflect the parties' intention, misguided though they both may have been.

Is this imaginary context suggestive of what Schwartz and Scott would include as "the interpreter's experience and understanding of the world?" Perhaps. The interpreter's experience and understanding, however, would consist of the interpreter's implicit context, not everyone's, and not likely the parties'. Corbin strongly and rightly objected to interpretation using the interpreter's context instead of the parties'.[14] Using the interpreter's context injects arbitrariness into the process; it bears no reliable relation to the parties' intention and, indeed, may be quite foreign to them.

An important difference between literalism, on one hand, and objectivism or subjectivism, on the other, is that literalism hides the contextual elements it employs only implicitly. It precludes proof of, or argument about, those elements. The legal rules implementing the other theories, by contrast, expose their contextual elements to view. Under the other

---

[12] *Id.* at 661 ((quoting Ease Crossroads Center, Inc. v. Mellon-Stuart Co., 205 A.2d 865, 866 (Pa. 1965)).

[13] *Id.* (emphasis added).

[14] Corbin, *supra* note 7, at § 542.

theories, parties must offer proof of the facts constituting the relevant context and have to prove them (unless judicial notice is appropriate). Parties can argue about the existence and significance of those facts. And interpreters can interpret consciously and deliberately in light of those facts. These three features make objectivism and subjectivism superior to literalism because the Rule of Law requires non-arbitrary and predictable settlements of disputes. Hiding contextual elements is incompatible with this goal.

§ 2.2. Objectivist Elements

Objectivism significantly expands the set of interpretive elements to include (in addition to the contract's governing term, the dictionary, and rules of grammar) the contract as a whole, the objective circumstances at formation, the document's purpose(s), ordinary meanings, trade usages and customs, legal precedents, and any practical construction. This extent of context is sufficient to give apt meanings to contract terms if one accepts that the parties' intention as revealed to a reasonable person by their manifestations of intention—not their mental intentions—should ground the meaning(s) of a contract's terms. Many courts accept this view.[15]

§ 2.2.1. The Whole Contract

Even in jurisdictions sometimes thought to employ literal interpretation, such as New York and Pennsylvania, the courts will take into account, to use New York's formulation, "the contract as a whole to determine its purpose and intent."[16] Recent New York precedent provides that:

> A written contract will be read as a whole; and every part will be interpreted with reference to the whole; and if possible it will be so interpreted as to give effect to its general purpose.... The meaning

---

15 *E.g.*, *Williams*, 132 F.3d at 947.

16 W.W.W. Assoc., Inc. v. Giancontieri, 566 N.E.2d 639, 642 (1990). *See also* Kinek v. Paramount Communications, Inc., 22 F.3d 503, 509 (2d Cir. 1994); *Steuart*, 444 A.2d, at 661; Aron v. Gillman, 128 N.E.2d 284, 288 (N.Y. 1955); Nau v. Vulcan Rail & Constr. Co., 36 N.E.2d 106, 110 (N.Y. 1942).

of a writing may be distorted where undue force is given to single words or phrases.[17]

In a well-known passage in *Central Hanover Bank & Trust Co. v. Commissioner*,[18] Judge Learned Hand explained:

> There is no more likely way to misapprehend the meaning of language—be it in a constitution, a statute, a will or a contract—than to read the words literally, forgetting the object which the document as a whole is meant to secure. Nor is a court ever less likely to do its duty than when, with an obsequious show of submission, it disregards the overriding purpose because the particular occasion which has arisen was not foreseen. That there are hazards in this is quite true; there are hazards in all interpretation, at best a perilous course between dangers on either hand; but it scarcely helps to give so wide a berth to Charybdis's maw that one is in danger of being impaled upon Scylla's rocks.[19]

Thus, the whole contract is the target for interpretation—the intrinsic context for each provision or word.

The whole contract also is important because a word, sentence, paragraph, or more; or the contract's structure and relationships among its terms, may shed light on the reasonable meaning(s) of a governing word or term.[20] For the same reasons, the courts treat several writings that are parts of the same transaction as one writing for the purpose of interpretation,[21] at least when they are executed at the same time.[22] A reasonable interpretation treats the contract as a harmonious whole, if possible.

§ 2.2.2. Objective Circumstances

Distinguishing between literalism and objectivism permits us to include the circumstances element within objectivism and to distinguish objective from subjective circumstances. The objective circumstances provide a context of use that, together with the conventions of language use

---

17 Westmoreland Coal Co. v. Entech, Inc., 794 N.E.2d 667, 670 (N.Y. 2003).
18 159 F.2d 167 (2d Cir. 1947).
19 *Id.* at 169.
20 For an extended illustration, see § 5.2.2.
21 Gordon v. Vincent Youmans, Inc., 358 F.2d 261, 262–63 (2d Cir. 1965).
22 Talley v. Talley, 566 N.W.2d 846, 851 (S.D. 1997).

within that context, generate the reasonable meaning(s) of the parties' manifestations of intention when the contract was made. Subjective circumstances, by contrast, lay a basis for drawing inferences about what the parties had in mind when writing or reading, speaking or hearing, the relevant contract language. An objectivist court would believe something like the following statement by the Supreme Court of Connecticut:

> The intention of the parties to a contract is to be determined from the language used interpreted in the light of the situation of the parties and the circumstances connected with the transaction. The question is not what intention existed in the minds of the parties but what intention is expressed in the language used.[23]

Crone v. Amado[24] is a simple illustrative case. The owners of a guest ranch contracted with a builder to build an addition. The owners' mortgage agreement, which the builder also signed, provided that $8,700 of the borrowed $25,000 would be used to pay off the existing mortgages on the property; the remaining amount would be held by a realtor, the owners' agent, to pay the builder's weekly bills for materials and labor. The contract did not say whether the builder would be paid on a fixed price or cost-plus basis, making it ambiguous. When the cost of construction exceeded the amount held by the realtor, the builder refused to continue, contending that the parties had a cost-plus agreement. The owners, by contrast, contended that the builder had agreed to a fixed price of $16,300, representing the amount of the borrowed money ($25,000) less the amount that the contract required be used to pay off existing mortgages ($8,700). In addition to considering the parol evidence rule and the parties' practical construction, the Supreme Court of Arizona considered the circumstances when the contract was made. The court wrote:

> [N]either of the parties had seen any plans or specifications; no survey had been made of the proposed building site; building materials were scarce; and what were available were rationed under O.P.A. regulations.[25]

---

[23] Barnard v. Barnard, 570 A.2d 690, 696 (Conn. 1990); *see* Dome Petroleum Ltd. v. Employers Mut. Liability Ins. Co. of Wisc., 767 F.2d 43, 47 (3d Cir. 1985).

[24] 214 P.2d 518 (Ariz. 1950).

[25] *Id.* at 523.

The court concluded that no reasonable builder would have agreed to a fixed-price contract under these circumstances. Accordingly, the court affirmed the trial court's interpretation finding the contract to be a cost-plus contract.

In *Crone*, the appellate court reported circumstances consisting of facts existing in the objective context of the contract when it was made. They involved both the parties in particular and the broader economic and legal situation as well. The court did not infer from the facts what the parties had in mind when contracting. Rather, it looked to what a reasonable person would have understood under the circumstances. By focusing on a reasonable person, the court gave effect to the objective meaning of the parties' intention as manifested under the circumstances.

§ 2.2.3. Purpose(s)

A contract's or a term's purpose(s)—normally together with the whole contract and the circumstances—often help an interpreter to decide how the parties' used the language in question. Indeed, some courts consider purpose(s) to be of great importance.[26] Contracting parties can use language for many purposes, including describing the world of the contract, making commitments to bring it into existence by their actions, and more generally guiding their conduct. How they use language makes a difference to what the language means. Consider a clause providing: "The seller shall deliver the widgets to the buyer at the buyer's place of business on March 1, 2008." In the abstract, *shall* is ambiguous, as the dictionary indicates, because it can mean *will*, a prediction; or *must*, a commitment or obligation.[27] In the context of an enforceable contract, the parties no doubt used it for the purpose of signifying the seller's commitment and creating an obligation. It therefore means *must* and creates an obligation for the seller to deliver the widgets under the described circumstances. The parties did not use the clause, however, to describe the empirical world, as though it would have a truth-value that can be established by observation. It is not a scientific or social scientific proposition, which would involve a different purpose. Instead, the clause describes part of

---

[26] *See* Falkowski v. Imation Corp., 33 Cal.Rptr.3d 724, 732–33 (Cal.App. 2005); Teig v. Suffolk Oral Surgery Associates, 769 N.Y.S.2d 599, 600–01 (App.Div. 2003).

[27] *See* Concise Oxford English Dictionary 1316 (10th ed., J. Pearsall, ed. 2002).

the imaginary world of the contract and the seller's commitment to make it real. It guides the seller's conduct in contract performance.

To illustrate the use of purpose, in *Fishman v. LaSalle National Bank*,[28] the meaning of a prepayment term in a promissory note was in issue. The note permitted prepayment with the payment of a premium that was the greater of one percent of the outstanding balance or a yield maintenance prepayment calculation. The yield maintenance calculation could be performed as a single calculation applied to the outstanding balance (producing a prepayment of $11,514). In the alternative, it could be performed as a series of calculations to determine the present value of what the lender would lose as a result of the prepayment ($393,852). The US Court of Appeals for the First Circuit concluded that the latter method of calculation should be used, reflecting the clause's purpose in the contract. As reasonable parties and others in the same or similar circumstances would understand, the purpose was for the holder of the note to take the risk that interest rates would rise, while the borrower would take the risk that the rates would fall. Using the series of calculations would implement this purpose.[29]

§ 2.2.4. Ordinary Meanings

Many courts say that an interpreter should give contract language its ordinary meaning unless this meaning is unreasonable, does not yield a sensible result, or leads to "some absurdity, or some repugnance or inconsistency with the rest of the instrument."[30] Many of the same courts also include the whole contract, circumstances, and purpose(s). The ordinary meaning, then, is a factor to be weighed with other factors. This combination makes sense because an interpreter cannot give contract language its ordinary meaning without considering at least some of the context in which the parties used the language.[31] Once we know the words in issue, the whole document, the circumstances, and the contract's purpose(s), we have a context for attributing apt ordinary meanings to the words.

---

[28] 247 F.3d 300 (1st Cir. 2001).

[29] *Id.* at 302–03.

[30] Ravetto v. Triton Thalassic Technologies, Inc., 941 A.2d 309, 323–24 (Conn. 2008); *USA Life One Ins. Co.*, 682 N.E.2d at 539.

[31] *Cf.* Iowa Fuel & Minerals, Inc. v. Iowa State Bd. of Regents, 471 N.W.2d 859, 863 (distinguishing ordinary meanings as used in the contract from dictionary definitions of individual words); § 2.1.3.

The dictionary may provide candidates for ordinary meaning(s). Selecting the correct meaning from the lists of meanings in a dictionary, however, depends explicitly or implicitly on the conventions of language in the context of use.

It should be emphasized that the interpretive issue in a case is not like the question, "What is a tomato?" This kind of question probably will have more than one answer in ordinary English. (A tomato may be a fruit, a vegetable, or *sui generis.*) Instead, the question should be, "Is a tomato a *vegetable* within the meaning of this contract?" The parties are not bound to use *vegetable* in the sense in which botanists use it, if there is one such sense. Contract parties can use the word differently. Objectivism holds that the goal of respecting the contractual freedoms requires legal interpreters to pursue the reasonable meaning of the parties' manifestations of intention, taking into account the contract's purposes, the objective circumstances, and other objective elements.

We may suspect that many courts appear to rely on ordinary meanings alone when interpretive questions are easy. It then would be pedantic to explain how other interpretive elements give context to the words. For example, in one case, an automobile insurance policy provided coverage for personal or bodily injury to an insured "because of an auto accident."[32] The court found that the insured

> fell down a hill as a result of slipping on ice or snow. The automobile in question did not cause or contribute to the fall. Indeed, [the insured] had completely alighted from the vehicle. Falling after one has exited a parked car does not constitute an "auto accident." This is a slip-and-fall case, not an auto accident.[33]

Nonetheless, the parties often are speakers of ordinary English. They can be expected to cast their contracts in ordinary English in most situations. When they do, their manifestations of intention normally should be interpreted accordingly. Thus, even the generally subjectivist Restatement (Second) of Contracts [Restatement (Second)] makes ordinary meanings a key consideration (unless the parties have manifested a different intention or the words have a technical meaning).[34] If, however, an ordinary meaning would lead to unreasonableness, harshness, absurdity,

---

[32] Nat'l Gen. Ins. Co. v. Felty, 2007 WL 689544 (E.D.Ky. 2007).

[33] *Id.* at *3.

[34] RESTATEMENT (SECOND) OF CONTRACTS § 202(3)(a) (1981).

or some repugnance or inconsistency with the rest of the document, a court should reject the ordinary meaning.[35]

§ 2.2.5. *Trade Usages and Customs*

Contract parties do not always use words in their ordinary senses. They may give words special definitions stated in the contract. Sometimes they use technical terms or terms of art within a profession or industry, as when they participate in a specific trade and reasonably expect each other to employ special usages in the trade. They may reasonably understand words with more particularity or generality than a dictionary meaning provides. On all of these occasions and others, a word or phrase in a contract may have an unusual (but nonetheless conventional) meaning. This is especially true of trade usages and customs, which exist within a context that is more particularized to the parties than ordinary English and where the conventions of the relevant practice may give some terms special or technical meanings.

The Uniform Commercial Code (UCC) encourages reliance on trade usages for cases within its scope of application, including transactions in goods.[36] Trade usages commonly are employed in insurance cases.[37] The UCC defines a trade usage very broadly as follows:

> A "usage of trade" is any practice or method of dealing having such regularity of observance in a place, vocation, or trade as to justify an expectation that it will be observed with respect to the transaction in question.[38]

There are, however, much narrower definitions of a trade usage or custom, requiring that both parties know of the usage or that it be of long standing, notorious, well-established, and invariable, at the time when and place where the contract was made, so that they should have known.[39]

---

35 *USA Life One Ins. Co.*, 682 N.E.2d at 539; Simeone v. First Bank Nat. Ass'n, 971 F.2d 103, 107 (8th Cir. 1992).

36 UCC §§ 1-102, 2-102 (2001).

37 *E.g.*, City Fuel Corp. v. National Fire Ins. Co. of Hartford, 846 N.E.2d 775, 776 (Mass. 2006); Quinlivan v. EMCASCO Ins. Co., 414 N.W.2d 494, 497 (Minn.App. 1987).

38 UCC § 303(c) (2001). *See also* Restatement (Second) of Contracts § 222(1) (1981).

39 *E.g.*, SR Intern. Business Ins. Co., Ltd. v. World Trade Center Prop., LLC, 467 F.3d 107, 134 (2d Cir. 2006); Mullinnex LLC v. HKB Royalty Trust, 126 P.3d 909, 918–22 (Wyo. 2006).

According to the UCC, a usage of trade in the vocation or trade in which the parties are engaged, or of which they are or should be aware, is relevant in interpretation even if a contract is not ambiguous.[40] Some courts, however, require a finding of ambiguity on the basis of ordinary meaning before considering evidence of a trade usage.[41] Though the UCC provides that express terms, any course of performance, and any course of dealing have priority over a usage of trade,[42] the courts often have occasion to allow fact-finders to employ such usages when interpreting a contract.[43]

§ 2.2.6. Legal Precedents and Statutory Definitions

A few courts consult legal precedents or statutory definitions when interpreting a contract.[44] A term that appears in the disputed contract may have a definition or an interpretation in such legal sources—a legal meaning. These courts sometimes apply legal meanings presumptively to the same words in the contract in the case at hand, as when an insurance policy provides coverage for liability for "unfair competition," which is a legal cause of action.[45] The evidence, however, may show that an ordinary meaning should prevail over a legal meaning because the ordinary meaning better reflects the parties' intention. Much care is needed to avoid taking definitions or interpretations out of context, producing an arbitrary result in the case at hand in relation to the parties' intention.[46] Thus, the parties' intention, as revealed by the contract's purpose, the circumstances, and other elements special to the case in question, may prevail over a legal meaning in many cases.[47]

In *Petula Associates, Ltd. v. Dolco Packaging Corp.*,[48] a lease of commercial property gave the lessee an option to purchase the property for fair market value. The lease required the parties to agree on the *fair market*

---

[40] UCC § 303(d); § 2-202, com. 1(c) (2001).

[41] *E.g.*, Langer v. Bartholomay, 745 N.W.2d 649, 656 (N.D. 2008); Milonas v. Public Employment Relations Bd., 648 N.Y.S.2d 779, 784 (App.Div. 1996).

[42] UCC § 303(e) (2001). *See also* Restatement (Second) of Contracts §203(b) (1981).

[43] *E.g.*, Nanakuli Paving & Rock Co. v. Shell Oil Co., 664 F.2d 772 (9th Cir. 1981).

[44] *E.g.*, In re Estate of Uzelac, 114 P.3d 1164, 1168–69 (Utah 2005).

[45] Bank of the West v. Superior Court, 833 P.2d 545, 552 (Cal. 1992).

[46] *See, e.g.*, World Trade Center Props., L.L.C. v. Hartford Fire Ins. Co., 345 F.3d 154, 186–87 (2d Cir. 2003).

[47] Utica City Nat. Bank v. Gunn, 118 N.E. 607, 608 (N.Y. 1918) (Cardozo, J).

[48] 240 F.3d 499 (5th Cir. 2001).

value, and it defined the term by setting forth a list of factors for the parties to take into account.[49] A dispute arose when the lessee exercised the option, but the parties failed to agree on the price. The US Court of Appeals for the Fifth Circuit, applying Texas law, looked to Texas precedents that defined fair market value as "the price a piece of property would receive on the open market if the seller and buyer were not compelled to enter into the transaction."[50] It ruled broadly that,

> [c]onsequently, when the term "fair market value" is used in a contract governed by Texas law, it may be presumed that the parties intended the term to be understood according to this meaning, absent a clear indication to the contrary.[51]

The Texas precedent that the court consulted, however, involved a condemnation proceeding.[52] The court did not consider whether the contract's listed factors were consistent with the meaning of fair market value in such a proceeding. Nor did the court consider whether an option to purchase under a lease presents a different context requiring a different interpretation. Perhaps it would so require when the lessee paid for improvements to the property, which improvements raised its fair market value under the condemnation definition. The lessee should not have to pay for those improvements twice. It is conceivable, then, that the difference in the contexts should make a difference in the meaning. Moreover, the court's presumption that the parties (objectively or subjectively) *intended* the term to have the meaning it had in a condemnation proceeding is far-fetched. The Restatement (Second) wisely disapproves of the use of legal meanings drawn from other contexts.[53]

Nonetheless, there is a kind of contract that some courts will, and the Restatement (Second) suggests they should, interpret in light of legal precedent among other elements.[54] This is the standardized agreement, such as a typical insurance policy. (A standardized agreement may or may not be a contract of adhesion, but this makes no difference on a question

---

49 *Id.* at 502.

50 *Id.* at 503.

51 *Id.*

52 State v. Windham, 837 S.W.2d 73 (Tex. 1992).

53 Restatement (Second) of Contracts § 201, cmt. c. (1981); *see* Flintkote Co. v. General Acc. Assur. Co., 410 F.Supp.2d 875, 887 (N.D.Cal. 2006); Della Ratta, Inc. v. American Better Community Developers, Inc., 380 A.2d 627, 634–35 (Md.App. 1977).

54 Restatement (Second) of Contracts § 211(2) (1981).

of contract interpretation.[55]) In a departure from its generally subjectivist perspective, the Restatement (Second) says,

> [a standardized agreement] is interpreted wherever reasonable as treating alike all those similarly situated, without regard to their knowledge or understanding of the standard terms of the writing.[56]

This provision strips the parties' mental intentions from the interpretation of a standardized contract. It indicates that a court should give the words in such a contract their legal meanings in the precedents when the precedents involve the same words in a similar standardized agreement between similarly situated parties.

In a very abstract way, legal meanings are a part of the objective context within which the parties contract. They often are too remote from the parties' minds, however, to shed light on their subjective intentions. It also should be asked whether they are too remote to be part of the context in which the parties used the words, as when a reasonable person in the parties' shoes would be unaware of the legal meaning and have no reason to be aware of it. When too remote, a legal meaning of a word is outside the contract's context and the scope of objective interpretation.

§ 2.2.7. Practical Construction (Course of Performance)

A practical construction, which the UCC calls a *course of performance*,[57] concerns the parties' conduct *after* a contract was formed and before a dispute arises. It usually involves conduct in the performance of the contract. To count as a practical construction, one party must engage in repeated conduct over a considerable period of time, and the other party must accept or acquiesce in it with knowledge of the conduct and an opportunity to object to it.[58] For example, in *Coliseum Towers Associates v. County of Nassau*,[59] a lease was unclear as to whether the landlord or the tenant was obligated to pay the real property taxes. The tenant, not under protest and without objection by the landlord, paid the taxes for seven years. The court

---

[55] Rory v. Continental Ins. Co., 703 N.W.2d 23, 41 (Mich. 2005).

[56] RESTATEMENT (SECOND) OF CONTRACTS § 211(2) (1981).

[57] UCC § 303(1) (2001).

[58] *Id.*; Coliseum Towers Assoc. v. County of Nassau, 769 N.Y.S.2d 293, 296 (App.Div. 2003); Georgiades v. Glickman, 75 N.W.2d 573, 576–77 (Wis. 1956).

[59] *Coliseum Towers Assoc.* 769 N.Y.S.2s at 296.

held that the lease obligated the tenant to pay the taxes. The meaning of an ambiguous contract thus can be determined by the subsequent conduct of one party, acquiesced in by the other, before a dispute arises. Such interpretation is objective because it is based on conduct—a manifestation of intention, though an *ex post* one—that indicates how the parties' used ambiguous language on the point in question. (A practical construction also may ripen into a waiver or modification.[60])

§ 2.3. Subjectivist Elements

The difference between objective and subjective elements lies primarily in the kinds of inferences that an interpreter draws from the contract's text and contextual facts. Both theories take into account, for example, the circumstances surrounding the making of the contract in question. Subjectivism draws inferences, from all of the circumstances, past and present, and any other relevant evidence, to what the parties had in mind when speaking or hearing, writing, or reading the contract's language. The Supreme Court of Oklahoma expressed the subjectivist's credo this way:

> In considering this transaction we must place ourselves as far as possible in the position of the parties when the contract was entered into and consider the instrument itself as drawn, its purposes and the circumstances surrounding the transaction, and, from a consideration of all the elements, determine upon what sense or meaning of the terms used their minds actually met.[61]

Objectivism, by contrast, infers *reasonable* meaning(s) from the parties' manifestations of intention in the light of the circumstances, whether or not the meaning(s) reflect what the parties had in mind as the meaning of the terms they used. Objectivism holds that reasonable meanings stem from the parties' use of language in the objective context and the conventions of language use within that context. It excludes elements that bear only on the parties' states of mind.[62] Subjectivism, by contrast, considers all relevant evidence, including evidence of the elements discussed above

---

[60] UCC § 303(f) (2001).

[61] Altshuler v. Malloy, 388 P.2d 1, 4 (Okl. 1964); *see* Burkons v. Ticor Title Ins. Co. of Calif., 813 P.2d 710, 716 (Ariz. 1991).

[62] *See, e.g.*, Ginsberg v. Mascia, 182 A.2d 4, 6 (Conn. 1962).

in this chapter and below in this section. Subjectivism assumes that more context gets an interpreter closer to the parties' subjective intentions.

§ 2.3.1. Prior Course of Dealing

Especially in commercial relationships, parties may deal with each other through a sequence of similar contracts over time. Prior contracts, and the parties' conduct in performance of them, may establish a course of dealing that is relevant to interpreting a later agreement in the sequence.[63] The UCC defines a *course of dealing* as follows:

> A "course of dealing" is a sequence of conduct concerning previous transactions between the parties to a particular transaction that is fairly to be regarded as establishing a common basis of understanding for interpreting their expressions and other conduct.[64]

Unlike a usage of trade—which concerns what parties like those to the contract in question generally understand or do in similar situations—a course of dealing concerns what the parties to the contract in question did together before it was formed. Unlike a practical construction—which concerns what the parties did after concluding the contract in question—a course of dealing concerns what the parties did before the contract in question was concluded. Like a practical construction, however, a course of dealing must be a sequence of conduct over time, accepted without objection.[65]

For example, in *American Federation of State, County and Municipal Employees v. City of Benton, Arkansas,*[66] a union contract with the City of Benton provided that:

> The Employer [the City] shall continue to provide health, accidental death and dismemberment, disability, life and retirement insurance. Employee and employee dependent's health insurance coverage is set forth in Appendix B.[67]

---

[63] Ray Tucker & Sons v. GTE Directories Sales Corp., 571 N.W.2d 64, 69 (Neb. 1997).

[64] UCC § 1-303(b) (2001). *See also* RESTATEMENT (SECOND) OF CONTRACTS § 223(1).

[65] Kern Oil and Refining Co. v. Tenneco Oil Co., 792 F.2d 1380, 1385 (9th Cir. 1986).

[66] 2007 WL 496760, *1 (E.D. Ark. 2007).

[67] *Id.*

Appendix B stated: "The City of Benton shall provide insurance coverage for each employee while employed with the City of Benton." The union argued that "continue to provide health . . . and retirement insurance" within the meaning of the contract meant that the City had to pay employees health insurance after retirement. The City argued to the contrary that Appendix B clearly stated that the insurance obligation applied only to current employees. Apparently, the City had provided health and retirement insurance to union-represented retirees for over thirteen years. The court held that, despite the language in Appendix B, this course of dealing entitled union-represented retirees to health insurance paid for by the City.[68]

Some courts will call other kinds of dealings between the parties a course of dealing and, consequently, take other kinds of evidence into account. In one case,[69] the contract called for a contractor to clean "debris and residue from pores and cracks" in a structure and to remove "asbestos-containing materials . . . to a degree that no traces of debris or residue are visible. . . ." The issue was whether the contract required the contractor to remove asbestos from the pores and cracks: Were asbestos-containing materials in pores and cracks "debris and residue" within the meaning of the contract? After finding that the plain language of the contract required the contractor to remove visible asbestos from within the pores and cracks, the court considered what it called the parties' "course of dealing" to confirm this interpretation. It indicated that the original specifications for the job distinguished between friable and non-friable materials. Friable materials were to be removed "to a degree that no traces of debris or residue are visible." Non-friable materials "shall be cleaned until no residue is visible other than that which is embedded in the pores, cracks, or other small voids below the surface of the material." The contractor's representative had noted the difference in a conference call, indicating that he understood the visibility standard to require that no asbestos remain in the pores and cracks. By the most common definition of a course of dealing, however, this evidence was not it. The court was considering the course of negotiations leading to the contract.

A course of dealing is a subjective element because it particularizes the inquiry to the contract parties and bears only on the parties' probable states of mind. It shows "a common basis of understanding" between the

---

[68] *Id.* at *3.

[69] *Teig-Paradigm Environmental*, 465 F.3d, at 1339–40.

parties, not what would be a reasonable interpretation of the language in its objective context when it was used. In this respect, it is different from a trade usage or practical construction, both of which may show both a reasonable interpretation and a common basis of understanding. A subjective element bears only on *the parties'* states of mind.

§ 2.3.2. The Course of Negotiations

Parol evidence, including evidence of the course of negotiations leading to the contract in question, generally is admissible for the purpose of resolving ambiguities.[70] If the evidence or its significance is contested, the question of meaning usually is for the fact-finder, often a jury.[71] Because jury deliberations are secret, it is hard to find reported cases that detail how to use evidence of the course of negotiations. Review on appeal is not *de novo*.

We can suppose, however, that deletions to a draft document can reveal the parties' subjective intentions when they agree to the text on a subsequently contested issue. If a word or clause or more was deleted, and the parties agreed on a final text omitting that language, the final text does not mean whatever the deleted text provided unless it was removed due to a redundancy. A deletion followed by the addition of substitute language also can reveal the parties' subjective intentions.[72] The addition may broaden or qualify the document's meaning, so the ambiguity can be resolved accordingly, all else being equal. Solely adding to a draft in itself probably is less significant. The final text contains the added language; there is no point to considering the course of negotiations. An addition takes on significance when the court allows a party to testify as to its intention in making an ambiguous addition, or when the court admits negotiating documents, such as a party's letter or email, explaining its reason for proposing or accepting an addition. Moreover, the give-and-take of negotiations, though not involving deletions or additions to the specific governing language, can ground inferences as to the parties' subjective intentions or purposes.[73]

---

[70] *See* § 3.1.1.

[71] *See* § 5.1.

[72] *See* Sound of Music Co. v. Minn. Min. & Mfg. Co., 477 F.3d 910, 916–17 (7th Cir. 2007); Stroud v. Stroud, 641 S.E.2d 142, 146 (Va.App. 2007).

[73] *See* United Rentals, Inc., v. RAM Holdings, Inc., 937 A.2d 810, 830–46(Del.Ch. 2007); Reardon v. Kelly Services, Inc., 210 Fed. Appx. 456, 462–62 (6th Cir. 2006).

A number of specific interpretive guidelines concerning the course of negotiations reflect a focus on subjective intentions. Thus, an interpreter should give separately negotiated or added terms more weight than standardized terms.[74] Handwritten terms prevail over typewritten or printed terms, while typewritten terms prevail over printed terms.[75]

A striking example using a course of negotiations is *Paul W. Abbott, Inc. v. Axel Newman Heating and Plumbing Co., Inc.*[76] A plumbing contractor and a plumbing insulation subcontractor sued a city for work done in insulating domestic water piping below finished ceilings in the city's fire stations. The contract said: "All domestic water piping and rainwater piping installed above finished ceilings under this specification shall be insulated."[77] This sentence was ambiguous because the phrase "installed above finished ceilings" might modify both "domestic water piping" and "rainwater piping," or instead only "rainwater piping." A dispute arose over this ambiguity. Prior to submitting its bid, however, the office of the city architect advised the contractor that the intent of the specification was that the contractor would insulate all domestic water piping, and also rainwater piping installed above finished ceilings. Without further ado, the contractor submitted its bid. The court held that the contractor was obligated to perform the work in conformity with this mutual understanding.[78] The subcontractor, however, was not so obligated because it was not a party to the conversation.[79] Consequently, the specification had one meaning as between the city and the contractor and a different meaning as between the contractor and the subcontractor.[80]

We should note three qualifications: (1) the negotiating history does not include information available to only one party, unless the information is relevant to prove that a party did or did not know of a trade usage or custom;[81] (2) that two provisions were added at different times, reflecting negotiations, might not be relevant;[82] and (3) the Restatement (Second) provides that written, integrated standardized agreements generally are

---

[74] Restatement (Second) of Contracts § 203(d) (1981).

[75] Bristol-Myers-Squibb Co. v. Ikon Office Solutions, Inc., 295 F.3d 680, 685 (7th Cir. 2002).

[76] 166 N.W.2d 323 (Minn. 1969).

[77] *Id.* at 324.

[78] *Id.* at 324–25.

[79] *Id.* at 325.

[80] *Id.*

[81] Gaydos v. White Motor Corp., 220 N.W.2d 697, 701 (Mich.App. 1974).

[82] *Kinek*, 22 F.3d at 509.

"interpreted wherever reasonable as treating alike all those similarly situated, without regard to their knowledge or understanding of the standard terms of the writing."[83] This provision adopts the objective standard and therefore excludes the course of negotiations in a particular case except with respect to non-standard terms.

§ 2.3.3. A Party's Testimony as to Its Intention

Many courts, taking a subjective approach for the purpose of resolving ambiguities, allow a party to testify in court as to its own intent when negotiating or signing the contract in question.[84] Obviously, such testimony may be self-serving, or otherwise false due to a faulty memory or fear of the consequences of testifying honestly, as in the case of a continuing corporate employee. Courts that allow a party's testimony probably believe that the fact-finder, usually a jury, is sufficiently capable of detecting and discounting unreliable testimony about past intentions. Others seriously doubt that this is so and exclude such testimony.[85] The latter courts may believe that detection is too difficult, especially when a party has convinced itself of the truth of its false testimony. These doubts do not apply when a party testifies against its interest.[86] No illustration is needed on this obvious element.

§ 2.3.4. Subjective Circumstances

Subjectivist interpreters take into account circumstances bearing only on the parties' subjective intentions, though not to the exclusion of the

---

[83] RESTATEMENT (SECOND) OF CONTRACTS § 211(2) (1981).

[84] *E.g.*, Flying J Inc. v. Comdata Network, Inc., 405 F.3d 821, 834 (10th Cir. 2005); American Bank of Commerce v. M & G Builders, Ltd., 586 P.2d 1079, 1082 (N.M. 1978); Public Service Co. of Okla. v. Home Builders Ass'n of Realtors, Inc., 554 P.2d 1181, 1185 (Okl. 1976); Int'l Ass'n Machinists and Aerospace Workers Lodge No. 1194 v. Sargent Industries, 522 F.2d 280, 283–84 (6th Cir. 1975).

[85] *Coliseum Towers Assocs.*, 769 N.Y.S.2d at 29. *See also* Posner, *supra* note 2, at 1593–95; Joseph M. Perillo, *The Origins of the Objective Theory of Contract Formation and Interpretation*, 69 FORDHAM L. REV. 427, *passim* (2000).

[86] *See* Metropolitan Area Transit, Inc. v. Nicholson, 463 F.3d 1256, 1260 (Fed. Cir. 2006); *Stroud*, 641 S.E.2d at 146.

circumstances described above, which bear on their objective intentions.[87] The latter circumstances also may bear on the parties' subjective intentions. Again, the distinction depends on the target of the inferences that an interpreter draws from the circumstances.[88] A subjectivist court may consider some of the elements discussed above, such as the parties' prior course of dealing and the course of negotiations, as a part of the circumstances.[89] When these elements are so considered, the circumstances bear only on the parties' subjective intentions. An objectivist interpreter, by contrast, would not consider the parties' prior course of dealing or the course of negotiations to be a part of the circumstances relevant to interpretation. These elements are specific to the parties and would not be taken into account by a reasonable person giving meaning to the contract's language.

§ 2.4. Guides to Interpretation

§ 2.4.1. "Standards of Preference in Interpretation"

The Restatement (Second) distinguishes between so-called "rules in aid of interpretation" and "standards of preference in interpretation." The distinction is obscure. We can make sense of it, however, by considering the specifics that fall under each of these rubrics in terms of elements, which are factual and susceptible to proof, and guides to interpretation, which are legally normative considerations. The Restatement (Second's) rules in aid of interpretation, which are not "rules" but factors to be considered, thus include the circumstances, the parties' principal purpose, a written document as a whole, the generally prevailing meaning of contract language, and the course of performance, all of which are elements.[90] The standards of preference in interpretation, by contrast, tell an interpreter how to weigh competing elements when several are evidenced in a

---

87 Matter of Riconda, 688 N.E.2d 248, 251–53 (N.Y. 1997); Muskingum Coal Co. v. Eastern Hocking Coal Co., 122 N.E.2d 408, 411 (Ohio App. 1953); Thermalito Irrigation Dist. v. California Water Service Co., 239 P.2d 109, 116 (Cal.App. 1951).

88 *See* § 2.3.

89 Mobil Exploration and Producing U.S., Inc. v. Dover Energy Exploration, L.L.C., 6 S.W.3d 772, 776–77 (Tex.App. 2001); Hamilton v. Wosepka, 154 N.W.2d 164, 171 (Iowa 1967).

90 Restatement (Second) of Contracts § 202 (1981).

case and are conflicting. The standards of preference are set forth in Section 203(a) as follows:

> In the interpretation of a promise or agreement or a term thereof, the following standards of preference are generally applicable:
>
> (a) an interpretation which gives a reasonable, lawful, and effective meaning to all the terms is preferred to an interpretation which leaves a part unreasonable, unlawful, or of no effect;
>
> (b) express terms are given greater weight than course of performance, course of dealing, and usage of trade, course of performance is given greater weight than course of dealing or usage of trade, and course of dealing is given greater weight than usage of trade;
>
> (c) specific terms and exact terms are given greater weight than general language;
>
> (d) separately negotiated or added terms are given greater weight than standardized terms or other terms not separately negotiated.[91]

Subsection (a) does not merely identify elements. It compactly bundles three components, each of which guides interpretation. It may enhance clarity if we unbundle them here. First, subsection (a) states the mere surplusage rule, which holds that all of the words in an agreement should be given some effect, if possible. This rule presumes that the parties did not intend any words in their contract to be idle. Second, the subsection prefers interpretations that give a reasonable meaning to all of the contract's terms. Third, the subsection prefers interpretations that give a lawful meaning to all of the contract's terms. Each component rests normatively on the goal of ascertaining the normal parties' intention by assuming that the parties intended all of their contract terms to be reasonable, lawful, and effective. The lawfulness component also may reflect overriding considerations of public policy.

Subsections (b) through (d) also do not merely identify elements, as do the rules in aid of interpretation. Rather, the subsections guide the weighing of elements otherwise identified, though only in a bipolar manner. (Three or four or more elements may compete in a case, requiring a more sophisticated guide for weighing elements.[92]) These standards of preference rest on the goal of implementing the parties' subjective intentions. Thus, the contract's express terms are supposed to reflect

---

[91] *Id.* at § 203.

[92] *See* § 6.2.1.

the parties' intention in a particular contract in question better than any course of performance, course of dealing, or usage of trade. Indeed, subsection (b)'s hierarchy consists of increasingly more general elements of interpretation, increasingly remote from the parties' minds when making the contract in question. Subsection (c) gives a preference to which of two conflicting terms the parties better focused on, *i.e.*, the more specific term, again reflecting the subjective theory. Subsection (d), yet again reflecting the subjective theory, gives the course of negotiations, which are particular to the parties, preference over standardized terms, which are not. Again, this preference focuses on that which the parties focused on, better implementing their subjective intentions.

§ 2.4.2. Canons of Interpretation

The whole contract lays a basis for bringing into play many of the canons of contract construction. They are guides to interpretation, not elements as the term is used here. It is easy to apply the canons of construction, so the main ones will be mentioned briefly. One canon holds that all of the words of an agreement should be construed wherever possible as consistent with one another—to produce a harmonious whole.[93] Another holds that all of the words in an agreement should be given effect if possible (the mere surplusage rule).[94] A third holds that specific terms prevail over general terms if there is a conflict.[95] A fourth, *expressio unis est exclusio alterius* (when one thing is expressed, all excluded things are omitted), is not often used.[96] *Ejusdem generis* provides that, when general, catch-all words (such as "all other causes") follow a sequence of specific words (such as a list of *force majeure* events), the general words have the discrete characteristics of the specific words.[97] *Noscitur a sociis* says that words or terms in a contract should be understood with reference to those that accompany them.[98] And a word's meaning in one part of a contract is

---

[93] *E.g.*, *Kinek*, 22 F.3d at 509; Coker v. Coker, 650 S.W.2d 391, 393 (Tex. 1983); RESTATEMENT (SECOND) OF CONTRACTS § 202(5) (1981).

[94] *E.g.*, Malleolo v. Malleolo, 731 N.Y. S.2d 752, 753 (App.Div. 2001); Fraternal Order of Police, Lodge No. 69 v. City of Fairmont, 468 S.E.2d 712, 718 (W.Va. 1996).

[95] *Iowa Fuel & Minerals*, 471 N.W.2d at 863.

[96] LaSalle Nat. Bank v. Triumvera Homeowners Ass'n, 440 N.E.2d 1073, 1084 (Ill.App. 1982).

[97] In re Enron Creditors Recovery Corp., 380 B.R. 307, 322–23 (S.D.N.Y. 2008).

[98] Resource Bank v. Progressive Cas. Ins. Co., 503 F.Supp.2d 789, 796 (E.D.Va. 2007).

presumed to be its meaning wherever it appears.[99] Most courts now reject (as they should) a canon which says that the first of two clauses set forth in a contract presumptively prevails over a conflicting later one.[100] A further rule that some think of as a canon of interpretation, though it is a default rule because it has nothing to do with the parties' intention, provides that ambiguities shall be resolved against the drafter.[101] (Note that, in a broad sense, all of the rules and standards of interpretation may be thought of as canons of construction. Note also that some courts treat the canons as discretionary, subordinating them to the parties' intention when otherwise shown.[102])

Some canons, though not canons of interpretation, reflect public policy rather than aids in ascertaining the parties' intention. These canons are available to an interpreter only when resolving an ambiguity. Thus, if a contract or term is relevantly ambiguous, and one meaning-branch of the ambiguity violates public policy, that branch obviously should be excluded, leaving the other meaning as the unambiguous meaning. Arguably, the resolution of ambiguities against the insurer in insurance contracts, special canons enacted by legislatures for specific kinds of contracts, and other similar canons, are based on public policy or other non-interpretive considerations.[103]

§ 2.4.3. Good Faith in Interpretation

In every contract, there is an implied covenant of good faith and fair dealing.[104] It sometimes controls the question of ambiguity. One meaning-branch of an ambiguity might allow a party to perform the contract in bad faith. When this is so, the other meaning-branch should be adopted as the unambiguous meaning:

> Every contract implies good faith and fair dealing between the parties to it, and where an instrument is susceptible of two conflicting

---

[99] ML Direct, Inc. v. TIG Specialty Ins. Co., 93 Cal.Rptr.2d 846, 850 (Cal.App. 2000).

[100] *Compare* Extermitech, Inc. v. Glasscock, Inc., 951 So.2d 689, 694 (Ala. 2006) *with* Mealey v. Kanealy, 286 N.W. 500, 502–03 (Iowa 1939).

[101] *See* §§ 5.3.1, 5.3.2.

[102] One South, Inc. v. Hollowell, 963 So.2d 1156, 1162 (Miss. 2007).

[103] 20th Century Ins. Co. v. Super. Ct., 109 Cal. Rptr. 2d 611 (Cal.App. 2001); Bullwinkel v. New Eng. Mut. Life Ins. Co., 18 F.3d 429, 431 (7th Cir. 1994).

[104] UCC § 1-304 (2001); RESTATEMENT (SECOND) OF CONTRACTS § 205 (1981).

> constructions, one [of] which imputes bad faith to one of the parties and the other does not, the latter construction should be adopted.[105]

This is not the place to elaborate on what good faith and fair dealing permit or require of a party.[106] Suffice it to say that the implied covenant is not an element but, instead, is a guide to interpretation (as well as an implied term). Like the Restatement (Second)'s standards of preference in interpretation, it helps an interpreter choose between conflicting meanings advanced by the parties.

§ 2.5. Relevant Non-Interpretive Rules

The Restatement (Second) prefers a different tack, though it is not followed by most courts. Adopting a strikingly subjective theory, its main provision on interpretation says that:

> Where the parties have attached the same meaning to a promise or agreement or a term thereof, it is interpreted in accordance with that meaning.[107]

There are, however, very few cases indeed in which a court has found that the parties both attached the same meaning.[108] The question of a shared meaning arises only when there is an interpretive dispute. Though it is possible for a party to contend for a meaning that is different from a meaning that both parties attached when the contract was formed, proof of the past shared meaning is likely to be difficult. Moreover, realistically, many interpretive disputes probably arise when neither party attached a relevant meaning to the contested language when the contract was formed. The language of contracts of even moderate complexity governs many disputes that the parties (and their lawyers, if any) did not think about.

---

[105] Martindell v. Lake Shore Nat'l Bank, 154 N.E.2d 683, 690 (Ill. 1958). *See also* Milstein v. Security Pac. Nat'l Bank, 103 Cal. Rptr. 16, 18–19 (Cal.App. 1972); Ryder Truck Rental, Inc. v. Central Packing Co., 341 F.2d 321, 323–24 (10th Cir. 1965).

[106] *See generally* 2 E. ALLAN FARNSWORTH, FARNSWORTH ON CONTRACTS § 7.17b (3d ed. 2004); STEVEN J. BURTON & ERIC G. ANDERSEN, CONTRACTUAL GOOD FAITH: FORMATION, PERFORMANCE, BREACH AND ENFORCEMENT (1995); RESTATEMENT (SECOND) OF CONTRACTS § 205 (1981); Steven J. Burton, *Breach of Contract and the Common Law Duty to Perform in Good Faith*, 94 HARV. L. REV. 369 (1980).

[107] RESTATEMENT (SECOND) OF CONTRACTS § 201(1) (1981).

[108] FARNSWORTH, *supra* note 106, at § 7.9, p. 279.

Pace the Restatement (Second),[109] the courts generally do not dismiss such cases due to a failure of mutual assent; rather, most courts apply the contract's language, interpreting it in light of the relevant elements.

What happens, though, under the Restatement (Second) when the parties attached different meanings to contested language? For these cases, which are common, it shifts from an interpretive rule ((§ 201(1)) to a fault principle:

> Where the parties have attached different meanings to a promise or agreement or a term thereof, it is interpreted in accordance with the meaning attached by one of them if at the time the agreement was made
>
> (a) that party did not know of any different meaning attached by the other, and the other knew the meaning attached by the first party; or
>
> (b) that party had no reason to know of any different meaning attached by the other, and the other had reason to know of the meaning attached by the first party.[110]

Put more simply, this provision penalizes the party that could have forestalled the dispute by drafting the contract more carefully. It favors the other party's meaning. In some jurisdictions, it is an important supplement to interpretation, though it can involve difficult problems of proof. But the rule, as a fault rule, does not aim to implement the parties' (objective or subjective) agreement based on the elements of contract interpretation. It is therefore a non-interpretive rule for resolving interpretive disputes.

There are other non-interpretive rules for resolving interpretive disputes. These are default or closure rules, which apply when the parties have not otherwise agreed—that is, when interpretation fails. The most prominent of these is the rule requiring, usually as a last resort, interpretation against the drafter when there is only one.[111] Again, this rule penalizes the party that could have forestalled the dispute by drafting the contract more carefully. It is based on a fault principle, not the parties' agreement, and is not an element of or guide for interpretation. There are a good many such default rules, especially under the UCC.[112]

---

[109] Restatement (Second) of Contracts § 201(3) (1981) (failure of mutual assent occurs when the parties attached different meanings and neither knew nor should have known of the meaning attached by the other).

[110] Restatement (Second) of Contracts § 201(2) (1981).

[111] *See* § 5.3.2.

[112] UCC § 1-302 (2001).

CHAPTER 3

Identifying the Terms

Before determining whether a contract is ambiguous or resolving any ambiguity that may be found, it is crucial to identify the text to be given meaning—the terms of the contract. Broadly speaking, the *terms* are the linguistic formulations, oral or written, manifesting the parties' agreement. The parties' contractual relations—their rights, duties, and powers—stem primarily from the agreed terms.

For oral contracts, there are few special problems when identifying the contract's express terms. The parties and any witnesses will testify to what was said when promises were made or exchanged. The identification of terms is a matter of fact. For written contracts, however, there are a number of special issues when a party offers parol evidence, including legal issues. The doctrine governing these issues is known as the parol evidence rule. Written contracts and this rule are the subjects of this chapter.

§ 3.1. The Parol Evidence Rule

Professor James Bradley Thayer famously said of the parol evidence rule: "[F]ew things are darker than this or fuller of subtle difficulties."[1]

---

1 James B. Thayer, *The "Parol Evidence" Rule*, 6 HARV. L. REV. 325, 325 (1893).

Indeed, judicial opinions stating and applying this rule can be confusing, and the treatises often are little better. There is one major reason for this—a failure to distinguish the parol evidence rule from the plain meaning and four corners rules.[2] The parol evidence rule governs the identification of a contract's terms when there is a writing.[3] It does nothing else. In particular, contrary to the views of some, the parol evidence rule is not the rule that excludes parol evidence whenever such evidence is excluded. The exclusion is a function of the four corners rule, which has this evidentiary function and may come into play *before* a court can apply either the parol evidence or the plain meaning rules.

§ 3.1.1. Statement of the Rule

The most widely endorsed version of the common law parol evidence rule may be stated in two parts as follows, synthesizing the authorities read for this study: (1) When an enforceable, written agreement is the final and complete expression of the parties' agreement, prior oral and written agreements and contemporaneous oral agreements (together, "parol agreements")[4] concerning the same subject as the writing do not establish contract terms when the parol agreement contradicts or adds to the terms of the writing; (2) in addition, when an enforceable, written agreement is the final, but not the complete, expression of the parties' agreement, a parol agreement may add to, but may not contradict, the written terms.[5] This doctrinal statement, as far as it goes, is a matter of wide consensus.[6] It hides, however, many complications.[7]

---

[2] *See* §§.3.1.1; 4.2.1; 4.2.4.

[3] *See generally* Mullinnex LLC v. HKB Royalty Trust, 126 P.3d 909, 920 (Wyo. 2006); Casa Herrera, Inc. v. Beydoun, 83 P.3d 497, 503 (Cal. 2004); Alstom Power, Inc. v. Balcke-Durr, Inc., 849 A.2d 804, 811 (Conn. 2004); Charles A. Burton, Inc. v. Durkee, 109 N.E.2d 265, 270 (Ohio 1952); 2 E. ALLAN FARNSWORTH, FARNSWORTH ON CONTRACTS § 7.2 (3d ed. 2004); JOSEPH M. PERILLO, CALAMARI AND PERILLO ON CONTRACTS § 3.2 (5th ed. 2003); Scott J. Burnham, *The Parol Evidence Rule: Don't be Afraid of the Dark,* 55 MONT. L. REV. 93, 109–20 (1994).

[4] *But see* UCC § 2-202 (2001) (not including contemporaneous written agreements).

[5] *See, e.g., Mullinnex,* 126 P.3d at 920; RESTATEMENT (SECOND) OF CONTRACTS § 213 (1981); RESTATEMENT (FIRST) OF CONTRACTS § 237 (1932); 2 FARNSWORTH, *supra* note 2, at § 7.3.

[6] *See* RESTATEMENT (FIRST) OF CONTRACTS §§ 237 *et seq.*(1932); RESTATEMENT (SECOND) OF CONTRACTS §§ 209 *et seq.* (1981).

[7] *See generally* John D. Calamari & Joseph M. Perillo, *A Plea for a Uniform Parol Evidence Rule and Principles of Contract Interpretation,* 42 IND. L.J. 333 (1967).

To elaborate on the statement, the rule applies when the parties conclude a final, or a final and complete, written contract.[8] When the contract is final but not complete, it sometimes is called a *partially integrated agreement*. When the contract is both final and complete, it sometimes is called a *completely integrated agreement*. Often, however, the courts write simply and less precisely of an *integrated agreement*. When the parties conclude an integrated agreement, they normally intend it to supersede parol agreements within its scope. That is, they *integrate* or *merge* parol agreements into the writing. The writing supplants them and becomes the sole repository of the contract's terms as of the time of contract formation.[9]

When it applies, accordingly, the rule discharges (renders ineffective and inoperative) some parol agreements that contradict or add to an integrated agreement's written terms, as the case may be. It, therefore, is a substantive rule of law, not a rule of evidence.[10] That is, it determines that the terms of an agreement are those in the written document and denies operative effect to parol agreements that are contradictory or additional to the integration. This is true whether or not evidence of the parol agreement has probative value or is prejudicial.[11] When offered to establish contract terms, the rule precludes the introduction of evidence of even relevant, probative, and non-prejudicial parol agreements, no matter what kind of evidence is involved. A rule of evidence, by contrast, typically forbids one kind of evidence—say, hearsay testimony—because it is thought to be unreliable or prejudicial. Evidence law, however, may allow proof of the same fact by another kind of evidence—say, a document. A *consequence* of the parol evidence rule is that, when the rule applies, evidence of a parol agreement is irrelevant when offered to establish an agreement's terms.[12] The rule itself, however, renders parol agreements inoperative: The terms of such agreements do not ground contract rights, duties, or powers.

---

[8] United States v. Clementon Sewerage Auth., 365 F.2d 609, 613 (3d Cir. 1966).

[9] *See Casa Herrera*, 83 P.3d at 502–03.

[10] *Id.* at 502; Abercrombie v. Hayden Corp., 883 P.2d 845, 850 (Or. 1994); 9 John Henry Wigmore, Evidence in Trials at Common Law § 2400 (Chadbourn rev. 1981) (1898); Thayer, *supra* note 1.

[11] *But see* Masterson v. Sine, 436 P.2d 561, 564 (Cal. 1968) (basing application of the parol evidence rule on the credibility of the evidence).

[12] *Alstom Power*, 849 A.2d at 811).

To avoid unnecessary confusion, note at the outset several points about the parol evidence rule. First, the predicate of the rule is that a written contract is integrated. The consequence of the rule precludes giving legally operative effect to parol agreements; put otherwise and less precisely, the rule discharges parol agreements.[13] Accordingly, simply put, the parol evidence rule says only that, *when* a contract is integrated, parol agreements are not operative. In many jurisdictions, a *four corners rule* comes into play in deciding *whether* a written contract is integrated. Thus, the four corners rule determines the relevant elements of interpretation in deciding whether the predicate of the parol evidence rule is satisfied. The parol evidence rule itself does not determine what elements a court may consider when deciding the question of integration. Therefore, the four corners rule is not the same as the parol evidence rule. Further, the parol evidence rule does not preclude the admission of parol evidence for purposes other than establishing contract terms, such as determining whether a contract is integrated or ambiguous, or for resolving an ambiguity.[14]

Second, it is often said that there are several exceptions to the parol evidence rule.[15] Examples given are that parol evidence may be admitted to prove that there was no acceptance or no consideration.[16] Such evidence may be admitted to prove fraud, mistake, illegality, unconscionability, and other invalidating causes.[17] It may be admitted to prove a condition precedent to the enforceability of a written contract.[18] Allowing proof of these matters, however, does not involve exceptions because the so-called exceptions do not implicate the parol evidence rule at all. The parol evidence in these cases is being offered for the purpose of contesting whether an enforceable contract exists, not for the purpose of establishing its terms. The rule comes into play after we have decided that the parties have made an enforceable contract.[19] The admissibility of formation

---

13 *Casa Herrera*, 83 P.3d at 503–04.

14 Berg v. Hudesman, 801 P.2d 222, 229 (Wash. 1990); Garza v. Marine Transport Lines, Inc., 861 F.2d 23, 27 (2d Cir. 1988); RESTATEMENT (SECOND) OF CONTRACTS § 214 (1981).

15 *See, e.g.*, Eric A. Posner, *The Parol Evidence Rule, The Plain Meaning Rule, and the Principles of Contractual Interpretation*, 146 U. PA. L. REV. 533, 534–35 (1998).

16 *See* § 3.3.2.

17 *See* § 3.3.2.1.

18 *See* § 3.3.2.2.

19 *E.g.*, King v. Fordice, 776 S.W.2d 608, 611–12 (Tex.App. 1989). *See also* Mark K. Glasser & Keith A. Rowley, *On Parol: The Construction and Interpretation of Written Agreements and the Role of Extrinsic Evidence in Contract Litigation*, 49 BAYLOR L. REV. 657, 720 (1997).

and invalidating parol evidence is not an exception because the parol evidence rule does not apply in the first instance.

Third, the Restatement (Second) of Contracts [Restatement (Second)] provides, and most courts hold, that parol evidence may be admitted for the purpose of showing that an agreement is or is not integrated.[20] Other courts determine whether a written agreement is integrated from the face of the document.[21] The parol evidence rule often poses no barrier to addressing the question of integration in light of relevant parol *evidence*, such as evidence of the circumstances at the time of signing. Parol agreements should be distinguished from parol evidence; the latter may not amount to an agreement and therefore would not bind either party. The parol evidence rule applies to render parol *agreements* inoperative when they are offered to establish contract terms. Moreover, parol evidence offered on the question of integration is not being offered to establish contract terms.

Fourth, a court may admit parol evidence for the purpose of giving meaning(s) to the contract's terms.[22] Evidence offered for this purpose is not being offered to establish terms. So the parol evidence rule does not apply at all; giving meaning to a term is not an exception to the rule. This can be a point of confusion in the case law and elsewhere. Hence, it should be emphasized that the parol evidence rule is not the basis for excluding parol evidence *whenever* a court excludes such evidence. In determining whether the plain meaning rule applies (*i.e.*, whether the contract is unambiguous), the four corners rule operates in many jurisdictions to preclude consideration of parol evidence. But the four corners rule is not the same as either the parol evidence or the plain meaning rules.[23]

Fifth, evidence of a subsequent written or oral agreement is parol evidence but will be admitted to show an agreement to modify a prior integrated contract.[24] Such an agreement is not a prior oral or written agreement or a contemporaneous oral agreement but, instead, is a subsequent one. Similarly, the parties' subsequent conduct is extrinsic to the document but may be effective as a practical construction to show

---

[20] Restatement (Second) of Contracts §§ 209, cmt. c, 210, cmt. b (1981).

[21] Gifford v. Gifford, 236 N.E.2d 892, 893 (Mass. 1968); Taylor v. More, 263 N.W. 537, 539 (Minn. 1935); Gianni v. R. Russel & Co., Inc., 126 A. 791, 792 (Pa. 1924).

[22] Restatement (Second) of Contracts § 214(c) (1981).

[23] *See* §§ 3.1.1; 4.2.1; 4.2.4.

[24] Material Movers, Inc. v. Hill, 316 N.W.2d 13, 17 (Minn. 1982); Indus. Nat'l Bank v. Peloso, 397 A.2d 1312, 1314 (R.I. 1979).

whether a document is integrated or to give meaning to an ambiguous term.[25] Again, a practical construction is not a prior oral or written agreement or a contemporaneous oral agreement. Further, under the parol evidence rule in Article 2 of the Uniform Commercial Code (UCC), evidence of a course of performance, course of dealing, or usage of trade, though extrinsic to a writing, is not affected by the rule.[26]

Sixth, to fall under the parol evidence rule's effect, a parol agreement must concern the same subject matter as the written contract. That is, it must be within the scope of the writing, considered as a whole.[27] Collateral agreements—those that add to a partial integration or concern unrelated matters—can have operative effect despite the rule.[28]

Seventh, some courts add that a parol agreement may not "vary" or "change" the written terms.[29] However, a variance or change would be either an addition or a contradiction. They are short-hand, less precise ways to say that a parol agreement cannot add to or contradict an integrated, written contract, as the case may be. The point is covered by the above statement of the rule.

Eighth, the rule does not operate when a party seeks reformation to correct a mistake.[30] This is a genuine exception to the rule.

Ninth, the above statement of the rule does not use the term *extrinsic evidence*, though it is in common usage. This term may be defined as evidence relating to a written contract that does not appear within the four corners of the contract.[31] It is a synonym for "parol evidence" and will be used from time to time in this book.

It should be apparent that the parol evidence rule is complex and difficult to state completely in brief. Accordingly, one should be wary of the courts' short, incomplete boilerplate statements. Often, the courts will state the rule in a short sentence and then ignore it as stated. Or they may state only those parts of the rule that are dispositive in the case at hand. Consequently, one can be misled by parsing the words in such boilerplate closely. Nonetheless, a synthesis of the specific holdings in the cases supports the rule as articulated above. In the particular, however,

---

25 J&B Steel Contractors, Inc. v. C. Iber & Sons, Inc., 642 N.E.2d 1215, 1219 (Ill. 1994).

26 UCC § 2-202 (2001).

27 *Alstom Power*, 849 A.2d at 811. *See* § 3.3.1.

28 Mitchill v. Lath, 160 N.E. 646, 647 (N.Y. 1928).

29 *E.g.*, First Data POS, Inc. v. Willis, 546 S.E.2d 781, 784 (Ga. 2001).

30 *See* § 3.3.2.3.

31 BLACK'S LAW DICTIONARY 578 (Bryant A. Gardner, ed., 7th ed. 1999).

there are significant differences among the authorities.[32] The differences will be discussed below.

§ 3.1.2. Goals of the Rule

Like any legal rule, the parol evidence rule is and should be understood, interpreted, and applied to further its goals. Several goals have been attributed to the rule. Chief among them are (1) implementing the parties' intention by giving their writing the effect they intended it to have,[33] (2) fostering the stability of contractual transactions,[34] (3) protecting the integrity and certainty of written contracts,[35] and (4) protecting writings because they are more reliable than the memories of the parties.[36]

Of these, implementing the parties' intention is the most important. It is the primary goal of contract interpretation generally. Subject to some exceptions, contract law allows the parties to make their own legal relations as an exercise of their autonomy. The exceptions to this general principle do not touch the parties' choices to integrate all of their operative agreements relating to a transaction into a final, or final and complete, written contract. When they do this, the courts should give effect to their intention to supersede the relevant parol agreements. That they do so is indicated by the universal legal principle that the question of integration turns on the parties' intention to integrate.[37] (As we saw in Chapter 1, ascertaining the parties' intention is an ambiguous goal.[38] However one resolves this ambiguity, though, the primary goal stands as a matter of abstract principle.)

An additional and also important goal is to foster the stability of contractual transactions.[39] This goal is often stated but rarely, if ever, explained. It presumes in part that some written contracts should be reliable in themselves. An integrated writing becomes the authoritative guide

---

[32] PERILLO, *supra* note 2, at § 3.2.

[33] Traudt v. Neb. Pub. Power Dist., 251 N.W.2d 148, 150–51 (Neb. 1977).

[34] Farmers Coop. Ass'n v. Garrison, 454 S.W.2d 644, 648 (Ark. 1970). *See also* Berman v. Geller, 90 N.E.2d 843, 845 (Mass. 1950).

[35] *Gianni*, 126 A. at 792.

[36] Garrett v. Ellison, 72 P.2d 449, 451–52 (Utah 1937). *See also Masterson*, 436 P.2d at 564.

[37] *E.g.*, Behrens v. S.P. Constr. Co., Inc., 904 A.2d 676, 682 (N.H. 2006).

[38] *See* § 1.1.1.

[39] Varner v. Eves, 990 P.2d 357, 361 (Or.App. 1999); Hercules & Co., Ltd. v. Shama Restaurant Corp., 613 A.2d 916, 928–29 (D.C. 1992).

to the parties' conduct under the contract. Moreover, many people and firms, not having access to evidence of parol agreements, rely on written contracts as such. Their reliance would be undercut if parol agreements could change the terms of integrated written contracts. In addition to implementing the parties' intention, two key goals of contract law are to protect reasonable expectations arising from, and reasonable reliance on, promises. Protecting integrated written contracts from change by parol agreements furthers these goals with respect to many parties.

Protecting the integrity of written contracts, as such, does not seem to be a goal in itself. Rather, it should be regarded charitably as a means of implementing the first two goals. The parol evidence rule does not protect the integrity of *all* written contracts. It protects only those that are integrated, and only as against prior or contemporaneous written parol agreements. Because the question of integration turns on the parties' intention to integrate their agreement, the rule is best understood to implement that intention. Courts that state the integrity goal may be mesmerized by the history of the law's treatment of written contracts, which regarded them as virtually talismanic. Modern legal practice, however, has left such attitudes toward writings behind.

Protecting writings, because they are more reliable than the parties' memories, is not an apt goal of the parol evidence rule. Everyone now agrees that it is a rule of substantive law, not evidence law. Concerns about the reliability of the parties' memories are concerns of evidence law. The rule, moreover, does not fit this reliability rationale. Again, the rule renders inoperative some written parol agreements. The reliability rationale is relevant only to oral parol agreements. Prior written agreements can be produced as evidence and may be as reliable as the final written agreement with respect to what they represent. What they may represent, however, is the state of the parties' negotiations at one point in time; as negotiations proceed, that agreement may fall by the wayside. One of the parties' principal reasons for integrating prior agreements into a final writing is to be sure that such agreements are superseded. This reason has nothing to do with the parties' memories.

§ 3.2. Integrated Written Contracts

As indicated above, the parol evidence rule applies when there is an integrated, written contract. The authorities agree on the requirement of a writing. One question that should be considered at this time is whether integrated electronic contracts, such as those made over the internet, should invoke the parol evidence rule. We will consider this question below. In addition, we will consider the kinds of integrated writings that invoke the rule—partial and complete integrations—and how to establish a document's state of integration.

§ 3.2.1. Writings and Electronic Records

The parol evidence rule applies to all enforceable, integrated, written agreements. It should not be confused with a Statute of Frauds. Like a Statute of Frauds, the rule involves a requirement of a writing.[40] A Statute of Frauds, however, requires the parties to put certain agreements into writing if they are to be enforceable. The parol evidence rule does not; it determines the terms of a contract.[41] Unlike a Statute of Frauds, moreover, the existence of a writing is only part of a predicate for application of the rule, which application depends also on the parties' intention to integrate. A Statute of Frauds, by contrast, requires a writing as a condition for the enforceability of some contracts regardless of the parties' intention. A Statute of Frauds, additionally, applies only when a contract falls within certain subcategories of contracts, such as contracts for the sale of land. By contrast, an integrated, written contract invokes the parol evidence rule whether or not the contract falls within a subcategory. Again, unlike a Statute of Frauds, the parol evidence rule does not require that the parties sign the writing. One reason for parties to integrate may be to exclude the possibility of false testimony as to oral agreements.[42] But the parol evidence rule applies also to prior written agreements.

Few courts have faced the question whether several contemporaneous writings may be pieced together to constitute a single integrated contract. One has held that they may be pieced together into one integration.[43] Another has held that, if no single writing embodies the whole of the party's understanding, the parol evidence rule has no application.[44] The former holding allows contemporaneous written contracts to have operative effect. Under Article 2 of the UCC, the parol evidence rule is

---

[40] Baysden v. Roche, 563 S.E.2d 725, 726–27 (Va. 2002).

[41] Sterling v. Taylor, 152 P.3d 420, 425 (Cal. 2007).

[42] Harry J. Whelchel Co. v. Ripley Tractor Co., 900 S.W.2d 691, 693–94 (Tenn.App. 1995).

[43] Sawyer v. Arum, 690 F.2d 590, 592–93 (6th Cir. 1982).

[44] Stern & Co. v. State Loan & Fin. Corp., 238 F. Supp. 901, 911 (D. Del. 1965).

not applicable to such contracts.[45] The Restatement (Second) allows a "writing or writings" to be a partially or completely integrated agreement.[46] However, if one of the writings is completely integrated, prior oral or written contracts should not establish contract terms unless they are outside the scope of that writing.[47] If one of them is partially integrated, the others may establish non-contradictory additional terms even though they are within the scope of that writing. The existence of a side letter or agreement should be evidence that a written contract is integrated only partially. Such letters or agreements often are useful to the parties and may indicate their intent that the main agreement not be the complete agreement.

As of the date of this writing, no cases have been found that address the question whether an integrated electronic contract invokes the parol evidence rule. In light of the advent of widespread computerized contracting, it is inevitable that the question will be adjudicated. When it is, the parol evidence rule should be applied.

Parties can make an electronic contract in several ways. For example, they may contract by e-mail much as they might contract by paper correspondence, with a final text represented by the last two e-mails sent. They may negotiate by e-mail over a text in an attached computer file with the negotiations culminating in a final computer file that is saved to the parties' hard drives. They may contract on terms contained on a website on the internet, whether or not a human being reviews the file. Or they may exchange a computer file on a disc or a memory stick.

Electronic contracts might be left in the form of computer files and never be printed on paper. If the parties do this, the contract is not "written" in the usual sense of the word. It can be argued that the parol evidence rule applies only when a contract is written because that is how the courts state it. An electronic contract is not written, the argument continues, so the parol evidence rule does not apply.

This argument should be rejected. It is somewhat like arguing that a printed or typewritten contract is not "written," for purposes of the parol evidence rule, as though only handwritten contracts satisfy the writing requirement. Such an argument would be absurd. It is, moreover, a fine

---

[45] UCC § 2-202 (2001).

[46] Restatement (Second) of Contracts §§ 209(1), 210(1) (1981); *see* Steinke v. Sungard Fin. Sys, Inc., 121 F.3d 763, 771 (1st Cir. 1997).

[47] TRINOVA Corp. v. Pilkington Bros., 638 N.E.2d 572, 575 (Ohio 1994). *See* § 3.3.1.

example of how a rule crafted for a purpose can be misused in a new situation, due solely to the happenstance of the language used to state it, so that its purpose is defeated. At this writing, the question is without legal precedent. It is open to the courts to hold that integrated electronic contracts invoke the parol evidence rule.

As indicated above, the chief purpose of the parol evidence rule is to implement the parties' intention to integrate their agreement in a final, or final and complete, writing.[48] A second important purpose is to protect the security of written contracts so that people and firms may rely on them without having to discover parol agreements.[49] These purposes support applying the parol evidence rule when there is an integrated, electronic contract because, as with written contracts, the parties may intend to integrate their agreement. They and others, moreover, may rely on a contract in a computer file in the same way that they rely on a written contract. In particular, they may, and should be able to, rely on an integrated electronic contract without having to discover parol agreements.

This argument draws support by analogy to a number of laws concerning electronic contracting. The federal Electronic Signatures in Global and National Commerce Act[50] generally places electronic contracting on an equal footing with other kinds of contracting. It applies to contracts in interstate and foreign commerce. In addition, as of 2006, forty-six states had done substantially the same thing by adopting the Uniform Electronic Transactions Act.[51] Moreover, the argument draws support from the Amendments to Article 2 of the UCC, promulgated in 2003 by the National Conference of Commissioners on Uniform State Laws and the American Law Institute. Article 2's amended parol evidence rule will be found in Section 2-202. It protects "records," which are defined in Section 2-103(1)(m) as "information that is inscribed on a tangible medium or that is stored in an electronic or other medium and is retrievable in perceivable perform." Therefore, the amendment clearly would apply the parol evidence rule to electronic contracts. (It is not expected that the amendments to Article 2 will be widely adopted for reasons unrelated to the parol evidence rule or electronic contracting. Hence, the amendment to Section 2-202 to include records is only persuasive authority for

---

[48] *See* § 3.1.2.

[49] *Id.*

[50] 15 USC §§ 7001-7006 (2000).

[51] *See* UETA § 6 (1999).

holding that the parol evidence rule applies when there is an enforceable integrated electronic agreement.)

§ 3.2.2. *Kinds of Integrated Agreements*

The legal authorities say that the parol evidence rule applies—with different consequences—when there is a partially integrated writing, completely integrated writing, and sometimes a written integrated agreement, the last without differentiating between partial and complete integrations. In this section, we will elaborate these concepts of integration. The following section will consider how to establish a document's state of integration.

§ 3.2.2.1. Partial Integration

The concept of a partial integration is not difficult to understand, though some authoritative statements of it are confusing and awkward. It is simply a written contract that expresses the parties' final agreement on the points covered, without also being complete. The parol evidence rule does not apply if the parties' agreement is not at least partially integrated; that is, the rule does not apply if the agreement is not final, even if it is complete. A tentative written agreement would be a draft and not binding on the parties at all.

The Restatement (Second) adopts this concept, though in a more complicated and awkward way. It first says, "[A]n integrated agreement is a writing or writings constituting a final expression of one or more terms of an agreement."[52] The subject of this definition of *integrated agreement* does not distinguish between partial and complete integrations. The Restatement (Second) goes on, however, to define a completely integrated agreement as "an integrated agreement adopted by the parties as a complete and exclusive statement of the terms of the agreement."[53] Because an integrated agreement is a final expression, and the definition of a completely integrated agreement uses the term "integrated agreement," the effect of the two definitions is to define a completely integrated agreement as a final and complete expression of the parties' agreement. This is confirmed

---

[52] RESTATEMENT (SECOND) OF CONTRACTS § 209(1) (1981).
[53] *Id.* § 210(1).

by a third definition: "A partially integrated agreement is an integrated agreement other than a completely integrated agreement."[54] By process of elimination, then, there are two types of integrations, partial and complete. Why the drafters of the Restatement (Second) went about their job in this indirect and confusing way is a mystery.

Section 2-202 of the UCC, applicable to transactions in goods, also is unduly awkward, but employs the same concept of integration (without using the term). It provides in relevant part:

> Terms with respect to which the confirmatory memoranda of the parties agree or which are otherwise set forth in a writing intended by the parties as a final expression of their agreement with respect to such terms as are included therein may not be contradicted by evidence of any prior agreement or of a contemporaneous oral agreement . . . but may be supplemented
>
> (b) by evidence of consistent additional terms unless the court finds the writing to have been intended also as a complete and exclusive statement of the terms of the agreement.

The first part of this provision concerns partially integrated agreements. It states a predicate for applying the parol evidence rule when there are confirmatory memoranda, which by definition express the parties' final agreement, or otherwise a final agreement. The consequence attached to this predicate is that additional terms may supplement (add to) the writing, as with any partially integrated agreement. This much is relatively straightforward. The provision, however, almost smuggles in its predicate for applying the parol evidence rule when there is a completely integrated agreement. The predicate is the same as that of the common law. The second part of subsection (b), together with the last part of the first section, establishes that a complete and exclusive statement of the parties' agreement cannot be supplemented by additional terms. The first part of the provision, oddly, is the source of the requirement that a complete and exclusive statement must be final to have this effect. Consequently, what amounts to a completely integrated agreement cannot be supplemented by consistent additional terms, as is the case under the common law. (There are other aspects of Section 2-202 that do not mimic the common law,

---

[54] *Id.* § 210(2).

to be sure. In particular, Section 2-202 does not appear to bar the use of a contemporaneous oral agreement.)

§ 3.2.2.2. Complete Integration

The concept of a complete (sometimes called an exclusive, total, or entire) integration also is not difficult to understand. It is simply a written contract that expresses the parties' final and complete agreement.

The Restatement (Second) again is in accord with this definition, but again it is a little bit awkward: "A completely integrated agreement is an integrated agreement adopted by the parties as a complete and exclusive statement of the terms of the agreement."[55] To see that, according to this definition, a completely integrated agreement is one that is final and complete, we must consult another provision that defines an integrated agreement as one that is final.[56] Moreover, that a completely integrated agreement is both a complete and an exclusive statement would appear to involve a redundancy. This usage does not track the usage of most courts. When these courts use the term *integration* or its cognates, without specifying whether the integration is partial or complete, they do not mean that a written agreement is final but not complete. They usually use it without differentiating between partial and complete integrations.

As indicated above, Article 2 of the UCC, though confusing and awkward, adopts in practical effect the common law's concept of a complete integration.

§ 3.2.2.3. Undifferentiated Integration

Many courts use the term *integration* without differentiating between partial and complete integrations. This usage is an imprecise and confusing way of referring to both or either a partial or a complete integration. Consequently, undifferentiated use of the term may refer to either a partial integration or a complete integration. This ambiguity is can produce confusion. The two concepts should be kept distinct.

The Restatement (Second), as indicated above, employs the concept of an integrated agreement, but defines the term as a "final expression of

---

[55] RESTATEMENT (SECOND) OF CONTRACTS § 210(1) (1981).

[56] *Id.* § 209(1).

one or more terms of an agreement."[57] An "integrated agreement," in Restatement (Second) parlance, therefore is a partially integrated agreement, but it is not a completely integrated agreement. This is not consistent with judicial usage. Article 2 of the UCC does not use the term, undifferentiated or otherwise.

Use of "integration," without differentiating between partial and complete integrations, should be regarded as a short-hand expression. We should bear in mind that there are two concepts here. As indicated by the statement of the parol evidence rule above,[58] the rule has two branches. One concerns partially integrated agreements, and the other concerns completely integrated agreements. The courts attach different consequences to each. (In this book, *integration* will be used to simplify the text with the intent that it refer to partial and/or complete integrations, as the case may be.)

§ 3.2.3. Establishing a Document's State of Integration

The courts hold that the question of integration turns on the parties' intention to integrate their agreement. Most often, it is an interpretive question to be decided by the court as a matter of fact based on all relevant evidence at an evidentiary hearing.[59] As indicated in Chapter 1, there are three main theories by which to understand a question of contractual intention—literalism, objectivism, and subjectivism.[60] Accordingly, there are three main ways courts allow a party to establish the state of integration of their document. First, literalism holds that the parties' intention is best reflected in the document itself. Literalism requires a court to determine whether a document is partially or completely integrated by looking at a merger clause in the document, if any, without considering any evidence of the clause's context, such as the whole document or the circumstances. Second, objectivism holds that the parties' intention is best reflected in the contracts' evident purpose and the document as a whole, understood in a limited context. The elements allowed as proof of context, however, are mainly the objective circumstances at the time that the

---

[57] *Id.*

[58] *See* § 3.1.1.

[59] Emrich v. Connell, 716 P.2d 863, 866–67 (Wash. 1986); Hatley v. Stafford, 588 P.2d 603, 608 (Or. 1978).

[60] *See* § 1.3.

contract was made. Third, subjectivism holds that a full review of the context, including all relevant parol evidence, is necessary to determine the parties' intention to integrate. The courts employ all three approaches at different times, even within a particular jurisdiction. Subjectivism, however, appears to be the emerging trend.

§ 3.2.3.1. Literalism and Merger Clauses

Many courts suppose that the parties' intention to integrate their agreement into a writing is best revealed by the document's clauses themselves, considered apart from any context, including any parol evidence.[61] In particular, these courts focus on the presence or absence of a merger clause, also called an *integration clause.* A boilerplate merger clause for a completely integrated agreement might read along the following lines:

> This Agreement represents the parties' entire agreement. It supersedes any prior or contemporaneous, oral or written, agreements. There are no other agreements or statements, oral or written, expressing the parties' agreement.

On their faces, such clauses indicate the parties' intention to integrate their agreement and the extent to which they intend to do so. Put otherwise, a merger clause expresses the parties' intention to merge extant parol agreements into a final, or a final and complete, writing.

In many jurisdictions, the presence of a clear merger clause raises a conclusive presumption that the agreement is integrated.[62] Hence, "a merger clause acts . . . to require full application of the parol evidence rule to the writing in question."[63] According to literalism, the parties' intention to integrate is best revealed by the literal meaning of the merger clause itself.[64] Extrinsic evidence certainly is not admissible to establish

---

[61] Armstrong Paint & Varnish Works v. Continental Can Co., 133 N.E. 711, 713 (Ill. 1922) (limited to the common law, by contrast with the UCC, in *J&B Steel Contractors*, 642 N.E.2d at 1218).

[62] Thayer v. Dial Indus. Sales, Inc., 85 F. Supp. 2d 263, 269 (S.D.N.Y. 2000); UAW-GM Human Res. Ctr. v. KSL Recreation Corp., 579 N.W.2d 411, 418 (Mich.App. 1998); *see* Nelson v. Elway, 908 P.2d 102, 107 (Colo. 1995).

[63] Bank Julius Baer & Co. v. Waxfield Ltd., 424 F.3d 278, 283 (2d Cir. 2005).

[64] Primex Int'l Corp. v. Wal-Mart Stores, Inc., 679 N.E.2d 624, 627 (N.Y. 1997).

the document's state of integration.[65] Strictly speaking, even the document as a whole cannot be consulted.

Considering merger clauses exclusively and literally, however, can produce arbitrary results at odds with the parties' objective and subjective intentions on the question of integration. There may be many contracts of different kinds, all made prior to the contract in question. The parties may not intend to supersede all of them even when the clause says that the last agreement "supersedes all prior agreements."[66] In such a case, a court should hold that *all* does not mean all. For example, in *Bank Julius Baer & Co. v. Waxfield Ltd.*,[67] the parties first entered into an arbitration agreement providing for the arbitration of all disputes between them. Later, they concluded a pledge agreement containing a merger clause providing that it "supersede[d] all prior agreements."[68] The question before the court was whether the pledge agreement superseded the arbitration agreement. The court held that pledge agreement did not supersede it, but conceded that a literal reading of the merger clause would have that effect.[69] Upon consulting the written document as a whole, the court found an incorporation clause providing that "[w]ithout exception, all the rights and remedies provided in this Agreement are cumulative and not exclusive of any rights or remedies provided under any other agreement."[70] The court read the two clauses together to give meaning to both, as required by objectivist principles of contract interpretation and as allowed by subjectivism.[71] Giving the merger clause its literal meaning, the court reasoned, would render the incorporation clause nugatory. To avoid rendering the merger clause pointless, the court held, the pledge agreement superseded previous agreements only to the extent they were in conflict; that is, the merger clause established only that the pledge agreement was partially integrated.[72] Consequently, *all prior agreements* did not mean, literally, *all* prior agreements. The arbitration agreement continued in force.

---

65 *J&B Steel Contractors*, 642 N.E.2d at 1220.

66 *See* Mark V, Inc. v. Mellekas, 845 P.2d 1232, 1237 (N.M. 1993).

67 424 F.3d 278. *See also* Sec. Watch, Inc. v. Sentinel Sys., Inc., 176 F.3d 369, 372 (6th Cir. 1999); *Primex Int'l Corp.*, 679 N.E.2d at 626–27.

68 *Bank Julius Baer*, 424 F.3d at 283.

69 *Id.*

70 *Id.*

71 *Id.*

72 *Id.*

The result in *Bank Julius Baer* implements the parties' probable intentions on the question of integration. Parties may have a web of contracts between them on a host of subjects. When this is so, it rarely is their intention to wipe the slate clean each time they conclude a contract, whether or not it contains a merger clause, and especially when the merger clause is boilerplate. Thus, the incorporation clause in *Bank Julius Baer* preserved the prior agreement.

Assume, however, that there had been no incorporation clause. Still, the question in *Bank Julius Baer* would be whether the pledge agreement superseded the arbitration agreement as required by the literal meaning of the pledge agreement's merger clause. Still, the arbitration agreement should not be discharged because doing so would not implement the parties' probable intentions. Under the common law parol evidence rule, even if the pledge agreement is completely integrated, the arbitration agreement should be unaffected because it is outside the scope of the pledge agreement.[73] Merger clauses should not have a broader effect. They are not reasonably understood to reach remote or unrelated contracts even when they use the words *all prior agreements*. Rather, *all prior agreements* is reasonably understood and most probably intended only to reach other agreements within the scope of the contract containing the clause, especially predecessor agreements and agreements reached in the course of negotiations but not contained in the document. The parties, of course, are free by contract to discharge any of their agreements. But a standard merger clause in one contract is not the way to do it with respect to agreements outside that contract's scope. They were probably out of sight and out of mind, and a reasonable person reading the clause would so conclude.

Another problem with literalism is that a merger clause may turn out to be ambiguous. Assume, for example, a common kind of merger clause that says simply, "This contract represents the parties' entire agreement." The precedents suggest that such a clause may be ambiguous because it is not clear whether the contract is partially or completely integrated. Thus, in *Parrot v. Guardian Life Insurance Co. of America*,[74] a merger clause providing only that the contract was the parties' "entire contract" was held to effect a partial integration.[75] Other courts have held that similar merger

---

[73] *See* § 3.3.1.
[74] 866 A.2d 1273 (Conn. 2005).
[75] *Id.* at 1281.

clauses establish that the contract is complete on its face.[76] In cases of ambiguous merger clauses, literalism offers no resources for resolving the ambiguity by interpretation. It limits the decision-maker to the literal meaning of the terms employed. An ambiguous term has no literal meaning. To avoid this problem with literalism, the drafter should be careful to say more than that the contract is "entire." Under literalism, the absence or ambiguity of a merger clause will lead a decision-maker to conclude that the contract is not integrated.

Merger clauses also are significant under the objective and subjective approaches. They are, however, given less than conclusive effect. They will be considered again below.

§ 3.2.3.2. Objective Intention to Integrate

Objectivism treats the question of integration as an interpretive question. It (objectivism) is a sometimes-followed approach. An objectivist court seeks the intention of the parties to integrate or not as revealed by their whole written contract, interpreted as a reasonable person would interpret it. By contrast with literalism, such a court will look not only at a merger clause, if any, but also at least at the allegation of a parol agreement and the document as a whole on its face. Among the objective circumstances that rarely are considered are custom and usage,[77] the parties' relative bargaining strength,[78] and whether a party was represented by counsel.[79] The goal is to determine whether an alleged parol agreement "naturally" would have been included in the writing had the parties made it and intended to keep it alive.[80] *Naturally* in this context should be understood to require that the interpreter consider whether a reasonable person looking at the whole document and the alleged parol agreement would think that the parties would have included the latter in the writing had they intended to keep it in force. Unlike subjectivism, however, an objectivist court will not look at all relevant evidence.

---

[76] *E.g.*, Howard v. Perry, 106 P.3d 465, 467 (Idaho 2005).

[77] *See* Conway v. 287 Corporate Ctr. Assocs., 901 A.2d 341, 347 (N.J. 2006).

[78] *Hatley*, 588 P.2d at 609.

[79] *Id.*

[80] Kimbell Foods, Inc. v. Republic Nat'l Bank of Dallas, 557 F.2d 491, 495–97 (5th Cir. 1977); Braten v. Bankers Trust Co., 456 N.E.2d 802, 805 (N.Y. 1983).

Under objectivism, a merger clause is not necessary to integrate an agreement.[81] Such a clause is only one way of proving that an agreement is integrated, and it is not conclusive when present in a contract.[82] A merger clause nonetheless is of great significance: It raises a rebuttable presumption of integration[83] or places a "heavy burden" on a party to prove that the contract was not integrated.[84] Overcoming such a presumption or burden can be accomplished based on the same elements that objectivism makes relevant to the question of integration when there is no merger clause. However, to overcome the presumption, at least one jurisdiction requires a showing of fraud, bad faith, unconscionability, negligent omission, or mistake in fact.[85] (This odd requirement represents a misunderstanding of contract law.)

Because a merger clause is not necessary, the document as a whole may be integrated on its face or on the basis of the circumstances at formation, its purpose(s), and other objective elements. Again, the question concerns the parties' intention to integrate their agreement based on how these elements together would be understood by a reasonable person. Thus, many courts hold that all apparently complete writings are presumed to be integrated.[86] A few go further, holding that all written agreements are presumed to be integrated.[87] The general thrust of objectivism is to determine whether the alleged parol agreement would naturally have been included in the written contract if it had been made and not superseded.[88] If it would have been included, a reasonable person would understand the written contract to be integrated.

In the classic case of *Gianni v. R. Russel & Co.*,[89] the court addressed the question of integration by limiting its inquiry to the alleged parol agreement and the four corners of a written lease and possibly including

---

81 Steinke v. Sungard Fin. Sys., Inc., 121 F.3d 763, 771 (1st Cir. 1997); Bank Leumi Trust Co. of N.Y. v. Wulkan, 735 F. Supp. 72, 78 (S.D.N.Y. 1990).

82 Kimbrough v. Reed, 943 P.2d 1232, 1235 (Idaho 1997).

83 Madey v. Duke Univ., 336 F. Supp. 2d 583, 605 (M.D.N.C. 2004); Hawes Office Sys., Inc. v. Wang Labs., Inc., 524 F. Supp. 610, 613–14 (E.D.N.Y. 1981).

84 McAbee Constr., Inc. v. United States, 97 F.3d 1431, 1434 (Fed. Cir. 1996); Shevel's, Inc.-Chesterfield v. Southeastern Assocs., Inc, 320 S.E.2d 339, 344 (Va. 1984).

85 *Madey*, 336 F. Supp. 2d at 606.

86 *Hatley*, 588 P.2d at 609; Hall v. Process Instruments & Control, Inc., 890 P.2d 1024, 1027 (Utah 1995).

87 Jack H. Brown & Co., Inc. v. Toys "R" Us, Inc., 906 F.2d 169, 173 (5th Cir. 1990).

88 Mellon Bank Corp. v. First Union Real Estate Equity and Mortg. Invests., 951 F.2d 1399, 1406 (3d Cir. 1991).

89 126 A. 791 (Pa. 1924).

the objective circumstances under which it was made. The lessee had signed a lease that provided him with a room in the lessor's office building from which he could sell tobacco, fruit, candy, soda water, and soft drinks. When the lessor allowed another tenant to sell soft drinks in the building, the lessee claimed that the lessor breached. Prior to signing the lease, the lessee alleged, the parties had agreed orally that he (the lessee) would have an exclusive right to sell soft drinks. The lessor set up the parol evidence rule as a defense.

The Supreme Court of Pennsylvania reversed the trial court's judgment for the lessee, holding that the lease was a completely integrated agreement and that the parol agreement, if it was made, was within the scope of the lease. The court compared the alleged oral agreement with the lease, asking whether "parties, situated as were the ones to the contract, would naturally and normally include the one in the other if it had been made."[90] It cited a provision of the lease document to support its conclusion that the parties would have done so: The lease covered the uses to which the room could be put and what the lessee could and could not sell there. But the court did not confine itself to the four corners. It also considered the "situation of the parties," reporting that the lease was signed after it had been left in the lessee's hands and, the lessee admitted, had been read to him by two persons, one of whom was his daughter. Had there been a not-superseded agreement for an exclusive for soft drinks, the court concluded, it presumably would have been included in the cited provision of the lease.

The court in *Gianni* included some context in its reasoning—the alleged parol agreement, the document as a whole, and the parties' situation. It compared the written lease with the alleged parol agreement. *Gianni* consequently is not vulnerable to the Corbinian counterargument to objectivism—that "a writing cannot of itself prove its own completeness."[91] The case is not an example of literalism. The critical question is whether the court failed to take into account enough context to give an appropriate answer to the question of integration. This depends basically on how one conceives of a contract. If a contract is constituted by the parties' objective manifestations, whatever their subjective intent, the allegation of a parol agreement, the document as a whole, and the circumstances at formation, are enough. More context presumably is

---

[90] *Id.* at 792.

[91] Restatement (Second) of Contracts § 210, cmt. b (1981).

needed, however, if a contract is constituted by the parties' mutual mental intentions, as evidenced by their manifestations of intention and other evidence to infer their subjective intent. More is needed, that is, if we suppose that the parties had relevant intentions and that more context gets us closer to those intentions.

If one presupposes subjectivism, there might be a problem with *Gianni*. There might really have been an oral agreement giving the lessee an exclusive on soft drinks. (The lessee produced a witness to a prior oral agreement, but the lessor's agent denied it.) The parties may not have (subjectively) intended to supersede it. If so on both counts, the oral agreement arguably was denied its rightful effect. In choosing between objectivism and subjectivism, however, the presupposition begs the question. For reasons given in Chapter 6, the parties' objective intentions—those manifested in the lease as it would be understood by a reasonable person under the circumstances—may be more important. For the reasons the court gave, it is plausible to suppose that a reasonable person would expect an agreement giving the lessee an exclusive on soft drinks, if there was one, to be included in the written lease. If so, the lessee justifiably can be held responsible for the apparent state of integration of the lease he signed after reviewing it twice.

In *Myskina v. Conde Nast Publications, Inc.*,[92] a more recent case, the court similarly looked at some context while still taking an objective approach. It considered the allegation of a parol agreement, the document as a whole, the circumstances when it was signed, and the document's purpose. The written document in question was a release that allowed a magazine to publish photographs of a model.[93] The model claimed that an oral agreement limited her consent to publication in a single issue of a certain magazine.[94] The court held that, under New York law, the release was an integrated agreement, so the parol evidence rule made the alleged oral agreement ineffective.[95] There was no merger clause.[96] The court relied on six factors.[97] First, the release did not mention the alleged oral agreement. Second, the transaction was straightforward. Third, the release plainly stated that the model consented to the

[92] 386 F. Supp. 2d 409 (S.D.N.Y. 2005).
[93] *Id.* at 412.
[94] *Id.*
[95] *Id.* at 416.
[96] *Id.* at 412.
[97] *Myskina*, 386 F. Supp. 2d at 415–16.

magazine's use of all photographs taken on the day of the shoot. Fourth, the release's language purported to treat the issue of consent comprehensively ("I, the undersigned, hereby irrevocably consent. . . ."). Fifth, the alleged oral agreement contemplated a condition fundamental to the model's consent such that the parties would not have omitted it had they intended to adopt it. Sixth, though represented only by an administrative assistant from her publicity firm, she was represented. Consequently, the written release was held to be fully integrated.[98]

Of these six factors, the first, second, third, and fourth were contained within the document as a whole. The fifth goes outside the document to consider a counterfactual question: Had the parties intended to adopt the oral agreement, would they have omitted it from the writing? This question bears on whether a reasonable person would expect the parties to include the asserted parol agreement in the writing had they intended it to survive.[99] The sixth also goes outside the four corners, taking into account the objective circumstances under which the release was signed. These factors together provided a context indicating that the release was integrated. Notably, the court did not ask whether the alleged oral agreement was made and subjectively was intended to survive the writing, and it did not trace the history of any negotiations that might have occurred nor allow testimony by a party about its own intent. The context was limited to the document as a whole, the document's apparent purpose, and the circumstances at the signing.

Myskina indicates that it is not a sound objection to its objective approach that the court used the parol evidence rule to impose an unjustified obligation on the model. Assume that the model subjectively understood her consent to be limited to publication of the photographs in one issue of one magazine. Perhaps there were discussions centered on that one issue and no others, leaving her with an impression to that effect. She nonetheless signed the written release, which did not incorporate such an understanding. Assume further that she was imposed upon from a subjective point of view. Nonetheless, the goal of implementing the parties' subjective intentions, if this is a goal, is not the only goal. Holding parties responsible for their manifestations of intention, when fair, also is a goal. The latter goal argues for considering the question objectively, determining whether the document is integrated by asking how a reasonable

---

98 *Id.*

99 Bourne v. Walt Disney Co., 68 F.3d 621, 627 (2d Cir. 1995).

person would understand it under the circumstances. Moreover, the photographer and his employer, and magazines considering publication of the photographs, could be expected to rely on the release without investigating the model's subjective intention. Protecting such reliance also is a goal of contract interpretation. Even if there was some imposition on the model in *Myskina*, it might be justified by the weight of the other goals.

An important question is whether, in addition to the alleged parol agreement, and the document and its circumstances, objectivism allows other parol evidence to be admitted on the question of integration. Many authorities appear to follow an objective approach generally but to allow extrinsic evidence of subjective intent on this question.[100] Many, however, like *Myskina*, require that the question be resolved based on the document viewed in light of the objective circumstances. Among the elements that most objectivist courts would allow on the question of integration are the parties' practical construction with respect to integration,[101] statements at the time of signing that a clause was inoperative and meaningless,[102] whether the writing was signed,[103] whether the writing contained a merger clause,[104] and the silence of the document on a critical point.[105]

Allowing a party to introduce extrinsic evidence of a parol agreement on the question of integration might seem as a practical matter to defeat the purpose of the parol evidence rule—to make such agreements ineffective and, therefore, irrelevant and inadmissible to establish contract terms. Once a parol agreement is in evidence, it will be difficult for the finder of fact—especially a jury—to disregard it for other purposes. In particular, a jury would find it difficult to distinguish between parol evidence introduced on the question of integration from parol evidence introduced to establish the contract's terms. There is a simple response to this criticism. Most courts hold that the question of integration is for the court, not the jury.[106] The jury need not be present when the question of

---

[100] *E.g.*, Hamade v. Sunoco, Inc., 721 N.W.2d 233, 248 (Mich.App. 2006).

[101] *J&B Steel Contractors*, 642 N.E.2d at 1219.

[102] McEvoy Travel Bureau, Inc. v. Norton Co., 563 N.E.2d 188, 191 (Mass. 1990).

[103] Conn. Acoustics, Inc. v. Xhema Constr., Inc., 870 A.2d 1178, 1183 (Conn.App. 2005).

[104] Founding Members of the Newport Beach Country Club v. Newport Beach Country Club, Inc., 135 Cal. Rptr. 2d 505, 512–13 (Cal.App. 2003).

[105] Society of Lloyd's v. Bennett, 182 Fed. Appx. 840, 845 (10th Cir. 2006).

[106] *E.g.*, *TRINOVA*, 638 N.E.2d at 576. *See also* Restatement (Second) of Contracts § 209(2) (1981). *See generally* Charles T. McCormick, *The Parol Evidence Rule as a Procedural Device for Control of the Jury*, 41 Yale L.J. 365 (1932).

integration is alleged or argued, or even when evidence on it is offered or introduced. The jury may be present later, if the document is determined not to be integrated, when parol evidence is introduced to establish terms.[107]

The objective approach may seem impure when a court's reasoning is read as a whole. In *McAbee Construction, Inc. v. United States*,[108] for example, the court held that, to determine whether an agreement is integrated, the writing and the circumstances surrounding its execution should be taken into account.[109] The merger clause in that agreement was clear and, the court wrote, it placed an "extremely heavy burden" on the party asserting that the agreement was not completely integrated.[110] In discussing the circumstances, however, the court took into account the several months of negotiations that preceded execution of the document, which negotiations are not circumstances at the time of execution. During those negotiations, the content of the proffered parol agreement was discussed, and the party advancing the parol agreement had requested that it be set forth in a "statement of understanding."[111] This was not done.[112] In finding that the document was completely integrated, the court reasoned that that party either should have stricken the merger clause from the document or incorporated the statement of understanding by reference in the merger clause.[113] By taking into account prior negotiations, the court seems to have sought the parties' subjective intentions, even though its statement of the law was objectivist.

Appearances can be deceiving. Notably, the lynchpin of the court's reasoning in *McAbee Construction* was its insistence that the merger clause should have been stricken, or the statement of understanding incorporated into the final written contract, if the parol agreement existed and parties intended to keep it alive. Insisting on one of these measures supports the court's conclusion because the requirement furthers the goal of holding parties responsible for the reasonable meaning of their manifestations, even when their subjective intentions are different. This goal supports the objective theory and is not a major goal of the subjective theory.

---

107 *See* Haggard v. Kimberly Quality Care, Inc., 46 Cal.Rptr. 2d 16 (Cal.App. 1995).
108 97 F.3d 1431 (Fed.Cir. 1996).
109 *Id.* at 1434.
110 *Id.*
111 *Id.*
112 *Id.*
113 *McAbee Constr.*, 97 F.3d at 1434.

The main thrust of the court's opinion, accordingly, should be understood to follow the objective theory. Its discussion of the negotiations should be understood to amount to the following assertion: Even if there was a parol agreement during the parties' negotiations, and there may have been, it has no effect (to establish contract terms) due to the writing's state of integration, evidenced most clearly by the merger clause.

§ 3.2.3.3. Subjective Intention to Integrate

Most courts follow a more subjective theory on the question of integration.[114] This approach takes into account all evidence relevant to the parties' intention to integrate in an effort to ascertain what the parties had in mind. Literalism and objectivism, by contrast, limit the evidence relevant to the question. To review, literalism confines the court's consideration to the presence or absence of a merger clause in the written contract. Objectivism may consider, in addition, the allegation of a parol agreement, the document as a whole, the objective circumstances under which the document was signed and the document's evident purpose(s), to determine whether the proffered parol agreement would have been included in the writing had the parties intended to keep it alive. Subjectivism considers, in addition, evidence of the parol agreement,[115] the course of the parties' prior negotiations,[116] statements by a party of its own intention during negotiations,[117] testimony by a party in court of its intention,[118] and any other evidence relevant to the parties' intention on the question of integration.

Recall that, under literalism, a merger clause raises a conclusive presumption that the document is integrated; under objectivism, such a clause raises a rebuttable presumption or has "great weight." Under subjectivism, a merger clause is merely evidence that the contract is integrated.[119]

---

[114] *E.g.*, Fed. Deposit Ins. Corp. v. First Mortgage Investors, 250 N.W.2d 362, 365–66 (Wis. 1977).

[115] Cook v. Little Caesar Enters., Inc., 210 F.3d 653, 656 (6th Cir. 2000); *Masterson*, 436 P.2d at 565.

[116] Town & Country Fine Jewelry Group, Inc., v. Hirsch, 875 F.Supp. 872, 876 (D. Mass. 1994).

[117] Connell v. Aetna Life & Cas. Co., 436 A.2d 408, 412 (Me. 1981).

[118] *See* Hibbett Sporting Goods, Inc. v. Biernbaum, 375 So.2d 431, 434–35 (Ala. 1979).

[119] *E.g.*, Behrens v. S.P. Constr. Co., 904 A.2d 676, 682 (N.H. 2006); State v. Triad Mech., Inc., 925 P.2d 918, 924 (Or.App. 1996).

Subjectivism treats the question of integration as a question of contract interpretation, not as a special issue. The aim is to find the parties' subjective intentions to integrate or not.

With notable exceptions, the Restatement (Second) prefers a subjectivist approach to contract interpretation issues. The question whether an agreement is integrated (final, as the Restatement (Second) defines it) or completely integrated (final and complete) is for the court,[120] even though it is described as a question of fact.[121] There is no restriction on the relevant evidence that a party may introduce on the question of integration.[122] Rather,

> a writing cannot of itself prove its own completeness, and wide latitude must be allowed for inquiry into circumstances bearing on the intention of the parties.[123]

The court may receive the evidence at a preliminary hearing.[124] This avoids confusing a jury when parol evidence is introduced for the purpose of determining a document's state of integration, but the court concludes that it is not admissible to add to or contradict the document's terms.

In a nod to the objective theory, the Restatement (Second) provides that a writing which

> in view of its completeness and specificity reasonably appears to be a complete agreement . . . is taken to be an integrated agreement unless it is established by other evidence that the writing did not constitute a final expression.[125]

On its face, this black-letter provision makes it a presumption that apparent completeness and specificity indicate that the writing is a final expression, but not a final and complete expression. However, a complete integration may be shown presumptively in the same way as in the case of a partial integration, without excluding any relevant evidence.[126]

---

120 Restatement (Second) of Contracts §§ 209(2), 210(3) (1981).
121 *Id.* § 209, cmt. c.
122 *Id.* §§ 209(2), 210(3).
123 *Id.* § 210, cmt. b.
124 Gerdlund v. Elec. Dispensers Int'l, 235 Cal. Rptr. 279, 282 (Cal.App. 1987).
125 Restatement (Second) of Contracts § 209(3) (1981).
126 *Id.* § 210, cmt. b.

In a further nod to the objective theory, the Restatement (Second) would treat many standardized agreements objectively on the question of integration, with a minor exception. To paraphrase, it provides that, where a party manifests assent to a writing with reason to believe that it is a standardized agreement, he or she adopts the writing as an integrated agreement, but not as a completely integrated agreement.[127] The exception applies if the user of the standardized agreement has reason to believe that the other party would not assent to the agreement if he or she knew that the writing contained a particular term. In that case, the term in question is not part of the agreement.[128] Outside of Arizona,[129] however, very few cases have been found that follow these provisions.

Article 2 of the UCC also takes a generally subjectivist approach to contract interpretation issues. Thus, the parol evidence rule never precludes a party from introducing extrinsic evidence of a course of performance, course of dealing, or usage of trade "in order that the true understanding of the parties as to the agreement may be reached."[130] Presumably for the same reason, by contrast with objectivism's focus on whether the parol agreement on additional terms "naturally" would have been included in the writing, Article 2 excludes such a parol agreement only if it "certainly" would have been included.[131] Article 2 thus allows much more parol evidence to show the full context of a written agreement. It seeks to give the parties' agreement "the meaning which arises out of the commercial context in which it was used."[132]

The best known case expounding the subjective theory on the question of integration is *Masterson v. Sine*.[133] Recall that a grant deed reserved to the grantors an option to repurchase a property for the selling price. The grantees were the grantor's sister and brother-in-law. The grantor went bankrupt, and the trustee in bankruptcy sought to exercise the option. Based on extrinsic evidence, the grantees argued that the parties

---

[127] *Id.* § 211(1).
[128] *Id.* § 211(3).
[129] *See* Darner Motor Sales, Inc. v. Universal Underwriters Ins. Co., 682 P.2d 388, 396 (Ariz. 1984).
[130] UCC § 2-202, cmt. 2 (2001).
[131] *Id.* § 2-202, cmt. 3.
[132] *Id.* § 2-202, cmt. 1.
[133] 436 P.2d 561 (Cal. 1968).

had made an agreement to keep the property in the family; therefore, the option was personal to the grantor and could not be exercised by the trustee in bankruptcy. Over a strong dissent,[134] the California Supreme Court, per Justice Traynor, held that the trial court erred by applying the parol evidence rule to keep extrinsic evidence of the alleged parol agreement from the jury. The court took into account the following factors: There was no merger clause, the deed was silent on the question of assignability, it would be difficult to put the personal agreement into the formal structure of a deed, it was a family transaction, the parties had no apparent experience in land transactions or otherwise had any warning of the disadvantages of failing to put the whole agreement in the deed, and the reservation of the option might have been put into the deed solely to preserve the grantor's rights as against possible future purchasers.[135] On this basis, the court concluded that the alleged oral agreement "might [n]aturally be made as a separate agreement."[136] Consequently, the trial court erred by excluding the parol evidence that bears on these and any other relevant factors.

Justice Traynor might be thought in *Masterson* to have eviscerated the parol evidence rule by turning it from a rule of substantive law into a rule of evidence. It is aimed, he wrote, at finding "the true intent of the parties."[137] Accordingly,

> [e]vidence of oral collateral agreements should be excluded only when the fact finder is likely to be misled. The rule must therefore be based on the credibility of the evidence.[138]

The opinion is not altogether clear *as to what* the fact finder might be mislead—the existence of a parol agreement or the parties' intention to supersede it. Because the "true intent" of the parties may have been for the deed to supersede the parol agreement (or not), the thrust of the opinion should be read to target the parties' intent to integrate. If it is so read, the parol evidence rule was not eviscerated but, instead, was placed on a radically subjective basis.

---

134 *Id.* at 567 (Burke, J. dissenting).
135 *Id.* at 565–67.
136 *Id.* at 564.
137 *Id.*
138 *Id.*

Some cases in California subsequent to *Masterson* seem to take a more objectivist approach. Thus, one intermediate appellate court wrote:

> In considering whether a writing is integrated, the court must consider the writing itself, including whether the written agreement appears to be complete on its face; whether the agreement contains an integration clause; whether the alleged parol understanding on the subject matter at issue might naturally be made as a separate agreement; and the circumstances at the time of the writing.[139]

The focus here is on the writing in a limited context. It does not reflect *Masterson's* main point, that evidence of a parol agreement "should be excluded only when the fact finder is likely to be misled."[140] That point presumptively opens the door to all relevant evidence.

The roles of judge and jury may be different under subjectivism in some jurisdictions. Literalism and objectivism treat the question of integration as a question of law for the court.[141] The Restatement (Second) does the same.[142] Some subjectivist courts, by contrast, shift decision-making authority to the jury. *Masterson* does this. So does *Hall v. Process Instruments & Control, Inc.*,[143] in which the court wrote that the question of integration was a factual question for trial. The court also allowed the plaintiff to introduce parol evidence on that question, subject to exclusion, thus manifesting a subjectivist approach. Of course, a typical jury is unlikely to distinguish between parol evidence offered on the question of integration and the same evidence offered to establish the contract's terms. Even if the parol evidence introduced on the question of integration is later excluded, it is in evidence, and the jury is unlikely to disregard it. Like *Masterson*, then, *Hall* weakens the parol evidence rule considerably.

The subjective approach overlaps with the objective approach. In *Haggard v. Kimberly Quality Care, Inc.*,[144] the contract stated that an employee could be terminated "at will, at any time, with or without cause

---

139 *Founding Members of the Newport Beach Country Club*, 135 Cal. Rptr. 2d at 512 (citing *Masterson*).

140 *Masterson*, 436 P.2d at 564.

141 *See* §§ 3.2.3.1; 3.2.3.2.

142 Restatement (Second) of Contracts §210(3) (1981).

143 890 P.2d 1024 (Utah 1995).

144 46 Cal. Rptr. 2d 16 (Cal.App. 1995).

or advance notice."[145] It also contained an unambiguous merger clause stating specifically that there were no agreements contrary to the at-will provision. The court held that the contract was integrated with respect to the termination provision; that is, it was partially integrated. It reasoned that the merger clause's content was supported by the circumstances surrounding execution of the contract. Thus, the employee had read the agreement, including the termination provision, and had expressed reluctance to sign it but did so anyhow. The court here focused on the document and its circumstances without taking into account prior negotiations or other evidence. This focus seems like the objective approach. The subjective approach, however, encompasses the literal import of the document, if any, and the objective circumstances.[146] It encompasses more elements if relevant evidence is available. If there is no more, the inference as to subjective intention will be drawn from the document as a whole, its purpose(s), and its objective circumstances.

§ 3.3. Non-Consequences of Integration

We have already stated the consequences under the parol evidence rule of integrating an agreement: In brief, if a contract is completely integrated, parol agreements cannot contradict or add to the written terms; if a contract is partially integrated, parol agreements cannot contradict but may add to the written terms.[147] Here, to avoid confusion, we will consider several consequences that the parol evidence rule does *not* have. The rule makes parol agreements inoperative *only if* evidence of the parol agreement is offered for the purpose of contradicting or adding to an integrated contract's terms. Parol evidence is admissible if offered for other purposes.[148] It is a mistake to believe that the parol evidence rule precludes the admission of any extrinsic evidence whatsoever, even when the writing is fully integrated. All depends on the purpose for which the evidence is offered.

---

[145] *Id.* at 21, 23.

[146] *Berg*, 801 P.2d at 229.

[147] *See* § 3.1.1.

[148] *Alstom Power*, 849 A.2d at 811; RESTATEMENT (SECOND) OF CONTRACTS § 214 (1981); RESTATEMENT (FIRST) OF CONTRACTS § 238 (1932).

§ 3.3.1. Collateral Agreements

Under the collateral agreement rule, a collateral parol agreement is operative, and proof of it is admissible, notwithstanding the parol evidence rule. Confusion may set in—needlessly—due to an ambiguity in *collateral agreement* as the term is used by the courts. Some cases use this term to refer to a parol agreement that adds to, but does not contradict, a partial integration. But other cases use the term to refer to a parol agreement that is made for a separate consideration and does not contradict and is outside the scope of a completely integrated agreement.[149] The first usage is superfluous because the parol evidence rule allows non-contradictory additional terms for partially integrated agreements in any event, without resort to the collateral agreement rule. In this discussion, the term will encompass only the second usage.

The collateral agreement rule, thus understood, makes good sense. Not all parol agreements are made in the course of negotiations leading up to an integrated contract. Parties may have a web of contracts between them—each involving a separate consideration—on a host of subjects. If this is so, it may not be their intention to wipe the slate clean of all earlier contracts each time they conclude an integrated contract, whether or not it contains a merger clause, and whatever a merger clause may say.[150] Again, earlier agreements beyond a later contract's scope were probably out of sight and out of mind when the later contract was concluded. The parties would not intend to discharge such independent contracts. In many cases, however, it is difficult to say whether a parol agreement is independent. As we shall see, some agreements made during negotiations leading to an integrated contract are held to be collateral because they are independent. The question turns on the parties' intention as determined by the court, looking at the whole document at the least.[151]

A case in which there was a collateral agreement is *Lee v. Joseph E. Seagram & Sons, Inc.*[152] The plaintiffs, a father and two sons, owners of a

---

[149] Stimac v. Wissman, 69 N.W.2d 151, 154 (Mich. 1955); *see* Mitchill v. Lath, 160 N.E. 646, 647 (N.Y. 1928).

[150] *See* Brennan v. Carvel Corp., 929 F.2d 801, 808 (1st Cir. 1991). *But cf.* Childers Oil Co., Inc. v. Exxon Corp., 960 F.2d 1265, 1270 (4th Cir. 1992) (taking into account a merger clause along with other, determinative factors).

[151] *Brennan*, 929 F.2d at 808; Restatement (Second) of Contracts § 213(2), cmt. c (1981).

[152] 552 F.2d 447 (2d Cir. 1977).

fifty-percent interest in a liquor distributorship in Washington, DC, offered to sell their interest to a distiller on condition that the distiller agree to relocate the sons in a new distributorship in a different city. Following negotiations, a written contract for a sale of the interest was signed, but it did not contain the agreement for the distiller to relocate the sons. When the distiller failed to relocate the sons, the sellers claimed that it breached an oral contract to relocate them. The distiller relied on the parol evidence rule to deny the sellers' claim.

The court, applying New York law, held that the oral agreement was enforceable as a collateral agreement due to six factors. First, the parties to the two agreements were different—the sellers personally were the parties to the oral agreement and their corporation was the party to the written agreement.[153] Second, as with many sales of corporations, side agreements (such as consulting agreements) would be anticipated. Third, there was a close relationship of confidence and friendship over many years between the father and the president of the distiller; from this, it may be inferred that a handshake would suffice between them. Fourth, the president had made the oral promise, but negotiations were conducted for the distiller by others who may not have had the two transactions together in their minds. Fifth, there was no merger clause. Sixth, there was no contradiction between the oral and written agreements. Together, the document and its circumstances indicated that the oral agreement was not one that the parties "would ordinarily be expected to embody in the writing"[154] had they made it and meant to keep it alive.

A court will hold that the allegedly collateral agreement was within the scope of the writing, and therefore inoperative, when the topic of the parol agreement was treated in the integrated writing.[155] Thus, in *Rainey v. Travis*,[156] an integrated prenuptial agreement provided that the wife would have an unconditional right to live in the couple's home for the rest of her life after her husband's death. Against a claim that a collateral agreement required the wife to live alone and not to use the house for any immoral purpose, the court held that the alleged collateral agreement

---

153 *Accord*, Marinelli v. Unisa Holdings Inc., 655 N.Y.S.2d 495, 496 (App.Div. 1997).

154 *Lee*, 552 F.2d at 451.

155 *See* Quorum Health Resources, Inc. v. Carbon-Schuykill Community Hospital, Inc., 49 F.Supp.2d 430 (E.D.Pa. 1999).

156 850 S.W.2d 839 (Ark. 1993).

"relate[d] directly" to the unconditional right and, therefore, was precluded by the parol evidence rule.[157]

A leading and controversial case is *Mitchill v. Lath*.[158] A prospective buyer of a farm objected to the presence of an icehouse on adjacent land owned by someone other than the seller. The seller promised orally to remove the icehouse after the conveyance, in consideration of the purchase of the farm by the buyer. The buyer relied on this promise and concluded a written contract for the sale of the farm. The buyer paid, and the seller conveyed. The seller, however, did not remove the icehouse, and the buyer brought an action for breach of contract. The New York Court of Appeals held that the icehouse agreement was not collateral to the land sale contract and, consequently, would not be enforced.

Mitchill established New York's doctrinal law of collateral agreements. To have operative effect,

> (1) [t]he [parol] agreement must in form be a collateral one; (2) it must not contradict express or implied provisions of the written contract; (3) it must be one that parties would not ordinarily be expected to embody in the writing. . . .[159]

The court affirmed that the icehouse agreement was collateral in form and that it did not contradict the provisions of the contract of sale. Moreover, the allegedly collateral agreement was one that parties ordinarily would be expected to embody in the writing.[160] It considered the written contract and its surrounding circumstances. The contract contained all of the standard terms in the typical land sale contract and therefore appeared to be complete. The presence of the icehouse on adjacent land and the buyer's objection to it, the court said, would not lead one to believe that there was a separate agreement.

In dissent, Judge Lehman accepted the court's doctrinal statement but argued that it did not apply to the case so as to render the icehouse agreement unenforceable.[161] He conceded that the written agreement was completely integrated. He wrote, however, that the land sale contract covered a limited field that did not include the icehouse agreement. He relied mainly on the fact that the written contract was for the sale of the

---

[157] *Id.* at 841. *See also Gianni*, 126 A. at 792.

[158] 160 N.E. 646 (N.Y. 1928).

[159] *Id.* at 647.

[160] *Id.*

[161] *Id.* at 648–50.

farm while the icehouse was on other land. Consequently, in his view, the icehouse agreement would not ordinarily have been included in the writing.

The majority's reasoning and the result in *Mitchill* should be criticized. The majority relied entirely on the document and the circumstance that the buyer had objected to the icehouse. There is no basis here, and it is a *non sequitur*, to infer an intention—objective or subjective—to negate the icehouse agreement. The document, moreover, contained terms only for the sale of identified real property, the farm. It contained nothing relating to the adjacent land. The written contract was complete with respect to the sale of the farm, but there was no indication in the document or surrounding circumstances that its scope went beyond that land. Its contents were those of a standard land sale contract, whose scope normally is limited to the land to be conveyed and the price to be paid, on various conditions, not services to be performed. Consequently, the icehouse agreement normally would have been left out of the land sale contract and should have been given effect. (Nonetheless, *Mitchill's* doctrinal force has been strong in New York.[162])

§ 3.3.2. Formation, Invalidating Causes, and Conditions

The parol evidence rule comes into play only when there is an enforceable, integrated, written agreement. Parol evidence consequently is admissible to show that there was no binding agreement.[163] Thus, parol evidence can be admitted to show that there was no acceptance or a want or failure of consideration,[164] that the parties did not intend an agreement to be legally binding,[165] that the contract was invalid due to fraud,[166] duress,[167] illegality,[168] unconscionability,[169] or public policy,[170] that the

---

162 *See, e.g.*, Fogelson v. Rackfay Const. Co., 90 N.E.2d 881 (N.Y. 1950).

163 Ensign Painting Co. v. Alfred A. Smith, Inc., 188 N.W.2d 534, 535–36 (Mich. 1971); Kitley v. Abrams, 299 F.2d 341, 345 (2d Cir. 1962); RESTATEMENT (SECOND) OF CONTRACTS §§ 213, 214(d) (1981).

164 Coast Bank v. Holmes, 97 Cal. Rptr. 30, 35 (Cal.App. 1971).

165 National City Bank, Akron v. Donaldson, 642 N.E.2d 58, 61 (Ohio App. 1994).

166 Ernst Iron Works v. Duralith Corp., 200 N.E. 683, 684 (N.Y. 1936).

167 Jones v. Franklin, 168 S.E. 753, 754 (Va. 1933).

168 Commonwealth v. Weinfield's, Inc., 25 N.E.2d 198, 200 (Mass. 1940).

169 Bassler v. Bassler, 593 A.2d 82, 88 (Vt. 1991).

170 Schara v. Thiede, 206 N.W.2d 129 (Wis. 1973).

agreement was a sham,[171] or that the parties agreed by parol that the contract should become binding only on the occurrence of a condition precedent.[172] Of these, only the fraud and conditions cases need be discussed because the other issues are transparent.

§ 3.3.2.1. Fraud

Most authorities hold that claims of fraud, based on parol agreements, representations or promises, are allowed.[173] In such cases, the parol evidence is not being offered to establish the terms of the contract. Instead, it is being offered to show that the contract was void or voidable. Consequently, the parol evidence rule should not come into play.

The result may be different in a few jurisdictions if the claim is promissory fraud and the parol promise contradicts a promise in the written contract. Thus, the Supreme Court of California has held that the parol evidence rule precludes proof that an integrated contract was fraudulently induced by a parol promise made with knowledge that it could not be kept.[174] The written contract was one for the sale of an oven and related equipment. It contained a promise that the oven would produce a certain quantity of tortillas per hour. After ten days of testing and correctional measures, the buyer signed an acceptance stating that it had observed the oven in operation and was satisfied with its production capacity. Sometime later, the buyer brought an action against the seller for breach of contract and fraudulent misrepresentation. It argued that the seller had made an oral promise—knowing it could not be kept—that the oven would produce a greater quantity of tortillas than that spelled out in the written contract. It lost that lawsuit on appeal. In the seller's subsequent action against the buyer for malicious prosecution, the court considered whether the seller had satisfied the favorable termination element of a malicious prosecution claim. The court rejected the buyer's argument on the basis that the parol evidence rule, as a rule of substantive law,

---

[171] Herzog Contracting Corp. v. McGowen Corp., 976 F.2d 1062, 1067–71 (7th Cir. 1992).

[172] Hicks v. Bush, 180 N.E.2d 425, 427 (N.Y. 1962).

[173] Restatement (Second) of Contracts § 214(d) (1981); 2 Farnsworth, *supra* note 2, at § 7.4. *But see* Ungerleider, M.D. v. Gordon, 214 F.3d 1279 (11th Cir. 2000) (to make out an exception to the parol evidence rule, a representation that induced entry into contract must not contradict the written contract).

[174] *E.g.*, *Casa Herrera*, 83 P.3d at 503. *See also* HCB Contractors v. Liberty Place Hotel Assocs., 652 A.2d 1278, 1279–80 (Pa. 1995).

rendered the alleged parol promise "non-existent."[175] The rule, it said, "establishes, as a matter of law, the enforceable and incontrovertible terms of an integrated written agreement."[176] Further, California courts had "consistently rejected promissory fraud claims premised on prior or contemporaneous statements at variance with the terms of a written integrated agreement."[177]

The court's reasoning should be challenged. The parol evidence rule does not render a parol promise "non-existent." Such promises are not legally operative to ground the parties' contractual rights, duties, and powers. But they continue to exist as a matter of fact. A claim of promissory fraud rests in part on the *fact* that a party made a promise without a present intention to keep it.[178] When such a claim is recognized, the promise is not given legal effect; that is, there is no action for breach of it. A better rationale rests on the reliance element of a claim of promissory fraud. A contract term that is inconsistent with a parol agreement or promise arguably makes reliance on the parol commitment unreasonable. If so, an action for fraud will not succeed.[179]

To probe more deeply, the reliance argument also can be challenged. Consider another case in which there is a claim of promissory fraud based on a parol promise. The defendant relies on a merger clause in an integrated, written contract to argue that any reliance on that promise would be unreasonable. If the merger clause makes the written contract an integrated one, the parol promise is non-existent under the California Supreme Court's reasoning. No fraud action then is possible. By contrast, the New York Court of Appeals has held that a general merger clause integrating an agreement does not cut off a claim of promissory fraud on reliance grounds.[180] The Supreme Court of New Hampshire has held that a contractual disclaimer providing that a party "makes no representations" as to specific matters does not cut off such a claim.[181] To have that effect, the parties must agree to a specific "no reliance clause," stipulating that "a party is not relying on any representations as to the very

175 *Casa Herrera*, 83 P.3d at 504.

176 *Id.* at 503.

177 *Id.* at 504.

178 Sabo v. Delman, 143 N.E.2d 906, 908 (N.Y. 1957); Prosser and Keeton on the Law of Torts § 109 (W. Paige Keton, *et al.*, eds., 5th ed. 1984).

179 Hamade v. Sunoco, Inc., 721 N.W.2d 233, 249–50 (Mich.App. 2006).

180 *Sabo*, 143 N.E.2d at 906 ((as distinguished in Danaan Realty Corp. v. Harris, 157 N.E.2d 597, 598–99 (N.Y. 1959)).

181 Van Der Stok v. Van Voorhees, 866 A.2d 972, 975–76 (N.H. 2005).

matter as to which it . . . claims it was defrauded."[182] If general merger clauses, disclaimers of representations, and general no-reliance clauses do not cut off such a claim, it seems *a fortiori* that a mere inconsistency between a parol promise and a written promise should not have that effect. The law should not "provide a blueprint for defrauding parties to shield their wrongdoing,"[183] especially through the use of boilerplate clauses.

§ 3.3.2.2. Conditions Precedent

Notwithstanding the parol evidence rule, it is well settled that evidence of a parol agreement is admissible for the purpose of establishing a parol condition precedent to the legal effectiveness of an integrated, written contract.[184] Again, the parol evidence rule does not come into play. Such evidence is not being offered to establish contract terms but, rather, to show that the written agreement never became enforceable. For parol evidence of a condition to be allowed, the relevant condition must be to the legal effectiveness of the agreement and, therefore, to both parties' obligations.[185] A party cannot, however, prove such a parol agreement if it contradicts the explicit terms of the written contract. Thus, a written contract providing that the parties consent to it "irrevocably and unconditionally" will not be undermined by a parol condition to its effectiveness.[186] A court might not allow evidence of an oral promise not to enforce an arbitration clause in a contract because such a promise does not constitute a condition precedent to the legal effectiveness of the contract but, instead, of a clause in the contract.[187]

Absent such clearly contradictory language, however, matters can become murky. The leading case on the question is *Hicks v. Bush*.[188] The written contract provided for a merger of two corporations into a

---

[182] Danaan Realty Corp. v. Harris, 157 N.E.2d 597, 598–99, 606 (N.Y. 1959); *see* Travelodge Hotels, Inc. v. Honeysuckle Enters., Inc., 357 F.Supp. 2d 788 (D.N.J. 2005); Slack v. James, 614 S.E.2d 636, 640–41 (S.C. 2005).

[183] American Hardware Manufacturers, Ass'n v. Reed Elsevier, Inc., 2005 WL 3236590, at *5 (N.D. Ill. 2005).

[184] RESTATEMENT (SECOND) OF CONTRACTS § 217 (1981).

[185] 2 FARNSWORTH, *supra* note 2, at § 7.4.

[186] *Bank Leumi Trust*, 735 F.Supp. at 78; *Braten*, 456 N.E.2d at 805.

[187] Glazer v. Lehman Bros., Inc., 394 F.3d 444, 454–59 (6th Cir. 2005).

[188] 180 N.E.2d 425 (N.Y. 1962).

new corporation. Owners of the two corporations were to subscribe for stock in the new one within five days after the written agreement was made. The agreement provided:

> If within twenty-five days after the date hereof [the new corporation] shall have failed to accept any of said subscriptions delivered to it . . . then and in any such event the obligations of all of the parties hereto shall be terminated and cancelled.[189]

One of the two corporations subscribed, but the other did not, and the deal fell through. In an action for specific performance, the defendant offered testimony that the written agreement was signed "upon a parol condition" that it "was not to operate" as a contract and that the contemplated merger was not "to become effective" until they acquired funding in a certain amount.[190] The trial judge admitted the testimony, and the plaintiff appealed.

The New York Court of Appeals ruled, first, that parol evidence is admissible to prove an "oral condition precedent to the legal effectiveness of a written agreement."[191] Second, however, such a condition precedent must not contradict the express terms of that agreement. On the facts, the defendant argued that the parol condition would contradict the contract provision quoted above. The court rejected this argument. It held that the parol condition was "simply a further condition—a condition added to that requiring the acceptance of stock subscriptions within 25 days."[192] The court did not rest its holding on logical analysis of the question of contradiction. That might have shown that the parol condition contradicted the express words "then and in any *such* event" the parties' obligations would be canceled. Those words may signal that cancellation would occur *only if* the new corporation failed to accept a subscription. Instead, the court reasoned that the parol condition was the sort of condition that the parties would not be inclined to incorporate into a written agreement intended for the public.[193]

---

189 *Id.* at 426.
190 *Id.*
191 *Id.* at 427.
192 *Id.*
193 *Hicks*, 180 N.E.2d at 428.

§ 3.3.2.3. Reformation

The parol evidence rule does not discharge a parol agreement when a party seeks reformation of a contract.[194] This is a true exception to the rule. To get reformation, the party seeking it must prove that, unknown to either party, their true agreement differed materially from the written agreement.[195] Examples are typographical and transcription errors, or the parties' inattention to the writing.[196] Alternatively, the party seeking reformation can prove that, unknown to her but known to the other, who has mislead her with respect to the writing's contents, the written contract does not express the agreement.[197] Either way, parol evidence is essential to justice. This exception is based mainly on the premise that the parties' intend to replace their subjective agreement with an accurate written contract.[198] They do not intend to supersede it.

It might be thought that a party can simply allege a mutual mistake of the kind that would entitle it to reformation and thereby require the court to admit evidence of a parol agreement. This move would end-run the parol evidence rule. In practice, however, the reformation exception normally does not end-run the rule as a practical matter. Two features of reformation law make the remedy difficult to obtain. First, to survive a motion for summary judgment, a party seeking reformation must offer much more than an unsupported allegation that the writing does not reflect the true agreement.[199] The burden of proof is high: "[T]o be entitled to reformation, a party must establish that the undisputed material facts fully, clearly, and decisively show a mutual mistake."[200] Second, reformation is an equitable doctrine. A court may withhold it as a matter of discretion, as when it thinks a party seeks reformation as a strategic pretext.[201] No jury is involved. Consequently, courts frequently apply the parol evidence rule despite the reformation exception.

---

[194] Patton v. Mid-Continent Sys., Inc., 841 F.2d 742, 746 (7th Cir. 1988).

[195] Chimart Assocs. v. Paul, 489 N.E.2d 231, 233–34 (N.Y. 1986).

[196] OneBeacon America Ins. Co. v. Travelers Indem. Co. of Illinois, 465 F.3d 38, 41–42 (1st Cir. 2006).

[197] Hempel v. Nationwide Life Ins. Co., Inc., 370 A.2d 366, 371 (Pa. 1977).

[198] *See* Patton v. Mid-Continent Sys., Inc., 841 F.2d 742, 746 (7th Cir. 1988).

[199] *Chimart Assocs.*, 489 N.E.2d at 235–36.

[200] *OneBeacon America*, 465 F.3d at 41 (internal quotation marks omitted).

[201] Restatement (Second) of Contracts § 155, cmt. d (1981).

§ 3.3.3. *Finding and Resolving Ambiguity*

Contrary to some views,[202] the parol evidence rule does not preclude the admission of parol evidence for the purpose of giving meaning to an integrated, written contract's terms. Objectivism and subjectivism both hold this to be true. Thus, the (first) Restatement of Contracts, representing a broadly objective approach, provides that parol evidence is admissible "to establish the meaning of the integration when this is required for the application of the standards stated in §§ 230, 231." Section 230, in turn, provides:

> The standard of interpretation of an integration, except where it produces an ambiguous result, . . . is the meaning that would be attached to the integration by a reasonably intelligent person acquainted with all operative usages and knowing all the circumstances prior to and contemporaneous with the making of the integration, other than oral statements by the parties of what they intended it to mean.[203]

Note that the enumerated elements of interpretation come into play before an ambiguity appears. The Restatement (Second) provides simply:

> Agreements and negotiations prior to or contemporaneous with the adoption of a writing are admissible in evidence to establish . . .
> (c) the meaning of the writing, whether or not integrated.[204]

A court need not find an ambiguity before admitting contextual evidence. The second Restatement, however, allows a broader range of contextual evidence than does the first Restatement. It allows, in particular, a party's statement of its intention.[205]

To be sure, notwithstanding the "restatements," almost all jurisdictions disallow parol evidence when the written contract is unambiguous, and parol evidence is offered to give meaning to the writing.[206] The substantive basis of the exclusion, however, is the so-called plain meaning rule, not the parol evidence rule. There is an important distinction here.

---

202 *E.g.*, Peter Linzer, *The Comfort of Certainty: Plain Meaning and the Parol Evidence Rule*, 71 Fordham L. Rev. 799, 801 (2002).
203 Restatement (First) of Contracts § 230 (1932).
204 Restatement (Second) of Contracts § 214 (1981).
205 *Id.* at § 212, cmt. b.
206 *See* § 4.2.1.

The function of the parol evidence rule is *only* to identify the terms of a contract when there is an integrated writing. When applicable, its consequence is to discharge some parol agreements, leaving the integrated writing's terms as *the* terms of the parties' contract. The plain meaning rule, by contrast, comes into play whether or not a contract is integrated and only *after* the contract's terms have been identified. When applicable, its consequence is to prevent a finding on the basis of parol evidence that the terms are ambiguous.[207] We will consider the plain meaning rule, and distinguish it more completely from the parol evidence rule, in Chapter 4.[208]

[207] *Id.*
[208] *See* § 4.2.4.

CHAPTER 4

The Ambiguity Question

After identifying the terms of a contract, the next task in contract interpretation is to determine whether to admit extrinsic evidence, if any is offered, to give meaning to the terms. As we saw in Chapter 3, when there is a written contract, the parol evidence rule determines only what the *terms* of a written contract are and whether *they* can be contradicted or added to by a parol agreement. That rule, however, does not determine what evidence a court should allow for the purpose of giving *meaning* to the terms.[1] This determination usually is the province, in the first instance, of the so-called plain meaning rule. The rule, simply put, bans extrinsic evidence to prove the parties' intention when a written contract is unambiguous in the contested respect. In the absence of ambiguity, courts conclude that a document's meaning is "plain," and the plain meaning becomes the contract's meaning as a matter of law. The plain meaning rule is the common law in "an overwhelming majority" of jurisdictions.[2] It is not, however, the rule in the Restatement (Second) of Contracts [Restatement (Second)] or in Article 2 of the Uniform Commercial Code (UCC).[3]

A court determines whether a contract document is ambiguous in the contested respect. This determination is solely a question of whether

---

[1] *See* §§ 3.1.1; 3.3.3.

[2] 2 E. ALLAN FARNSWORTH, FARNSWORTH ON CONTRACTS § 7.12 (4th ed. 2003).

[3] UCC § 1-303 (2001); UCC § 2-202(a) (2001); *see* RESTATEMENT (SECOND) OF CONTRACTS § 201 (1981).

the contract language fails to resolve the dispute before the court.[4] If it thus fails, the court allows extrinsic evidence as relevant to resolving the ambiguity in accordance with the parties' intention. Chapter 5 considers how the law allows fact-finders to resolve any ambiguities that appear.

§ 4.1. The Nature of Ambiguity

A contract or term commonly is said to be ambiguous if it is susceptible to more than one reasonable meaning.[5] This definition of *ambiguity* is correct semantically but not quite accurate as a practical legal matter. A contract as a whole or a contract term may bear three, four, or more reasonable meanings (especially if it is drafted poorly). Usually, only two are advanced by the parties in litigation, each meaning favoring the party who advances it. The court's job is described most accurately as determining whether the contract is ambiguous as between these two meanings and, therefore, in the contested respect. A third or fourth meaning is irrelevant to the case at hand, as are ambiguities in contract terms that are not disputed; "a contract may be ambiguous when applied to one set of facts but not another."[6] Accordingly, "ambiguity is detected claim by claim."[7] As a consequence of this, Professors Arthur L. Corbin and E. Allan Farnsworth missed their marks when they argued that we should dispense with the question of ambiguity because all language is infected with ambiguity.[8] If one of the two contested meanings in the case is unreasonable, the contract is not ambiguous as a practical legal matter whatever other meanings the language might bear.

---

[4] *See* E. Allan Farnsworth, *"Meaning" in the Law of Contracts*, 939 Yale L.J. 939, 962 (1967).

[5] *E.g.*, McAbee Const., Inc. v. U.S., 97 F.3d 1431, 1434–35 (Fed. Cir. 1996); Columbia Gas Trans. Corp. v. New Ulm Gas, 940 S.W.2d 587, 591 (Tex. 1996); Hutchison v. Sunbeam Coal Corp., 519 A.2d 385, 390 (Pa. 1986).

[6] Eternity Global Master Fund Ltd. v. Morgan Guar. Trust Co. of N.Y., 375 F.3d 168, 177 (2d Cir. 2004); *see* Dore v. Arnold Worldwide, Inc., 139 P.3d 56, 60 (Cal. 2006); Donoghue v. IBC USA (Publications), Inc., 70 F.3d 206, 215–16 (1st Cir. 1995); Bank of the West v. Superior Court, 833 P.2d 545, 552 (Cal. 1992).

[7] World Trade Center Props., L.L.C. v. Hartford Fire Ins. Co., 345 F.3d 154, 184 (2d Cir. 2003).

[8] 3 Arthur L. Corbin, Corbin on Contracts § 542 (1961); Farnsworth, *supra* note 4, at 965.

Courts generally recognize two kinds of ambiguity.[9] The first is called *intrinsic* or *patent* ambiguity. This kind of ambiguity appears from the face of a contract document, viewed only within its four corners. It may be that a word or sentence has two contested meanings, or that two provisions have inconsistent implications in the case. No extrinsic evidence is needed to see an intrinsic ambiguity—only knowledge of the dispute, the proffered meanings, the relevant language, the whole contract, and common sense.

The second general kind of ambiguity is called *extrinsic* or *latent* ambiguity. This kind of ambiguity does not appear from the face of the document, which may seem perfectly clear to the judge. Upon a consideration of extrinsic evidence, a proffer of extrinsic evidence, a party's contention, or an affidavit, however, the document can be seen to be ambiguous in the contested respect. It bears emphasis that an extrinsic ambiguity renders a document ambiguous even though the document appears on its face to have only one meaning.[10] If it did not so appear, there would be no point to the concept of extrinsic ambiguity.

Some courts may find an extrinsic ambiguity, for example, if the contract includes words with both ordinary and extraordinary meanings, the latter of which can be established by a trade usage.[11] In *Hurst v. W.J. Lake & Co.*,[12] a pre-UCC case, a contract called for the purchase and sale of horsemeat scraps. The specifications provided that the scraps must be a minimum of 50 percent protein. The seller delivered scraps with between 49.5 and 50 percent protein. The court held that, due to custom and usage in the horsemeat trade, greater than 50 percent protein could mean greater than 49.5 percent protein.[13] In such a case, the contract language is clear on its face mathematically, and evidence of the trade usage is extrinsic evidence. The usage, however, reveals the language to have an extraordinary meaning as well as an ordinary, mathematical meaning, the former in the language that the parties presumably used. The custom was to round up from 49.5 percent. Consequently, the contract term, as the parties used it, was extrinsically ambiguous.

---

[9] Friendswood Dev. Co. v. McDade & Co., 926 S.W.2d 280, 282–83 (Tex. 1996); Federal Deposit Ins. Corp. v. W.R. Grace & Co., 877 F.2d 614, 620–21 (7th Cir. 1989).

[10] *Id.*; Bache Halsey Stuart Shields, Inc. v. Alamo Savings Assoc. of Texas, 611 S.W.2d 706, 708 (Tex.App. 1980).

[11] Flying J Inc. v. Comdata Network, Inc., 405 F.3d 821, 833 (10th Cir. 2005).

[12] 16 P.2d 627 (Or. 1932).

[13] *Id.* at 630.

Judge Richard A. Posner and others think that courts should recognize extrinsic ambiguities, at least when the relevant extrinsic evidence is objective and compelling.[14] The reason is that:

> a judge who, ignorant of the technical meaning, took the ordinary to be the intended meaning would be fooled. He would be like a judge who tried to interpret a contract written in French without knowing the French language.[15]

Most courts, however, recognize intrinsic but not extrinsic ambiguities.[16] In Illinois, for example:

> An agreement, when reduced to writing, must be presumed to speak the intention of the parties who signed it. It speaks for itself, and the intention with which it was executed must be determined from the language used. It is not to be changed by extrinsic evidence.[17]

Some courts recognize both intrinsic and extrinsic ambiguities.[18]

Courts that recognize extrinsic ambiguities sometimes put limits on what they will consider when determining whether there is an ambiguity. For example, the United States Court of Appeals for the Third Circuit, applying Pennsylvania law, recognized extrinsic ambiguities but established four limitations. First,

> [t]o determine whether ambiguity exists in a contract, the court may consider the words of the contract, the alternative meaning suggested by counsel, and the nature of the *objective* evidence to be offered in support of that meaning.[19]

---

[14] PMC, Inc. v. Sherwin-Williams Co., 151 F.3d 610, 614–16 (7th Cir. 1998).

[15] *Id.* at 614.

[16] *E.g.*, Air Safety, Inc. v. Teachers Realty Corp., 706 N.E.2d 882, 884–86 (Ill. 1999); Shifrin v. Forest City Enterprises, Inc., 597 N.E.2d 499, 501 (Ohio 1992); Teitelbaum Holdings, Ltd. v. Gold, 421 N.Y.S.2d 556, 559 (N.Y. 1979); Lewis v. East Texas Finance Co., 146 S.W.2d 977, 980 (Tex. 1942).

[17] *Air Safety*, 706 N.E.2d at 884. ((quoting Western Illinois Oil Co. v. Thompson, 186 N.E.2d 285 (Ill. 1962)).

[18] *E.g.*, Pacific Gas & Elec. Co. v. G.W. Thomas Drayage & Rigging Co., 442 P.2d 641, 645 (Cal. 1968); McCarty v. Mercury Metalcraft Co., 127 N.W.2d 340, 344 (Mich. 1964); Atlantic Northern Airlines v. Schwimmer, 96 A.2d 652, 656 (N.J. 1953).

[19] Bohler-Uddeholm America, Inc., v. Ellwood Group, 247 F.3d 79, 93 (3d Cir. 2001) (in part quoting *Mellon Bank*, 619 F.2d at 1011) (emphasis added, internal quotation marks omitted).

Second, the extrinsic evidence must show that specific terms in the contract are ambiguous: There must be a "contractual hook" on which to hang the proffered meaning.[20] Third, the proffered meaning must be reasonable.[21] Fourth, the proffered meaning must not contradict the common understanding of the disputed term or phrase if there is another term that the parties easily could have used to convey the contradictory meaning.[22]

It might be thought that admitting extrinsic evidence to establish an extrinsic ambiguity is problematic. If, after admitting and reviewing that evidence, the judge decides that the contract document is unambiguous, the evidence is inadmissible under the plain meaning rule. This seems circular.[23] We will discuss this issue below when we consider the roles of judge and jury in deciding the question of ambiguity.[24]

§ 4.2. The Law of Ambiguity

As indicated above, the plain meaning rule is by far the most widely employed rule governing the question of ambiguity. It is easy to misunderstand. It requires much less than is commonly supposed. This section seeks to clarify the rule and present the alternatives to it. We will consider the rule, the decision procedures under the rule and the main alternative, the roles of judges and juries, and the important distinction between the parol evidence and plain meaning rules.

§ 4.2.1. The Plain Meaning and Four Corners Rules

The most widely adopted statements of the plain meaning rule say that "[a]n unambiguous contract will be given its plain meaning."[25] Such statements can be very misleading if not read carefully. They may appear to hold that a court always, or whenever possible, should give contract

---

[20] *Id.*

[21] *Id.*

[22] *Id.* at 94–95.

[23] *Air Safety*, 706 N.E.2d at 884–86.

[24] *See* § 3.2.3.

[25] *E.g.*, Mundey v. Erie Ins. Group, 893 A.2d 645, 649–50 (Md.App. 2006); Intermountain Eye and Laser Centers, P.L.L.C. v. Miller, 127 P.3d 121, 125 (Idaho 2005); Saleh v. Farmers Ins. Exchange, 133 P.3d 428, 434 (Utah 2006); Rose v. M/V "GULF STREAM FALCON," 186 F.3d 1345, 1350 (11th Cir. 1999).

language a literal, acontextual meaning. But this is not right. The statement says only that the plain meaning prevails *when the language is unambiguous*. Therefore, the rule—a tautology—simply requires a court to give an unambiguous contract term its unambiguous meaning. In other words, if contract language has only one relevant meaning, a court must afford it that meaning. If there were more than one relevant meaning, of course, the language would be ambiguous, and there would not be a plain meaning at all.

A secondary variation on the plain meaning rule provides that a contract term presumptively should be given its natural and ordinary meaning.[26] That is, the courts should refuse to "indulge in a forced construction ignoring provisions or so distorting them as to accord a meaning other than the one evidently intended by the parties."[27] This variation assumes that the parties normally use the language in an ordinary way. If they do, and the ordinary meaning is not ambiguous, the rule implements their intention. But determining even an ordinary meaning requires consideration of its context of use.[28]

The secondary variation, too, can be misleading. For a court to answer the question of ambiguity on this basis, the "natural and ordinary" meaning must be the same as the unambiguous meaning; otherwise, the contract would be ambiguous, and there would be no ordinary meaning that resolves the interpretive dispute. Understood charitably, the variation holds that the ordinary meanings of words have weight—sometimes much weight—when balancing them with other factors bearing on the parties' intention. Even the Restatement (Second), which rejects the plain meaning and four corners rules, emphasizes the importance of interpreting language in accordance with its generally prevailing meaning (unless the parties manifest a different intention or the language has a technical meaning).[29] The critical problem arises, not from the plain meaning rule but, rather, from the four corners rule when it is applied to the question of ambiguity.

---

[26] Sturman v. Socha, 463 A.2d 527, 532 (Conn. 1983); Transamerica Ins. Co. v. Rutkin, 218 So.2d 509, 511 (Fla.App. 1969); Highley v. Phillips, 5 A.2d 824, 828-29 (Md. 1939); Virginian Ry. Co. v. Avis, 98 S.E. 638, 639 (Va. 1919).

[27] Celebrate Windsor, Inc. v. Harleysville Worcester Ins. Co., 2006 WL 1169816, *17 (D. Conn. 2006); *see* Reliance Ins. Co. of Illinois v. Weis, 148 B.R. 575, 579 (E.D. Mo. 1992).

[28] *See* §§ 2.1.3; 2.2.4.

[29] RESTATEMENT (SECOND) OF CONTRACTS § 202(3)(a) (1981).

The plain meaning rule should be distinguished from the four corners rule. In this context, the latter rule can be stated as follows: "When deciding whether a contract is ambiguous, a court may consider only the contract on its face, excluding all extrinsic evidence." It thus requires a court to decide whether a contract is ambiguous on the basis of the contract document alone, without resort to extrinsic evidence of the parties' intention as to its meaning(s).[30] Notably, the four corners rule must be applied *before* the plain meaning rule can be applied. Consequently, the four corners rule, by excluding evidence of the context, may recognize the possibility of an intrinsic but not an extrinsic ambiguity. The rule prescribes the elements of contract interpretation that a court may take into account for deciding the question of ambiguity. It has an evidentiary function. The plain meaning rule, by contrast, is a substantive rule of law that prescribes the legal consequence of concluding that there is no ambiguity. It should be stated as follows: "When a contract is unambiguous in the contested respect, the court must give the contract its unambiguous meaning as a matter of law." The plain meaning rule itself does not foreclose a court from considering the contract document in its context, including extrinsic evidence, bearing on the question of ambiguity. Consequently, concluding that a contract has a "plain" or "unambiguous" meaning can follow a broad analysis of the document in its context.[31]

Because, for practical purposes, the plain meaning rule requires a court to give unambiguous contract language its unambiguous meaning, it seems too obvious to need stating. The action is all in the rule's predicate—the logically preceding question of whether there is an ambiguity. Here, the plain meaning rule does not prescribe the elements that can be considered. The four corners rule, however, does.

§ 4.2.2. Decision Procedures

On the question of ambiguity, there is significant controversy among the courts. The classical view is that a court should decide whether a contract is ambiguous by looking at the document alone—as a whole—and

30 *E.g.*, Fairbourn Commercial, Inc. v. American Housing Partners, Inc., 94 P.3d 292, 295 (Utah 2004).

31 *E.g.*, First Christian Assembly of God, Montbello v. City and County of Denver, 122 P.3d 1089, 1092 (Colo.App. 2005); Brinderson-Newberg Joint Venture v. Pacific Erectors, Inc., 971 F.2d 272 (9th Cir. 1992).

deciding whether it bears both contested meanings.[32] That is, a court may find that the contract is ambiguous only if it finds an intrinsic ambiguity. Such an ambiguity may arise from ambiguous words, sentence ambiguity, structural ambiguity, or vagueness.[33] This approach is based on the four corners rule.

Two rival views hold that a court should find a contract ambiguous only *after* reviewing the evidence, including extrinsic evidence. These views recognize the possibility of an extrinsic ambiguity. They reject the four corners rule. There are two versions, which differ over the kinds of relevant extrinsic evidence that a court should consider. These versions reflect the objective and subjective theories. One version confines the relevant extrinsic evidence to objective factors.[34] The other allows, in addition, evidence bearing on the parties' mental intentions with respect to the meaning of the contract language to which they agreed.[35]

Pacific Gas & Electric Co. v. G.W. Thomas Drayage & Rigging Co., Inc.[36] is the landmark case exemplifying the subjective theory's decision procedure for deciding the question of ambiguity. An electric utility agreed with a contractor that the contractor would furnish the labor and equipment needed to remove and replace the upper metal cover of the utility's steam turbine. The contractor agreed to perform the work at its own risk and expense and to

> indemnify [the utility] against all loss, damage, expense and liability resulting from . . . injury to property, arising out of or in any way connected with the performance of the contract.[37]

In the event, the cover fell and damaged the exposed rotor of the turbine. The utility brought an action to recover the amount it subsequently spent on repairs. In the trial court, the contractor offered to prove by extrinsic evidence that the indemnity clause was meant to cover injuries to third parties only, not to plaintiff's property. The proffered extrinsic evidence included admissions by the utility's agents, the parties' conduct under similar contracts, and more. The trial court observed that the quoted

---

[32] West, Weir & Bartel, Inc. v. Mary Carter Paint Co., 255 N.E.2d 709, 711–12 (N.Y. 1969); Farnsworth, *supra* note 2, at § 7.12 (describing the "restrictive view").

[33] *See* § 4.4.

[34] Restatement (First) of Contracts §§ 230; 235, cmt. e (1932).

[35] Restatement (Second) of Contracts § 212(1) and cmt. b (1981).

[36] 442 P.2d 641 (Cal. 1968).

[37] *Id.* at 643.

language was "the classic language for a third party indemnity provision" and that "one could very easily conclude that . . . its whole intendment [was] to indemnify third parties."[38] It held, however, that the quoted language had a plain meaning that required the contractor to indemnify the utility—presumably that *all loss* means all loss, including a loss to the utility.

The Supreme Court of California reversed. Justice Roger Traynor's opinion for the court is famous for its blistering attack on the possibility of a plain meaning of a contract, evident from the document alone. He rejected the idea that words have "absolute and constant referents" that would make it possible to discover contractual intention in the words of the contract themselves. Quoting Corbin, he wrote that:

> the meaning of particular words or groups of words varies with the . . . verbal context and surrounding circumstances and purposes in view of the linguistic education and experience of their users and their hearers or readers.[39]

Further,

> [t]he fact that the terms of an instrument appear clear to a judge does not preclude the possibility that the parties chose the language to express different terms. That possibility is not limited to contracts whose terms have acquired a particular meaning by trade usage, but exists whenever the parties' understanding of the words used may have differed from the judge's.[40]

Justice Traynor focused on the question whether the trial judge should have admitted the contractor's extrinsic evidence *before* deciding whether the contract language was "fairly susceptible to either one of the two interpretations contended for"—whether the language was ambiguous.[41] The court held that the judge, upon the utility's objection, should have admitted the extrinsic evidence conditionally pending such a decision, reserving his ruling on the objection or admitting the evidence subject to a motion to strike.[42] The judge then should allow the evidence unconditionally if the

---

38 *Id.*

39 *Id.* at 644 (internal quotation marks omitted) ((citing Arthur L. Corbin, *The Interpretation of Words and the Parol Evidence Rule*, 50 Cornell L.Q. 161, 187 (1965)).

40 *Id.* at 645 (footnote omitted).

41 *Id.* at 646, 646 n.8.

42 *Id.* at 644–45, 645 n.7.

language of the contract was reasonably susceptible to the utility's proffered meaning.

Underlying Justice Traynor's opinion is the subjective theory of contract interpretation. He wrote:

> Accordingly, the meaning of a writing can only be found by interpretation in the light of all the circumstances that reveal the sense in which the writer used the words. The exclusion of parol evidence regarding such circumstances merely because the words do not appear ambiguous to the reader can easily lead to the attribution to a written instrument of a meaning that was never intended.[43]

Accordingly, he believed, evidence of the writer's subjective intention can reveal a reasonable meaning of the contract language, rendering it extrinsically ambiguous.

A court can employ Justice Traynor's decision procedure using the objective theory. Neither the objective theory nor the plain meaning rule requires a court to determine ambiguity from within the four corners of the document. The court could consider the parties' allegations, contentions, arguments, affidavits, and proffers of extrinsic evidence of the objective context before determining whether the contract language is extrinsically ambiguous.[44] Hence, it would take into account, according to a California precedent preceding *P.G. & E.*, testimony as to the

> circumstances surrounding the making of the agreement . . . including the object, nature and subject matter of the writing so that the court can "place itself in the same situation in which the parties found themselves at the time of contracting.[45]

According to the United States Court of Appeals for the Second Circuit, the law is objective:

> An ambiguity exists where the terms of a contract could suggest more than one meaning when viewed objectively by a reasonably intelligent person who has examined the context of the entire integrated

---

[43] *Id.* at 645 ((citing Universal Sales Corp. v. Cal. Press Mfg. Co., 128 P.2d 665, 679 (Cal. 1942)) (concurring opinion of Traynor, J.) (internal quotation marks omitted).

[44] *E.g.*, Lupien v. Citizens Utilities Co., 159 F.3d 102, 104–05 (2d Cir. 1998); Ahsan v. Eagle, Inc., 678 N.E.2d 1238, 1241 (Ill.App. 1997).

[45] *Pacific Gas & Elec.* 442 P.2d at 645 ((quoting Universal Sales Corp. v. Cal. Press Mfg. Co., 128 P.2d 665, 671 (Cal. 1942)).

> agreement and who is cognizant of the customs, practices, usages and terminology as generally understood in the particular trade or business.[46]

Under the objective theory, however, the court would not consider, for example, proffers of testimony by a party of its own intention nor evidence of the course of negotiations.[47] The court would benefit from knowing the parties' context but not their minds.

Notably, the result in *P.G. & E.* would not have differed had Justice Traynor followed the objective theory. Insofar as appears from the case reports, the contractor did not offer evidence other than that of the objective circumstances.[48] In truth, the trial court misunderstood the nature of ambiguity and the plain meaning rule. It followed a literalist approach and the four corners rule, and it did not recognize the possibility of an extrinsic ambiguity. Literalism and the four corners rule are what Justice Traynor really ridiculed—the view that words have, in his words following Corbin, "absolute and constant referents, apparent from the face of a document."[49] His criticism is not applicable to objectivism, which may abandon the four corners rule and allow for the objective context to be considered.

There is a fourth position in addition to the four corners rule, objective contextualism, and subjective contextualism. A very few, though important, authorities dispense with any need to determine whether a contract is ambiguous. They allow the admission of all relevant extrinsic evidence to give meaning to the contract in any case.[50] The Restatement (Second) is representative, though this part of it has not been very influential. In effect, it substitutes for almost all cases a doctrine of fault for a

---

[46] *Eternity Global Master Fund*, 375 F.3d at 173. *See also* Leprino Foods Co. v. Gress Poultry, Inc., 179 F.Supp. 2d 659, 677 (M.D. Pa. 2005); *Friendswood Dev.*, 926 S.W.2d at 282. *Contra*, Milonas v. Public Employment Relations Bd., 648 N.Y.S.2d 779, 784 (App.Div. 1996) (evidence of custom or usage admissible only if written contract is ambiguous); Western Union Tel. Co. v. American Communications Ass'n, C.I.O., 86 N.E.2d 162, 166 (N.Y. 1949) (same).

[47] Clear Lakes Trout Co., Inc. v. Clear Springs Foods, Inc., 106 P.3d 443, 446 (Idaho 2005); Murphy v. Keystone Steel & Wire Co., a Div. of Keystone Consol. Industries, Inc., 61 F.3d 560, 567 (7th Cir. 1995); Restatement (First) of Contracts § 230 (1932).

[48] *Pacific Gas & Elec. Co.*, 442 P.2d at 643.

[49] *Id.* at 644.

[50] *E.g.*, Johnson v. Cavan, 133 P.2d 649, 651–52 (Ariz.App. 1987); Alyeska Pipeline Service Co. v. O'Kelley, 645 P.2d 767, 770 n.1 (Alaska 1982).

doctrine that interprets the language used by the parties. Its fundamental rules of "interpretation" are as follows:

> (1) Where the parties have attached the same meaning to a promise or agreement or a term thereof, it is interpreted in accordance with that meaning.
> (2) Where the parties have attached different meanings to a promise or agreement or a term thereof, it is interpreted in accordance with the meaning attached by one of them if at the time the agreement was made
>   (a) that party did not know of any different meaning attached by the other and the other knew the meaning attached by the first party, or
>   (b) that party had no reason to know of any different meaning attached by the other, and the other had reason to know the meaning attached by the first party.
> (3) Except as stated in this Section, neither party is bound by the meaning attached by the other, even though the result may be a failure of mutual assent.[51]

Here, the meaning of a term must be *attached* to a word by at least one party. Meaning, therefore, is in a party's mind, and the attachment of a meaning to language constitutes its meaning under the circumstances indicated.[52] There is no limitation on the meanings the parties may attach to a term, such as a requirement that the relevant language be ambiguous according to the conventions of language use in the context. A comment says:

> [i]t is sometimes said that extrinsic evidence cannot change the plain meaning of a writing, but meaning can almost never be plain except in a context. Accordingly, the rule stated in Subsection (1) is not limited to cases where it is determined that the language used is ambiguous. Any determination of meaning or ambiguity should only be made in the light of the relevant evidence of the situation and relations of the parties, the subject matter of the transaction, preliminary negotiations and statements made therein, usages of trade, and the course of dealing between the parties.[53]

---

[51] Restatement (Second) of Contracts § 201 (1981).

[52] *Id.* at § 201, cmt. a.

[53] *Id.* at § 212, cmt. b.

Accordingly, evidence of parol agreements and negotiations, and a party's statement of its intention during negotiations, would be admissible to interpret in accordance with the parties' or a party's subjective intention.[54] Again, no decision on ambiguity is required. Consequently, as indicated in Chapter 1,[55] the Restatement (Second) says that, if the parties orally agree that *buy* shall mean sell, and a party says "buy," the court should hold them to sell.[56] Article 2 of the UCC similarly dispenses with any requirement that an ambiguity be found before a court admits evidence of a course of performance, course of dealing, or usage of trade.[57]

In sum, there are three decision procedures for determining whether a contract is ambiguous. The first is based on the four corners rule, which requires a court to determine ambiguity from the document alone. Only an intrinsic ambiguity can be found in this way. The second requires a court to determine whether there is an extrinsic ambiguity in light of objective extrinsic evidence proffered before the question of ambiguity is considered. The parties' statements of their own intentions, and evidence of the negotiations, would be excluded. The third also requires a court to determine whether there is an extrinsic ambiguity in light of extrinsic evidence considered before the question of ambiguity is decided, but it allows evidence of both objective evidence and evidence of subjective intentions. In addition, a fourth decision procedure dispenses with any need for a court to decide whether the contract's language is ambiguous.

When determining which of the four decision procedures should be employed, the key question is: How much context is needed to decide the question of ambiguity appropriately? All four procedures allow a court to consider some degree of context. Speaking summarily, the first allows a court to take into account the document as a whole, not only the governing word or phrase. The second includes the whole document and the objective circumstances when the contract was made. The third and fourth allow the document as a whole and all relevant evidence of the parties' subjective intentions as to the meaning of the contract's language.

---

[54] *Id.* at §§ 214(c); 212, cmts. b & c.

[55] *See* § 1.3.3.

[56] Restatement (Second) of Contracts § 212, cmt.b, Ill. 4 (1981).

[57] UCC § 2-202, cmt. 1(c) (2001); *see* Campbell Farms v. Wald, 578 N.W.2d 96, 100 (N.D. 1998); Nanakuli Paving and Rock Co. v. Shell Oil Co., Inc., 664 F.2d 772, 796–97 (9th Cir. (1981); Columbia Nitrogen Corp. v. Royster Co., 451 F.2d 3, 8 (4th Cir. 1971). *But see* Deerfield Commodities, Ltd. v. Nerco, Inc., 696 P.2d 1096, 1110 (Or.App. 1985) (the document must be reasonably susceptible to the interpretation suggested by the course of dealing, course of performance, or usage of the trade).

These alternatives reflect the objective theory in two versions and the subjective theory. Objectivism either confines the inquiry to the four corners of the contract document, viewed as a whole, or expands the inquiry to include the document's evident purpose(s) and the objective circumstances. Subjectivism is concerned that the parties' subjective intentions can be realized only by including, in addition, evidence of the course of negotiations, the parties' prior dealings, a party's statement of its own intent, and any other relevant evidence. We will consider the key question of how much context is needed, normatively, in Chapter 6.

§ 4.2.3. Judge and Jury

Under the four corners rule, the role of the judge is straightforward. She decides whether a contract is ambiguous from the face of the document.[58] If the document does not appear to be ambiguous, the analysis ends; the plain meaning rule comes into play to require that the judge give the unambiguous meaning to the contract as a matter of law. No extrinsic evidence then is admissible for the purpose of giving meaning to the writing. If the contract is ambiguous on its face, extrinsic evidence is admissible for that purpose. The courts generally give the question of meaning to the jury, when it is the fact-finder and when answering the question depends on disputed extrinsic evidence.[59] When there is no such dispute, the judge decides.[60] A little authority gives a question of meaning to the judge also when "the form or subject-matter of a particular contract outruns a jury's competence."[61]

Matters are more complicated when a court must determine whether there is an ambiguity after admitting extrinsic evidence. According to *Pacific Gas & Electric Co.*, as indicated above,[62] the trial court would admit the extrinsic evidence conditionally, reserving its ruling on admissibility or admitting it subject to a motion to strike. If the court then finds the contract to be ambiguous, the evidence stays in. If the court finds the contract to be unambiguous, it rules the evidence out or grants a motion to strike and, in either event, gives the contract its unambiguous meaning

[58] Winegar v. Smith Inv. Co., 590 P.2d 348, 350 (Utah 1979).

[59] Hartford Acc. & Indem. Co. v. Wesolowski, 305 N.E.2d 907, 910 (N.Y. 1973). *See* § 5.1.

[60] *Id.*

[61] *E.g.*, Meyers v. The Selznick Co., 373 F.2d 218, 222 (2d Cir. 1966).

[62] *See* § 4.2.2.

as a matter of law.[63] It may appear that the jury or judge-as-fact-finder hears the evidence in any event. If the court finds that there is no ambiguity, it may not be humanly feasible for the fact-finder to disregard it. When there is or will be a jury, however, the court can protect it from contamination by holding an evidentiary hearing outside of its presence. If the court finds the contract to be ambiguous, the parties can replay the evidence before the jury. Such a two-step procedure is somewhat unusual and can be awkward.[64]

A more streamlined procedure is possible. There is no need to *admit* any evidence to meet Justice Traynor's concern that, without considering a contract's context, a judge may blindly follow misleading apparent meanings and miss extrinsic ambiguities. His concern, like Corbin's, centered on the way a judge who did not know of the parties' context would be interpreting in the context only of her own linguistic background and experience. Because the judge's personal context will not match the parties', this can lead her to find an unambiguous meaning at odds with the parties' subjective intentions.[65] In Traynor's view, that would be an unjustified imposition on the parties.[66] However, a judge can base the ambiguity decision on submissions, including allegations, contentions, affidavits, offers of proof, and arguments by counsel, on a motion for summary judgment or upon objection before admitting the evidence at trial.[67] These submissions can provide a context for the ambiguity decision—even a rich context—that is not the judge's own, but that would acquaint her with that of the parties. She then can see (as well as one ever can) the contract language from their point of view. No findings of fact need be made—only the usual assumptions on such motions. In the first instance, the court needs to determine only whether the contract is ambiguous. It can leave proof of the document's meaning to a later stage if one is appropriate.

Note that there is an important convergence between the substantive law of contracts and the law of civil procedure. If a court finds a contract to be unambiguous in the contested respect, there can be no material

---

63 *Pacific Gas & Elec. Co.*, 442 P.2d at 645 n.7.

64 *Alyeska Pipeline Service*, 645 P.2d at 770.

65 *Pacific Gas & Elec. Co.*, 442 P.2d at 643.

66 *Id.* at 645.

67 *See Dore*, 139 P.3d at 60-61; Local Union No. 1992, Int'l Brotherhood of Electrical Workers v. Okonite Co., 189 F.3d 339, 343 (3d Cir. 1999); *Mellon Bank*, 619 F.2d at 1011.

dispute of fact as to its meaning. A judge should decide the question of meaning on a motion for summary judgment. Similarly, if a contract is unambiguous, no reasonable jury could come to any conclusion but one. A judge should decide on a motion for a directed verdict or judgment notwithstanding the verdict. Consequently, it seems, the law of civil procedure would require a court to decide (upon motion) whether a contract is ambiguous, even if the substantive law of contracts did not.

§ 4.2.4. The Parol Evidence Rule Distinguished

Some courts say that, when a contract is unambiguous and integrated, the parol evidence rule precludes the admission of extrinsic evidence offered to give meaning to a contract's terms:

> The parol evidence rule "prohibits the admission of extrinsic evidence of prior or contemporaneous oral agreements, or prior written agreements, to explain the meaning of a contract when the parties have reduced their agreement to an unambiguous integrated writing."[68]

This statement of the law confuses the parol evidence and plain meaning rules in three respects. First, it says that the parol evidence rule applies when a contract is both unambiguous and integrated. This confuses the predicates of two separate legal rules. The parol evidence rule applies when an agreement is integrated, whether or not it is unambiguous. The plain meaning rule, by contrast, applies when an agreement is unambiguous. An agreement can be partially or completely integrated even though one or more of its disputed terms is ambiguous, or not completely integrated even though a term is unambiguous. Second, the statement confuses the legal consequences of the two rules. The parol evidence rule discharges prior and contemporaneous parol agreements. The plain meaning rule, by contrast, requires a court to give unambiguous contract language its unambiguous meaning. Third, the functions of the two rules are different. The parol evidence rule functions to identify a contract's terms. The plain meaning rule functions to give meaning to a contract's terms.

---

[68] Alpha Real Estate Co. of Rochester v. Delta Dental Plan of Minn., 664 N.W.2d 303, 312 (Minn. 2003) ((quoting RICHARD A. LORD, WILLISTON ON CONTRACTS § 33:1 (4th ed.1999)). *See* P & O Nedlloyd, Ltd. v. Sanderson Farms, Inc., 462 F.3d 1015, 1019 (8th Cir. 2006); Wittig v. Allianz, A.G., 145 P.3d 738, 745 (Haw.App. 2006).

In sum, the predicates for and consequences of the two rules are different, and the rules have different functions. It is not the case that the parol evidence rule is the rule that operates to exclude parol evidence whenever it is excluded. That would turn the rule into a rule of evidence, whereas it is a rule of substantive law.[69]

To elaborate, the three sequential tasks in contract interpretation reduce the confusion. First, an interpreter must identify the terms to be given meaning. Second, she must decide whether those terms are relevantly ambiguous. Third, she must resolve any ambiguity that appears. The first two decisions are for the judge, while the third may be for the finder of fact. The confusion identified in the preceding paragraph collapses the first and second steps.

It might be thought that the first and second steps should be collapsed.[70] Perhaps identifying terms and giving them meaning cannot be distinguished because terms and meanings are the same thing. But this would be a mistake. The distinction between terms and meanings is well established in the law.[71] The Restatement (Second), for example, draws the distinction in its definition of *interpretation*: "Interpretation of a . . . *term* . . . is the ascertainment of *its* meaning."[72]

The distinction between terms and meanings should be understood conceptually as follows. Terms designate classes of actions, objects, events, states of affairs, or persons. For example, the word *bar* designates the class of all bars. It is abstract because it can encompass any number of things that are bars. One can identify a word like *bar* (or a string of words) as a term without determining which kinds of objects fall within the class it designates. *Bar* is ambiguous because it encompasses a number of subclasses. Thus, a law student may want to join the bar but may be barred and end up tending bar, behind bars, or selling candy. Deciding that *bar* is ambiguous, consequently, is a distinct and second step. It involves identifying the subclasses within the class of all bars—a legal organization, a physical constraint, a place to drink alcohol, or something sweet to eat. The subclasses are the word's possible meanings (its referents). Accordingly, an unambiguous word bears one and only one meaning; it designates

---

[69] *See* § 3.1.1.

[70] Peter Linzer, *The Comfort of Certainty: Plain Meaning and the Parol Evidence Rule,* 71 Fordham L. Rev. 799, 801 (2002).

[71] *See, e.g.*, Walsh v. Nelson, 622 N.W.2d 499, 503 (Iowa 2001).

[72] Restatement (Second) of Contracts § 200 (1981) (emphasis added); *see id.* at § 212(1).

one relevant subclass within one relevant class. An ambiguous word bears an array of meanings; it designates more than one relevant class or subclass. If a term is ambiguous, giving meaning involves disambiguating it—selecting a meaning from the array.

In this light, we can see that the parol evidence rule functions to identify a written contract's terms, which may designate a class or classes of cases to which the contract might apply. The plain meaning rule, by contrast, functions to determine whether a disputed contract term requires disambiguation in order to settle the dispute. If there is one and only one relevant class, the plain meaning rule precludes the admission of extrinsic evidence to show a meaning that the term will not reasonably bear. If there is more than one relevant class or subclass, the term is ambiguous, and extrinsic evidence is admissible to help select a meaning from the term's array in accordance with the parties' intention.

The above analysis allows us to distinguish as well between *interpretation* and *application*, the latter of which is a fourth step but is outside the scope of this book. Having selected a meaning from within the array of meanings borne by a contract term, one still has a subclass that encompasses concrete cases. Application involves classifying a concrete case within the subclass designated by the unambiguous or disambiguated meaning of a term.

§ 4.3. Unambiguous Contracts

The courts frequently find that a contract is unambiguous. Upon reading many cases, this becomes understandable. It seems that, very often, one party advances a far-fetched interpretation of the document.[73] The court excludes that interpretation, leaving only one eligible meaning—that advanced by the other party. The court then finds that the contract is unambiguous, and extrinsic evidence is inadmissible to vary the unambiguous meaning.

The courts do not differ much on the elements of interpretation that may be considered when deciding whether a contract is ambiguous. We can best understand the judicial approaches if we view them in light of the four corners rule, which confines the inquiry to the document on

[73] *Accord*, Corbin, *supra* note 8; *See* § 1.2.1.

its face. Accordingly, the courts will consider at least the contract as a whole within its four corners.[74] Evidence of the context, whether objective or going to the parties' states of mind, however, will not render an ambiguous contract unambiguous for the purpose of deciding whether to admit extrinsic evidence at this stage of interpretation. Rather, in jurisdictions that recognize extrinsic ambiguities, extrinsic evidence can show that a facially unambiguous contract is, in context, ambiguous.

§ 4.3.1. Literal Meaning of a Word or Phrase

Recall that literalism holds that a contract should be interpreted according to the literal meaning of a governing word or maybe a phrase, as found in a dictionary.[75] Again, courts sometimes recite the following mantra or the equivalent:

> When the language of a contract is plain and unambiguous, the court must afford it its literal meaning, despite a party's contention that he had a different understanding of its meaning.[76]

As indicated above in relation to the plain meaning rule,[77] however, such a mantra can be misleading. To review, it amounts to saying, "if contract language has only one meaning, the court must afford it that meaning." If there were another meaning, the language would be ambiguous, and a literal meaning rule could not apply. The sentence as a whole equates the literal meaning with the unambiguous meaning, if any.

The courts seem to understand that the mantra does not necessitate literal, acontextual interpretation in any case. Thus, after reciting it, one court went on to read a reasonableness requirement into all contracts and to explain the requirement as follows:

> The language of a contract should be construed with reference to the situation of the parties, the business to which the contract relates, the subject matter of the agreement, the circumstances surrounding

---

[74] *See* CB & H Business Services, L.L.C. v. J.T. Comer Consulting, Inc., 646 S.E.2d 843, 844–45 (N.C.App. 2007).

[75] *See* § 2.1.1.

[76] Sofran Peachtree City, LLC v. Peachtree Holdings, LLC, 550 S.E.2d 429, 432 (Ga.App. 2001).

[77] *See* § 4.2.1.

> the transaction, and the construction placed on the contract by the parties in carrying out its terms.[78]

By entertaining these extrinsic, contextual elements, the court endorsed objectivism, not literalism, despite its recitation of the mantra. Many, though mostly minor, opinions can be cited to the same effect.[79] Few courts indeed employ literalism literally.

Judge Posner, writing for the US Court of Appeals for the Seventh Circuit, has come closest to endorsing true literalism:

> Disputes over the meaning of a written contract are ordinarily resolved by reference to the meaning of the contract as it would be gathered by a reader competent in English (if the contract is in English) and reasonably endowed with common sense. . . . This "literalist" approach is desirable because it gives contracting parties the security of knowing that their contract will be interpreted in the event of a legal dispute to mean what it says, rather than being interpreted to mean what a judge or jury, perhaps misled by self-serving testimony by one of the parties, might think it should have said."[80]

Nonetheless, Judge Posner treats literalism only as a presumption. The presumption can be overcome by objective evidence "that the contract does not mean what it says."[81] Allowing a party to overcome the presumption—even by contradicting its supposedly literal meaning—opens the door widely to objective evidence drawn from the contract's context. One comes closer to literalism if the objective contextual evidence must make out a "compelling case" for departing from the literal meaning (if there was one).[82] Even so, this is not an endorsement of true literalism.

---

[78] Harper-Wittbrodt Automotive Group, LLC v. Teague, 2006 WL 2706148 (Tenn.App. 2006); *see* Dunn v. Duncan, 2006 WL 1233046 (Tenn.App. 2006); Newman v. RAG Wyoming Land Co., 53 P.3d 540, 544–50 (Wyo. 2002).

[79] *E.g.*, Memphis-Shelby County Airport Authority v. Illinois Valley Paving Co., 2006 WL 2385300, *4–6 (W.D. Tenn 2006) (taking into account several provisions of the contract); United States v. Rand Motors, 305 F.3d 770, 775 (7th Cir. 2002) (taking into account the commercial context); Georgia Farm Bureau Mutual Insurance Co. v. Ray, 251 S.E.2d 34, 35 (Ga.App. 1978) (taking into account the whole contract).

[80] Airline Pilots Ass'n, Intern. v. Midwest Express Airlines, Inc., 279 F.3d 556, 556 (7th Cir. 2002).

[81] *Id.*

[82] PMC, Inc. v. Sherwin-Williams Co., 151 F.3d 610, 615 (7th Cir. 1998).

There are good reasons why, when determining whether a contract is ambiguous, the courts do not insist on giving a contract's language a literal, acontextual meaning. Advocates of the literalist approach never articulate what it is that should be interpreted literally—a word, a phrase, a paragraph, the contract as a whole, or more.[83] We should dismiss literal meanings of words in isolation because words too often are ambiguous, as any good dictionary will attest.[84] Some context—and a purpose—is required to select from a dictionary's array of meanings.[85] Consequently, a charitable view of literalism would point to a phrase or more. But a dictionary will not give the meaning of a phrase, a paragraph, or the contract as a whole.

In addition, literalism can give a contract an arbitrary meaning due to the mere happenstance of the language employed. A lease, for example, may state that the lessee shall be liable for harm to the premises caused "intentionally or non-intentionally."[86] A court should not hold the lessee strictly liable for harms that occur unintentionally and non-negligently—perhaps especially if the drafters testify that strict liability was not their intention.[87] Accordingly, the law eschews literalism by providing that no contract should be given an unreasonable or absurd meaning.[88] Further, even in objectivist jurisdictions, "to carry out the intention of a contract, words may be transposed, rejected, or supplied, to make its meaning more clear."[89] Judge Posner has written:

> [A] contract will not be interpreted literally if doing so would produce absurd results, in the sense of results that the parties, presumed to be rational persons pursuing rational ends, are very unlikely to have agreed to seek.[90]

---

[83] *See* Alan Schwartz & Robert E. Scott, *Contract Theory and the Limits of Contract Law*, 113 YALE L.J. 541, 572 (2003).

[84] Lorillard Tobacco Co. v. American Legacy Found., 903 A.2d 728, 740 (Del.Super. 2006); Gulf Metals Ind., Inc. v. Chicago Ins. Co., 993 S.W.2d 800, 806 (Tex.App. 1999).

[85] *See* § 2.1.3.

[86] Allstate Ins. Co. v. Watson, 195 S.W.3d 609 (Tenn. 2006).

[87] *Id.* at 612.

[88] Beanstalk Group, Inc. v. AM General Corp., 283 F.3d 856, 860–61 (7th Cir. 2002); Outlet Embroidery Co., Inc. v. Derwent Mills, 172 N.E. 462, 463 (N.Y. 1930) ("If literalness is sheer absurdity, we are to seek some other meaning whereby reason will be instilled and absurdity avoided.") (Cardozo, C.J.).

[89] Castellano v. State, 374 N.E.2d 618, 620 (N.Y. 1978).

[90] U.S. v. Barnett, 415 F.3d 690, 692 (7th Cir. 2005).

For a contract to be ambiguous, both proffered meanings therefore must be reasonable.[91] Were this not the law, literalism would lead to the very departure from the parties' intention that literalist advocates fear.

A contract may lack ambiguity in the contested respect, to be sure. But a lack of ambiguity is not due to literal, acontextual meanings in the governing term. Instead, as we shall see, it is due to evidence in the context established by the contract document as a whole and the contract's purpose(s).

§ 4.3.2. The Plain Meaning of a Document

In judicial usage, the literal meaning of a contract term, if any, is not the same as the plain meaning of a term or document.[92] A term or document has a plain meaning when it is unambiguous in the contested respect. The plain meaning may be a property and function of the document as a whole viewed objectively or in a larger context. The plain meaning usually is not the same as the ordinary meaning of a term, which meaning may be ambiguous.

Most courts follow the four corners rule when deciding whether a contract is ambiguous, sometimes confusingly under the guise of the parol evidence rule.[93] As we have seen, under the four corners rule, a court must determine whether there is an ambiguity from the document as a whole, without considering extrinsic evidence of any kind.[94] The whole document, usually viewed in light of rules of grammar and the canons of construction, provides a significant degree of context. Using the whole document can lead a court to find reasonably that there is no ambiguity when, from the governing term viewed in isolation, there appears to be an ambiguity.

---

[91] Daniel v. Hawkeye Funding, Ltd. Partnership, 843 A.2d 946, 948 (N.H. 2004); § 4.1.

[92] Lipson v. Anesthesia Services, P.A., 790 A.2d 1261, 1278 (Del.Super. 2001); Reliance Ins. Co. of Illinois v. Weis, 148 B.R. 575, 579–80 (E.D.Mo. 1992).

[93] *E.g.*, General Convention of New Jerusalem in the U.S. of America, Inc. v. MacKenzie, 874 N.E.2d 1084, 1087 (Mass. 2007); *Air Safety*, 706 N.E.2d at 884-86; Amfac, Inc. v. Waikiki Beachcomber Inv. Co., 839 P.2d 10, 31 (Haw. 1992); C.R. Anthony Co. v. Loretto Mall Partners, 817 P.2d 238, 242 (N.M. 1991).

[94] Murphy v. Duquesne University of the Holy Ghost, 777 A.2d 418, 429 (Pa. 2001); *Air Safety*, 706 N.E.2d at 884; Midway Center Associates v. Midway Center, Inc., 237 N.W.2d 76, 78 (Minn. 1975).

For instance, in *South Road Associates, LLC v. International Business Machines, Inc.*,[95] a lessor sued a lessee for failing to return the "premises" in "good order and condition," as required by Article 7 of the lease, because the property's soil and groundwater were chemically contaminated by leakage from underground tanks that the lessee had installed there. The lessee argued that "premises" in the lease referred only to the interior space of the leased buildings, not to the land on which the buildings were situated. Hence, Article 7 did not require it to return the land in good order and condition. The lessor argued that the lessee's conduct in using the land for storage tanks and in paying all of the real estate taxes created an (extrinsic) ambiguity. The Court of Appeals of New York held, however, that the lessee's meaning was correct as a matter of law.

"Premises" in Article 7, considered in isolation, appears to have been ambiguous. It could refer to the entire leasehold, including the land, as the trial court had held.[96] That would make sense in terms of the dictionary and Article 7's evident purpose.[97] However, the contract's other provisions rendered the word unambiguous to the contrary in this lease. Floor plans of the buildings were attached to the lease: A provision defining the specific leasehold interest stated that what was shown on the floor plans was "hereinafter called 'the premises.'"[98] The lease, moreover, repeatedly mentioned the "premises" separately from the land, as in a provision stating that signs could not be placed on the land or the outside of the building but could be placed on the entrance doors to the premises. The lessee's meaning would render the term *premises* superfluous in such a provision—a result disfavored by the mere surplusage rule of construction. Accordingly, the document as a whole rendered "premises" unambiguous as used in Article 7: The word referred to the buildings but not to the land. It plausibly could be said that the court found the plain meaning of the word, but this would be a *result* of its interpretive analysis, not a cause or justification.

A few courts would not rely on the canons of construction, as did the New York court in *South Road Associates*, when deciding in the first instance whether a contract is ambiguous. The Supreme Court of Tennessee, for

---

[95] 826 N.E.2d 806 (N.Y. 2005).

[96] *Id.* at 808.

[97] Webster's New Int'l Dictionary 1789 (3d ed. 1993).

[98] *South Road Assocs.*, 826 N.E.2d at 807 n.1.

example, favors a three-step approach.[99] The court first determines whether the contract is ambiguous on its face. If it is, the canons of construction come into play. If the contract remains ambiguous after taking into account the canons, the question of meaning is one for the fact-finder. Most courts, however, favor a two-step approach by which they consider the canons at the first step.[100] The two-step approach makes better sense.

§ 4.3.3. *Extrinsic Evidence*

In jurisdictions that recognize extrinsic ambiguities, as we have seen, the decision whether a contract is ambiguous follows judicial consideration of the proffered or provisionally allowed extrinsic evidence. Such evidence may consist of the objective circumstances only,[101] or of the objective circumstances together with evidence of the parties' subjective intentions.[102] However, in these jurisdictions, the court must decide after considering the extrinsic evidence whether the language of the contract document is reasonably susceptible to both meanings.[103] If not, the contract is unambiguous, the extrinsic evidence is excluded, and the judge decides the interpretive question as a matter of law. Little authority explains just how this question of reasonable susceptibility should be answered under this contextual approach.

§ 4.3.3.1. Need for Ambiguous Language

One possibility is that the court should decide the question of reasonable susceptibility after it reviews extrinsic evidence. It may turn out, in the light of that evidence, that the document's language is extrinsically ambiguous in that it bears an array of contested meanings, which array was not apparent from the face of the document alone. But it also may turn out that the document's language does not bear such an array even

---

[99] Planters Gin Co. v. Federal Compress & Warehouse Co., Inc., 78 S.W.3d 885, 890 (Tenn. 2002). *See also* Hillabrand v. American Family Mut. Ins. Co., 713 N.W.2d 494 (Neb. 2006); Eudy v. Universal Wrestling Corp., 611 S.E.2d 770, 773 (Ga.App. 2005).

[100] *E.g.*, DeWitt County Elec. Co-op., Inc. v. Parks, 1 S.W.3d 96, 100 (Tex. 1999).

[101] Williams v. Metzler, 132 F.3d 937, 947 (3d Cir.1997); Ahsan v. Eagle, Inc., 678 N.E.2d 1238, 1241 (Ill.App. 1997); Hamblen County v. City of Morristown, 656 S.W.2d 331, 334 (Tenn. 1983); Watkins v. Petro-Search, Inc., 689 F.2d 537, 538 (5th Cir. 1982).

[102] *Pacific Gas & Elec. Co.* 442 P.2d at 645–46.

[103] *Id.*

in the light of the extrinsic evidence. In the latter case, the contract is neither intrinsically nor extrinsically ambiguous, and the unambiguous meaning is the contract's meaning as a matter of law.[104]

Thus, in *Hearst Communications, Inc., v. Seattle Times Co.*,[105] the owner of a newspaper, the *Seattle Times* (*Times*), brought an action against a publishing company, Hearst Communications, for breach of a joint operating agreement (JOA) whereby the *Times* had agreed to publish both its own newspaper and one of Hearst's newspapers. The JOA contained a loss operations clause providing that either party could terminate after three consecutive years of operations losses when the "agency remainder"—the amount left after deducting agency expenses from agency revenues—was insufficient to pay a party's news and editorial expenses. The JOA also contained a five-page definition of agency expenses. And it contained a *force majeure* clause providing that

> [n]either party shall be liable to the other for any failure or delay in performance under this Agreement, occasioned by . . . strike, labor dispute . . . or any other cause substantially beyond the control of the party required to perform.[106]

Beginning in 2000, the newspaper union went on strike, causing significant increases in expenses and decreases in revenues for both papers. As a result, the *Times* was unable to cover its news and editorial expenses for two years, and it suffered a loss in the third year as well. Hearst sought a judgment declaring that the *Times* could not invoke the loss operations clause because its losses over the three years were the result of *force majeure* events, including the labor strike.

The issue in the case was whether "agency expenses," within the meaning of the contract, included losses occasioned by the labor strike. If it did not include them, there would not be three consecutive years of losses, and the *Times* could not invoke the loss operations clause to terminate the JOA. Hearst argued that the *force majeure* clause modified the loss operations clause so that losses from labor strikes were not agency expenses for the purpose of calculating agency revenues. The court rejected Hearst's argument on the basis of the wording of the *force majeure*

---

[104] *See* City of Pinehurst v. Spooner Addition Water Co., 432 S.W.2d 515, 518–19 (Tex. 1968).
[105] 115 P.3d 262 (Wash. 2005).
[106] *Id.* at 269.

clause, which said that neither party shall be "liable" for a "failure or delay in performance" occasioned by a labor strike. Liability, the court said, would flow from the *Times's* failure to print and distribute the newspapers because of a labor strike, and this liability would be excused if it occurred. By its terms, however, the *force majeure* clause did not affect the calculation of agency expenses, and the loss operations and *force majeure* clauses did not reference each other. Therefore, the five-page definition of agency revenues in the loss operations clause governed the calculation, and the three years of losses gave the *Times* the right to terminate as a matter of law.

Interestingly, the parties in *Hearst Communications* each had submitted extensive extrinsic evidence regarding the negotiation of the JOA and the parties' conduct under the agreement. A Hearst executive testified as to Hearst's subjective intent with respect to the relationship between the loss operations and *force majeure* clauses. The court "recognized that the meaning of a writing 'can almost never be plain except in a context.'"[107] A court, it said, should consider relevant evidence of the contract's subject matter and objective, the circumstances at its making, any practical construction, and the reasonableness of the parties' respective meanings.[108] However, the court required that

> the surrounding circumstances and other extrinsic evidence are to be used to determine the meaning of *specific words and terms used* and not to show an intention independent of the instrument.[109]

Its analysis of the ambiguity question took into account only the contract's written provisions—within its four corners—and concluded that it bore only one reasonable meaning. Further, Hearst's subjective intention was irrelevant. And even if the parties subjectively shared intentions, such intentions were irrelevant because the parties failed to express them within the written agreement.

The court thus allowed consideration of objective extrinsic evidence to provide a context for deciding whether the contract was ambiguous. It insisted, however, that the extrinsic evidence shed light on the written contract by showing that it was relevantly ambiguous. The light in this

---

107 *Id.* at 266 ((quoting Restatement (Second) of Contracts § 212, cmt. b (1981)).

108 *Id.*

109 *Id.*

case was too dim to show such an ambiguity, so the court gave the contract its plain meaning.

In the landmark *Pacific Gas & Electric Co.* case, discussed above,[110] Justice Traynor seemed to have this approach in mind. He wrote that, after considering the extrinsic evidence, the court must decide whether "*the language of a contract*, in the light of all the circumstances, is 'fairly susceptible of either one of the two interpretations contended for.'"[111] He gave the example of a trade usage or custom showing that *ton* in a lease can mean a long ton (2,240 pounds) or a statutory ton (2,000 pounds).[112] Hence, when extrinsic evidence is considered, it generally provides the context but does not displace the text.

§ 4.3.3.2. No Need for Ambiguous Language

A cautionary note: A very few courts do not seem to require that extrinsic evidence reveal an ambiguity in the contract's language, at least when the evidence makes out a compelling case contrary to the language, based on the parties' subjective intentions. One of these is *Bache Halsey Stuart Shields, Inc. v. Alamo Savings Assoc. of Texas.*[113] It involved a lease providing in an addendum that the lessor

> does hereby grant [the lessee] the right to exclude any company engaged in the securities brokerage business as Lessee from the Alamo Savings Tower and the Gunter Hotel premises.[114]

The lease described the "premises" as space

> on the ground Floor(s) of the Alamo Savings Tower (the 'Building'), located on Lot 28, Block 1, New City Block 12571 in the City of San Antonio . . . and having a street address of 901 N.E. Loop 410.[115]

During the negotiations, the lessor made public its plans to construct a second tower 100 feet away from the Alamo Savings Tower, also on Lot 28,

---

110 *See* § 4.2.2.

111 *Pacific Gas & Elec. Co.*, 442 P.2d at 645–46 ((quoting Balfour v. Fresno C. & I. Co., 44 P. 876, 877 (Cal. 1895)) (emphasis added). *See also C.R. Anthony*, 817 P.2d at 243; Hamilton v. Wosepka, 154 N.W.2d 164, 167 (Iowa 1967).

112 *Pacific Gas & Elec. Co.*, 442 P.2d at 645 n.6.

113 611 S.W.2d 706 (Tex.App. 1980).

114 *Id.* at 707.

115 *Id.* at 707–08.

with a street address of 903 N.E. Loop 410, the two buildings to be connected by an enclosed mall or atrium. After the lessee took possession of the leased premises, however, the lessor abandoned the plans for the enclosed mall or atrium and commenced construction on the second building. It leased space in the second building to another brokerage business. The lessee (under the first lease) objected that the lease to its competitor violated the exclusionary clause in the first lease.

The Court of Civil Appeals of Texas said that, standing alone, the exclusionary clause seemed unambiguously restricted to space in the first building. Under the extrinsic ambiguity doctrine, however, it considered the purpose of the clause as a part of the surrounding circumstances. It found that the lessee wanted to get away from the competitor, who had had offices close to the lessee's prior location. "Clearly," the court wrote, "one purpose of the clause in question was to allow [the lessee] to achieve this purpose."[116] It also pointed out that the second building was on the same lot as the first. Under these circumstances, it concluded, there was an issue of fact whether the parties intended that the lessor should be free to lease space in the second building to the lessee's competitor. It did not, however, point to any language in the lease that bore two relevant meanings.

Though the lot numbers of the two buildings were the same, the addendum defined the lessee's premises as located at 901 N.E. Loop 410. The second building was located at 903 N.E. Loop 410. The difference in the addresses indicates unambiguously that the lessor did not breach the express terms of the lease. The court did not say that the circumstances revealed an ambiguity in the lease's language. It decided on the basis of the parties' unexpressed intentions. But Texas law required it to find "the true intent of the parties *expressed in the agreement*."[117] Very few, if any, courts would hold that unexpressed intentions count.[118] (In other jurisdictions, the lessor may have breached the lease's implied covenant of good faith and fair dealing.[119])

---

116 *Id.* at 708.

117 *Id.* ((quoting Murphy v. Dilworth, 151 S.W.2d 1004 (Tex. 1941)) (emphasis added).

118 *E.g.*, *Hearst Communications*, 115 P.3d at 267; McCutchin v. SCA Services of Arizona, Inc., 709 P.2d 591, 592 (Ariz.App. 1985).

119 *See generally* STEVEN J. BURTON & ERIC G. ANDERSEN, CONTRACTUAL GOOD FAITH: FORMATION, PERFORMANCE, BREACH AND ENFORCEMENT (1995).

Another case that seems to have dispensed with the need for an ambiguity in the contract language is *Gillmor v. Macey*.[120] It involved a contract granting an easement to the grantor's neighbor. The contract stated:

> [The grantee] agrees that he will not allow use of and will not himself use any three-wheeled motorized All Terrain Vehicles or any two-wheeled motorcycles or motorized 'dirt bikes' on the Easement at any time.[121]

Later, the parties disagreed about whether the grantee could use or allow the use of four-wheeled all-terrain vehicles (ATVs) on the easement. The court recognized the extrinsic ambiguity doctrine and considered extrinsic evidence on a motion for summary judgment. The evidence showed, for example, that both parties were aware of the grantor's intention to limit the use of ATVs or dirt bikes on the easements because they caused noise and dust. The parties, moreover, were not aware that four-wheeled ATVs existed because such vehicles were new to the market when the contract was made.

It is tempting to think that the court held, in effect, that "three" means "four," and that this violates the requirement that an ambiguity appear in the contract language after considering extrinsic evidence. The case is not significantly like *Hurst v. W.J. Lake & Co.*, discussed above,[122] where the court interpreted "greater than 50%" to mean "greater than 49.5%" due to a trade usage of rounding up. There was no relevant usage concerning three- and four-wheeled ATVs, and here there was no rounding up or anything similar. The case also is not significantly like one in which the parties have agreed that "buy" in performance of their contract shall mean "sell," as discussed in Chapter 1.[123] There was no prior agreement creating a private code. It also is tempting, however, to think that the court got it right. The parties' subjective intentions when the contract was made apparently converged on the clause's purpose—to prevent noise and dust—which is caused as much by four- as by three-wheeled ATVs. The court employed the subjective theory in this case to support

---

120 121 P.3d 57 (Utah App. 2005).

121 *Id.* at 69.

122 *See* § 4.1.

123 *See* § 1.3.3.

ascertaining the parties' intention as to purpose by disregarding the contract's unambiguous language.[124]

§ 4.4. Ambiguous Contracts

As we have seen, a contract is ambiguous when it is susceptible to two or more reasonable meanings that are advanced by the parties.[125] Ambiguities may be intrinsic or extrinsic.[126] Intrinsic ambiguities take the forms of term ambiguities, sentence ambiguities, structural ambiguities, and vagueness.[127] Extrinsic ambiguities also take these forms because the relevant extrinsic evidence must show that the contract's language is ambiguous. In this section, we will look at several examples of ambiguous contracts in these forms. We will consider how a judge or fact-finder should resolve such ambiguities in Chapter 5.

§ 4.4.1. Term Ambiguity

Term ambiguities are the easiest to detect. They involve a single word or short phrase that reasonably bear the two contested meanings. In Chapter 1, we gave the following simple examples: The word *bank* refers to distinct things when it is used in descriptions of rivers and of financial institutions. When a commercial contract calls for the purchase and sale of *chicken*, can the seller fulfill its obligation by delivering stewing chickens rather than the younger and more expensive broilers and fryers?[128]

§ 4.4.2. Sentence Ambiguity

In Chapter 1, we gave the following simple example of a sentence ambiguity: In a land sale contract, the seller commits to "put in gas and electricity lines at no cost to the buyer; property also to be surveyed at once." Must the seller put in the gas and electricity at once?

---

[124] *See also* Radiation Sys., Inc. v. Amplicon, Inc., 882 F.Supp. 1101, 1123 (D.D.C. 1995); W.O. Barnes, Inc. v. Folsinski, 60 N.W.2d 302, 306 (Mich. 1953); RESTATEMENT (SECOND) OF CONTRACTS § 202(1) and cmt. c (1981).

[125] *See* § 4.1.

[126] *Id.*

[127] Farnsworth, *supra* note 4, at 952–57.

[128] Frigaliment Importing Co., Ltd. v. B.N.S. Intern. Sales Corp., 190 F.Supp. 116 (1960).

In *Shelby County State Bank v. Van Diest Supply Co.*,[129] a common kind of sentence ambiguity was at the center of the dispute. The parties entered into a security agreement that described the collateral as "[a]ll inventory, including but not limited to agricultural chemicals, fertilizers, and fertilizer materials sold to Debtor by [the seller]."[130] The court found that this sentence was ambiguous.[131] It could include as collateral all inventory whether or not supplied by the seller, including the listed agricultural goods supplied by the seller. Or it could include "[a]ll inventory . . . sold to Debtor by the seller," excluding inventory supplied by third parties.

Sentence ambiguities often involve a question whether a modifying word or clause pertains to a part of the sentence. Consider the following part of a *force majeure* provision in a contract for the manufacture and sale of goods:

> Neither party will be liable for delays or suspension of performance . . . caused by acts of God or governmental authority, strikes, accidents, explosions, floods, fires or the total loss of manufacturing facilities or any other cause that is beyond the reasonable control of that party ("Force Majeure") so long as that party has used its best efforts to perform despite such Force Majeure.[132]

The "reasonable control" clause might modify all of the listed *force majeure* events, or it might modify only "any other cause." Put otherwise, "or" preceding the "reasonable control" clause might be conjunctive or disjunctive.[133] It would matter, for example, when the manufacturer's plant was destroyed by an explosion within its control. (We will consider how a court can resolve this ambiguity in Chapter 5.[134])

A court found a more subtle sentence ambiguity in *Intermountain Eye and Laser Centers, P.L.L.C. v. Miller*.[135] The dispute concerned the duration of a non-competition agreement between a physician and his employer. The governing clause said that the agreement would continue

---

129 303 F.3d 832 (7th Cir. 2002).
130 *Id.* at 834–35.
131 *Id.* at 836.
132 The Pillsbury Co., Inc. v. Wells Dairy, Inc., Ruling on Wells Dairy Motion for Summary Judgment against Pillsbury, Iowa District Court for Plymouth County, Law Nos. LACV029916 & LACV029523, April 17, 2006. The author served as an expert consultant for Wells Dairy's attorneys in this case.
133 *See* FARNSWORTH, *supra* note 2, at § 7.2.
134 *See* § 5.2.
135 127 P.3d 121 (Idaho 2005).

> for the period of 2 years immediately following the termination of the Physician's employment with the company for any or no reason (. . . including the expiration of the term of this Agreement).[136]

The question was whether the parenthetical clause modified *reason* or *termination*. If it modified *reason*, the employer could argue that the two-year period commenced at the time that the physician's *employment* terminated even if the employment terminated after the expiration of the agreement. If, however, the parenthetical clause modified *termination*, the physician could argue that the period commenced earlier, when the *agreement* expired.

§ 4.4.3. Structural Ambiguity

Structural ambiguities involve incoherence or conflicts among the provisions of a contract. In Chapter 1, we gave the following simple example: Assume that the termination clause of a contract for the sale of goods provides that either party may terminate at any time but only with one year's notice. The *force majeure* clause, however, says that the buyer may terminate upon the occurrence of a *force majeure* event. If a *force majeure* event occurs, may the buyer terminate immediately?

In *Canam Steel Corp. v. Bowdoin Construction Corp.*,[137] a structural ambiguity appeared from two documents, one incorporating the other by reference. The first was a form contract between a general contractor and its structural steel subcontractor. It contained a pay-when-paid provision: "Receipt of payment by the Contractor shall be a condition precedent to any payment to the Subcontractor hereunder."[138] The subcontractor's steel supplier, wary of the subcontractor's credit, sought an assurance from the general contractor that payment would be made within sixty days of the steel supplier's invoice. The general contractor sent a letter to the steel supplier that said:

> It is our intent to issue a check made jointly to [the steel supplier and the subcontractor] for [the contract price for the steel supplied]. It will be paid 60 days from the date of your invoice. . . . Payment to

[136] *Id.* at 126.
[137] 613 N.E.2d 121 (1993).
[138] *Id.* at 122.

> be made under the terms and conditions of the contract between [the subcontractor and the general].[139]

When the general contractor refused to pay for supplied steel on the ground that the owner had not paid him, the steel supplier brought an action against it. The steel supplier reasonably rested its case on the provision requiring the general to pay within sixty days of the steel supplier's invoice. The general reasonably defended on the basis of the letter's incorporation by reference of the structural steel subcontract, which contained the pay-when-paid provision.

§ 4.4.4. Vagueness

In Chapter 1, we said that a word or phrase is vague when it has no distinct boundaries between its range of application and the range of neighboring words. Rather, there is a band in which reasonable people may differ over the proper use of the term; indeed, there is no single proper use within the band. For example, the range of application of "orange" shades into those for "yellow" and "red" with no lines of demarcation. A contract that calls for a delivery of goods of "fair and average quality" may lead to a dispute due to vagueness.

A common kind of vagueness problem is illustrated by *Elliot & Frantz, Inc. v. Ingersoll-Rand Co.*[140] A manufacturer and a distributor entered into a distribution contract in which the manufacturer agreed to "provide sales assistance, engineering and application advice, reasonable quantities of advertising materials, campaigns and instruction in sales and service."[141] After the manufacturer terminated, the distributor claimed that the manufacturer breached by failing to supply it with adequate services and support as required by this provision. The district court granted summary judgment for the manufacturer on the ground that the contract required a reasonable amount of support. The appellate court held that the district court erred because the clause was vague. It did not, by its terms, require a quantitative level of services and support and could be interpreted to require either a minimal amount or a reasonable amount. It did require reasonable quantities of advertising materials, but it did not

---

139 *Id.*

140 457 F.3d 312 (3d Cir. 2006).

141 *Id.* at 327.

by its terms require reasonable quantities of sales assistance, engineering, and application advice. It may be added that it was unclear due to a sentence ambiguity—whether *reasonable* modified only "quantities of advertising materials" or also "campaigns and instruction in sales and service." And, if reasonable services and support were required, *reasonable* obviously is a vague term. The question of meaning was given to the jury.

§ 4.5. No Need to Find Ambiguity?

Though the great majority of jurisdictions require a finding of ambiguity before or after considering extrinsic evidence, some secondary authorities would not. Chief among them are Corbin and Farnsworth, the Restatement (Second) of Contracts, and the UCC. The courts do not follow the former three authorities widely in this respect. The latter, however, is statutory law that courts have followed in some interesting cases.

§ 4.5.1. Corbin

Corbin, followed by Farnsworth, strongly opposed any need for a court to find an ambiguity before admitting all relevant evidence of subjective intention in order to interpret the relevant contract language. His arguments, however, depend on a questionable premise. The argument is as follows:

> There are, indeed, a good many cases holding that the words of a writing are too "plain and clear" to justify the admission of parol evidence as to their interpretation. In other cases, it is said that such testimony is admissible only when the words of the writing are themselves "ambiguous." Such statements assume a uniformity and certainty in the meaning of language that do not in fact exist; they should be subjected to constant attack and disapproval.[142]

Findings of plain meaning and ambiguity however, need not make these assumptions about the nature of language and meaning. Accordingly, one can accept that all language is ambiguous and retain the plain meaning and ambiguity rules. It is irrelevant whether the contract language is ambiguous in the abstract. What matters is whether it is ambiguous as

---

[142] CORBIN, *supra* note 8, at 108–10; Farnsworth, *supra* note 4.

between the (usually two) meanings advanced by the parties.[143] One of those meanings may well be outside the array of meanings that the language reasonably bears under the circumstances. When this is the case, a court properly holds that the contract is unambiguous (in the contested respect).

Corbin's argument is telling as against literal, acontextual interpretation. Very few courts, if any, however, employ this approach. The argument, moreover, is not effective against objective interpretation. Some courts interpret objectively and make the ambiguity decision only after considering the document as a whole, its evident purpose(s), the circumstances under which it was made, and other features of the objective context. This context makes the court's practice neither literalist, because meaning will vary with the context, nor acontextual, because the objective context matters.

§ 4.5.2. The Restatement (Second) of Contracts

The Restatement (Second) largely follows Corbin on interpretation. It does not say that a finding of ambiguity is required, before or after considering extrinsic evidence of subjective intention.[144] The best reading is that the Restatement (Second) does not require a finding of ambiguity, before or after. The comments make it clear that no such finding is needed when the extrinsic evidence concerns an agreed private code,[145] general usage,[146] trade usage,[147] or "the rules in aid of interpretation," several of which involve extrinsic evidence.[148] These specifics may be supported by more general provisions. For example, a term must be given a specific meaning when the parties both have attached that meaning to it; here, there is no linguistic limitation on the meaning that a party can attach.[149] In this light, reconsider the case of an agreed private code:

> A and B are engaged in buying and selling shares of stock from each other, and agree orally to conceal the nature of their dealings by using the word "sell" to mean "buy" and using the word "buy" to

---

[143] *See* § 4.1.
[144] By contrast, see Restatement (First) of Contracts §§ 230, 233 (1932).
[145] Restatement (Second) of Contracts § 212, cmt. b., illus. 4 (1981).
[146] *Id.* at § 220, cmt. d.
[147] *Id.* at § 222, cmt. b.
[148] *Id.* at § 202, cmt. a.
[149] *Id.* at § 201(1).

> mean "sell." A sends a written offer to B to "sell" certain shares, and B accepts. The parties are bound in accordance with the oral agreement.[150]

Certainly the word *buy* is not ambiguous in that its array of reasonable meanings includes sell. Under the Restatement (Second), this does not matter. Extrinsic evidence of the private agreement is admissible to give meaning to the express agreement.

Three additional provisions bolster the above reading. The Restatement (Second) provides that reasonable usages, trade usages, and courses of dealing may *qualify* the parties' express agreement.[151] As will be illustrated in the next section, qualifying an agreement may involve a partial contradiction of its terms. This means that, under these provisions, a term need not be ambiguous in order for evidence of these elements to be admissible. Even a partial contradiction entails that a meaning is being given to the express term that is not within its array of reasonable meanings.

There is, however, little support in the case law for dispensing with findings of ambiguity before admitting evidence of the parties' subjective intentions, as in the case of the private code. As indicated above, the great majority of jurisdictions follow the plain meaning rule.[152] It requires a finding of ambiguity before admitting extrinsic evidence for the purpose of giving meaning to the contract's terms. Even the landmark *Pacific Gas & Electric* case does not dispense with a requirement that the language be ambiguous before finally admitting extrinsic evidence for this purpose.[153] And ironically, as indicated above, dispensing with the need to find ambiguity ignores the procedural context in which the question arises.[154] Consequently, on this point, the Restatement (Second) does not restate the common law very well.

§ 4.5.3. The Uniform Commercial Code

The UCC also does not require a finding of ambiguity before allowing extrinsic evidence of a contract's commercial context—primarily, course

[150] *Id.* at § 212, cmt. b., illus. 4.
[151] *Id.* at §§ 221–23.
[152] *See* § 4.
[153] *See* § 4.2.2.
[154] *See* § 4.2.3.

of performance, course of dealing, and usage of trade.[155] A principal purpose and policy of the statute is "to permit the continued expansion of commercial practices through custom, usage and the agreement of the parties."[156] Consequently, the very concept of an agreement is liberated from the common's law's formalistic rules of offer and acceptance.[157] *Agreement* is defined as

> the bargain of the parties in fact, as found in their language or inferred from other circumstances, including course of performance, course of dealing, or usage of trade as provided in this Act.[158]

Because an agreement may be inferred from the commercial context, that context always is relevant to ascertaining the commercial meaning of the agreement, supplementing it, or even qualifying it.[159] No need to find ambiguity stands in the way.

The idea of qualifying an agreement requires some elaboration. On this basis, a few courts have held that the commercial context can trump a contract's unambiguous express terms.[160] One court has written that established practices and usages within a particular trade or industry are a *more* reliable indicator of the parties' "true intentions" than the "sometimes imperfect and often incomplete language of the written contract."[161] On these views, the contract language does not always control inferences from the commercial context.

In *Nanakuli Paving and Rock Co. v. Shell Oil Co.*,[162] a paving contractor, Nanakuli, contracted with a supplier of asphalt, Shell. An express provision of the contract said that the price for the asphalt was to be "Shell's Posted Price at the time of delivery."[163] Following the 1973 oil embargo, Shell's posted price rose significantly. Paying this price would hurt Nanakuli, which had bid for jobs it was bound to do in non-escalating contracts on the basis of Shell's posted price at the earlier time of the bid. Nanakuli claimed that Shell was contractually bound to "price protect" it; that is, Shell was bound to sell the previously committed asphalt to

---

155 UCC § 2-202(a) and cmt. 1(c) (2001); *Columbia Nitrogen*, 451 F.2d at 9.

156 UCC § 1-102(2)(b) (2001).

157 *E.g., id.* §§ 2-204; 2-206; 2-207.

158 *Id.* at § 1-201(b)(3).

159 *Id.* at § 1-303(d) (2001).

160 *Nanakuli Paving and Rock Co.*, 664 F.2d at 797; *Columbia Nitrogen*, 451 F.2d at 9–10.

161 Urbana Farmers Union Elevator Co. v. Schock, 351 N.W. 2d 88, 92 (N.D. 1984).

162 664 F.2d 772 (9th Cir. 1981).

163 *Id.* at 778.

Nanakuli at the (lower) posted price at the time when the bids were made. The jury found that Shell was so bound, and the US Court of Appeals for the Ninth Circuit upheld the verdict.

Nanakuli made one argument that is relevant here: There was a trade usage requiring price protection based on the practices of all materials suppliers to the asphalt paving trade in Hawaii. Shell argued in response that, even if there were a relevant usage of trade, price protection could not reasonably be construed as consistent with the express price term, in which case the UCC required that the express price term control. Shell's argument raised the question whether a usage of trade can prevail over an express term when they contradict each other. The court held that the usage of trade can prevail when the contradiction is only partial. The court wrote, quoting a law review article before applying its point to the case:

> Therefore usage may be used to 'qualify' the agreement, which presumably means to 'cut down' express terms although not to negate them entirely." Here, the express price term was "Shell's Posted Price at time of delivery." A total negation of that term would be that the buyer was to set the price. It is a less than complete negation of the term that an unstated exception exists at times of price increases, at which times the old price is to be charged, for a certain period or for a specified tonnage, on work already committed at the lower price on non-escalating contracts.[164]

The result in *Nanakuli* is not obviously correct. Perhaps the unambiguous express pricing term should have prevailed over any contrary usage of trade. This view draws support from Sections 1-205(4) and 2-208(2), as they were in force when the case was decided. They provide a hierarchy of contextual elements of interpretation:

> [T]he express terms of an agreement and any applicable course of performance, course of dealing, or usage of trade must be construed whenever reasonable as consistent with each other. If such a construction is unreasonable:
>
> (1) express terms prevail over course of performance, course of dealing and usage of trade. . . .[165]

[164] *Id.* at 805.
[165] UCC § 1-303(e)(1) (2001).

The hierarchy comes into play only when these contextual elements of interpretation cannot be harmonized reasonably with the express terms.[166] In *Nanakuli*, it may be argued, no reasonable harmonization was possible; therefore, the express pricing term should have prevailed.

Moreover, there might be a significant difference between the relevant provisions in Articles 1 and 2 of the UCC. In Article 1, upon which the *Nanakuli* court relied, the contextual elements can "explain, supplement or qualify the terms of the agreement."[167] In Article 2, however, when the agreement is integrated, the contextual elements can only explain or supplement the express terms.[168] There is no reference to qualifying express terms in Article 2. Because Article 2 applies specifically to transactions in goods,[169] and asphalt paving materials are goods, the text arguably draws a distinction here that undermines the holding in *Nanakuli*. That case is based on the "qualify" language that was missing from the more directly applicable part of the statute.

§ 4.6. Criticisms of the Plain Meaning and Four Corners Rules

Scholars—and an occasional judge—have subjected the plain meaning and four corners rules to sometimes blistering criticisms.[170] Some subjectivists claim that these rules are on the way out in an increasing number of jurisdictions,[171] though the research conducted for this study does not bear this claim out. With an eye to the future, when more courts might consider abandoning these rules, it may help to review the main criticisms and their rejoinders here.

---

166 *Id.* at § 1-303(a).
167 *Id.* at § 1-303(d).
168 UCC § 2-202(a) (2001).
169 *Id.* at § 2-102.
170 Corbin, *supra* note 8, at §§ 535, 542; Joseph M Perillo, Calamari & Perillo on Contracts § 3.10 (5th ed. 2003); James Bradley Thayer, A Preliminary Treatise on the Law of Evidence 428–29 (1898), 9 John Henry Wigmore, A Treatise on the Anglo-American System of Evidence in Trials at Common Law § 2470 (3d ed. 1940); Margaret N. Kniffin, *A New Trend in Contract Interpretation: The Search for Reality as Opposed to Virtual Reality*, 74 Oregon L. Rev. 643, *passim* (1995).
171 *Id.* at 649.

§ 4.6.1. Subjectivist Criticisms

Critics generally do not distinguish between the plain meaning and four corners rules. They advance three principal arguments against them together. Two of these arguments have considerable force. In this section, we will present the principal critical arguments in their strongest terms. In the next section, we will present the principal rejoinders.

The chief criticism of the plain meaning and four corners rules has been that there are no plain meanings that an interpreter can find on a contract document's face. Corbin, for example, insisted that plain meanings emerge from the words in their contexts: "[S]ome of the surrounding circumstances always must be known before the meaning of the words can be plain and clear."[172] Further, Professor John Henry Wigmore argued, the idea that a court can find a contract's words to be unambiguous, without consulting the context, rests on a fallacy: "The fallacy consists in assuming that there is or ever can be some one real or absolute meaning."[173] Corbin added:

> [W]hen a judge refuses to consider relevant extrinsic evidence on the ground that the meaning of written words is to him plain and clear, his decision is formed by and wholly based upon the completely extrinsic evidence of his own personal education and experience. . . . A word has no meaning apart from [its context]; much less does it have an objective meaning, one true meaning.[174]

We can call this the "argument from skepticism," noting again that it is directed against literalism, not objectivism, which these two scholars did not consider.

A second, related argument is founded on anti-formalism. Formalism, in this context, puts a burden on the parties to express themselves in the law's abstract forms or else to forgo the law's benefits. The plain meaning and four corners rules put a burden on the parties to express their intentions in the contract document clearly. Parties who do not express their intentions in this way fail to meet the law's requirements as to form. Professor Melvin A. Eisenberg favors, by contrast, what he calls *responsive contract law*. He believes that

---

[172] CORBIN, *supra* note 8, § 542, at p. 100.
[173] WIGMORE, *supra* note 170, at § 2461.
[174] Corbin, *supra* note 39, at 171.

> [i]f . . . contract law is viewed as a functional instrument whose purpose is to effectuate the objectives of parties to a promissory transaction, if appropriate conditions are satisfied and subject to appropriate constraints, then the principles of interpretation should be responsive, where appropriate, to subjective intentions.[175]

Accordingly, Eisenberg endorses individualized (dependent on particular circumstances) contract principles rather than standardized (formal, abstract) contract rules. More specifically, he prefers general principles of interpretation that depend for their applications on objective variables only when the variables provide reliable surrogates for the parties' states of mind.[176] He would disapprove of the plain meaning and four corners rules because they do not employ variables that are good surrogates.[177] We can call this *the argument from anti-formalism*.

A third, also related criticism stems from the principles of contractual freedom—freedom of contract and freedom from contract. It may be argued that these principles require a court to give a contract the meaning that the parties subjectively intended, when we can.[178] An objective decision on ambiguity from within the document's four corners will fail to implement the parties' subjective intentions in some cases, as when there is an extrinsic ambiguity and one party advances the meaning revealed by extrinsic evidence. Such a failure may deprive the parties of their freedom of contract. If a court limits its inquiries to intrinsic ambiguities, moreover, it will impose legal relations on the parties in some cases. Imposition deprives the parties of their freedom from contract. We can call this argument the *argument from principle*.

We can construct the way in which the three arguments work together. If words had absolute and constant referents, parties who merely know the language could use the words to communicate their subjective intentions on the face of a contract document. But words do not have such referents, so the faces of contract documents can be unclear, incomplete, or misleading as to the parties' subjective intentions. Interpreters should consult the contexts of the documents regularly. Consulting a rich context

175 Melvin A. Eisenberg, *The Emergence of Dynamic Contract Law*, in 2 THEORETICAL INQUIRIES IN LAW 1, 16 (2001).

176 Melvin A. Eisenberg, *The Responsive Model of Contract Law*, 36 STAN. L. REV. 1107, 1111 (1984).

177 *See id.* at 1120.

178 CORBIN, *supra* note 8, at §§ 538, 543.

will bring interpretive decisions closer to implementing the parties' subjective intentions. This should be the goal of contract interpretation due to the principles of contractual freedom.

§ 4.6.2. Objectivist Rejoinders

Before turning to the three corresponding rejoinders, note that the subjectivist critics generally do not distinguish between the plain meaning rule and the four corners rule.[179] The two rules are analytically distinct, and the distinction has consequences. To repeat, the four corners rule requires a court to decide whether a contract is ambiguous on the basis of the contract document alone—without resort to extrinsic evidence: It prescribes the elements of interpretation that a court may take into account when deciding the question of ambiguity. The plain meaning rule, by contrast, prescribes the legal consequence of a finding that a contract is unambiguous in the contested respect: It requires a court to give an unambiguous contract its plain (*i.e.*, unambiguous) meaning. On its own, the plain meaning rule does not foreclose a court from considering extrinsic evidence bearing on the question of ambiguity, which must be answered before the plain meaning rule can be applied.

The distinction's consequences are significant when we consider alternatives to the conflation of the two rules. An objectivist court might endorse the plain meaning rule and jettison the four corners rule. More elements of contract interpretation then could be considered when answering the question of ambiguity.[180] Evidence of a trade usage, for example, is objective extrinsic evidence that could reveal an extrinsic ambiguity. The law could allow the court to consider a proffer of evidence or evidence of a trade usage in a check for such an ambiguity. After jettisoning the four corners rule, the plain meaning rule still would require that the court find an ambiguity in the contract language before admitting evidence of a trade usage for the fact-finder.

With respect to the argument from skepticism, a defender of the plain meaning rule first would assert that, in the real world, there are many contracts whose terms are unambiguous *in the contested respect*. There may be clarity for the practical purpose at hand. As indicated in

---

179 *E.g.*, PERILLO, *supra* note 170; Kniffin, *supra* note 170.
180 *See Bohler-Uddeholm America*, 247 F.3d at 93.

Chapter 1, many appellate cases involve one party advancing a far-fetched meaning that can be dismissed easily, leaving the contract unambiguous in the contested respect.[181] Other cases, such as those involving factual disputes only or disputes that do not reach the courtroom, probably involve many, many more clear terms.[182] Second, *pace* the skeptics, the two rules do not assume that clarity in any case results from words with "some one real or absolute meaning" apart from some context. After all, the two rules fully recognize that language can be ambiguous and depend on context—at least the document as a whole—for its meaning. Third, the argument from skepticism itself is an abstract, philosophical argument about the nature of language. The argument, ironically, is not sensitive to the context in which judges address the question of ambiguity. In the judicial context, the judge's job is to consider only the reasonable meanings (usually two) that the parties advance. There may be plenty of ambiguity in a contract in the abstract while there is none as concerns the dispute before the court. Fourth, the argument from skepticism is better aimed at literalism, which focuses on single words or short phrases and the dictionary without attending to the context in which the parties used the words. The skeptical argument misses its target when aimed at the two rules as they generally are employed by the courts.

With respect to the argument from anti-formalism, a defender of the plain meaning rule might argue that the goals of fostering secure transactions, holding parties responsible for their expressions when fair, protecting third parties' interests, and ensuring administrability, support some degree of formalism. These goals support requiring the parties to express themselves in a way that the law (and contract parties) can recognize easily. They may outweigh the goal of respecting the contractual freedoms by ascertaining the parties' subjective intentions. For both parties and others, investigating the parties' subjective intentions can be costly, if such investigations are possible without rights to discovery and perhaps even then. In addition, the principle of responsibility justifies holding parties to their objective expressions when fair. Doing so poses an incentive for the parties to express themselves clearly, to the advantage of those who rely on the document and of courts who must decide the question of ambiguity. The three principles may justify implementing the parties' objective intention even though that intention does not track their subjectivities.

---

181 *See* § 1.2.1.

182 *Id.*

(To prevent jurisprudential misunderstanding, note that defending formalism in this context does not commit the objectivist to a conceptual or classical theory of contract law, such as one that sees the law as a system of formal rules from which results in cases can be deduced without more. Those versions of formalism, though historically supportive of the plain meaning and four corners rules, are indefensible today.[183] The defense of the present, contractual version rests mainly on a purposive policy analysis intended to advance contract interpretation's several goals, not on some ideal of science or something inherent in the idea of law or a contract. The defense, moreover, is consistent with a modern theory of law that permits judges to take into account purposively the legal principles and policies that justify the legal rules.[184])

With respect to the argument from principle, a defender of the two rules might argue that deciding the question of ambiguity from within the four corners of the contract document implements the parties' subjective intentions in most cases, *i.e.*, when the judge knows and uses the parties' common language, which in most cases will be standard English. This argument assumes, in effect, that material extrinsic ambiguities are unusual. Further, even a subjective theory will not implement the parties' subjective intentions in all cases due to the problems of proving those intentions. In addition, total responsiveness to the parties' subjective intentions makes sense only if the contractual freedoms were the sole principles at stake in contract interpretation. These principles, though important and weighty, are not absolute, as suggested above. Other relevant principles also have weight and may qualify the contractual freedoms. The balance of principles may require a compromise by the subjective view.

Both the subjectivist arguments and the objectivist rejoinders have considerable force. However, we may suggest here, the focus of further thought should not be on the need for context in order to give meaning to words. We should leave literalism behind. It offers no resources for resolving ambiguities in any event. Both objectivists and subjectivists insist on the need for context because literalism fails, and meaning varies with the context. We should focus on the key question: How much context

---

[183] *See generally* Steven J. Burton, Judging in Good Faith (1992).

[184] *See generally* Steven J. Burton, An Introduction to Law and Legal Reasoning (3d ed. 2007).

is needed to decide the question of ambiguity appropriately? Is the objective context adequate, or should a court consider all relevant evidence of intention? Does more context get us closer to the parties' subjective intentions? Does more context undermine other goals? We will examine these and similar questions in Chapter 6.

CHAPTER 5

Resolving Ambiguities

After identifying the terms of a contract and determining that the terms are ambiguous in the contested respect, the interpretive task becomes one of resolving the ambiguity to settle the contract's meaning. There is no simple way to do this, though we could dismiss all cases in which a relevant ambiguity appears, as literalism requires. No jurisdiction does that. In many cases, juries resolve ambiguities. We cannot get inside the jury room, and no known studies test mock juries on questions of contract interpretation. So we can say nothing about jury deliberations here. We will, however, consider the roles of judge and jury, and cases in which judges were the interpreters, focusing on the elements and guides to interpretation that bear on the meaning of a contract or a contract term. These cases provide examples of how an interpreter can use the elements and guides. As a practical matter, they also suggest how advocates can develop relevant facts and make appealing arguments including, by analogy, arguments to juries. It will be seen that the subjective theory dominates the law here.[1] In addition, we will consider briefly default rules that do not resolve an ambiguity in the contract language. Rather, these rules

---

1 *See* Rudman v. Cowles Comm., Inc., 280 N.E.2d 867, 872 (N.Y. 1972); Baladevon, Inc. v. Abbott Laboratories, Inc., 871 F.Supp. 89, 98 (D.Mass. 1994); Hadad v. Booth, 82 So.2d 639, 643 (Miss. 1955); Wick v. Murphy, 54 N.W.2d 805, 808–09 (Minn. 1952); 2 E. Allan Farnsworth, Farnsworth on Contracts § 7.9 (3d ed. 2004).

generally settle an interpretive dispute when no interpretive resolution of an ambiguity is possible.

§ 5.1. The Roles of Judge and Jury

The law is somewhat uneven across the jurisdictions when it comes to allocating decision-making authority for resolving an ambiguity as between judge and jury. It has been written that all questions of interpretation are exclusively for the court,[2] but the research conducted for this study does not bear this out. Most jurisdictions, by far, give the jury a relatively narrow role, assigning this authority to it only when extrinsic evidence is admissible, introduced, and contested.[3] A few jurisdictions appear to give the jury a broad role, asking it to resolve all ambiguities as a matter of fact.[4] And, with respect to insurance contracts, some jurisdictions do not give the question to the jury at all.[5] The law's unevenness in this respect probably stems from a tension between respect for the jury and doubts about a jury's competence to resolve ambiguities in sometimes long and complex contract documents. A number of judges and observers express a hostile attitude toward jury competence, at least in commercial cases.[6]

§ 5.1.1. Question of Law or Fact?

Common sense tells us that questions of meaning and intention are questions of fact. The law, however, often treats them as questions of law.[7] As a general rule, accordingly, the judge resolves relevant ambiguities in a

---

[2] Edwin W. Patterson, *The Interpretation and Construction of Contracts*, 64 COLUM. L. REV. 833, 836 (1964).

[3] *E.g.*, State of New York v. Home Indemnity Co., 486 N.E.2d 827, 829 (N.Y. 1985); Ryder Truck Rental, Inc. v. Central Packing Co., 341 F.2d 321, 323 (10th Cir. 1965).

[4] *E.g.*, Opportunity, L.L.C. v. Ossewarde, 38 P.3d 1258, 1261–62 (Idaho 2002); Guilford Transp. Inds. v. Public Utilities Com'n, 746 A.2d 910, 914–15 (Me. 2000); Coker v. Coker, 650 S.W.2d 391, 394–95 (Tex. 1983).

[5] Powerine Oil Co. v. Superior Court, 118 P.3d 589, 571–72 (Cal. 2005) (insurance contract); National Sun Indus., Inc. v. S.D. Farm Bureau Ins. Co., 596 N.W.2d 45, 46 (S.D. 1999) (same).

[6] Utica Mut. Ins. Co. v. Vigo Coal Co., Inc., 393 F.3d 707, 714 (7th Cir. 2004) (Posner, J.). *See also* William C. Whitford, *The Role of the Jury and the Fact/Law Distinction in the Interpretation of Contracts*, 2001 WISC. L. REV. 931, 943 *et seq.*

[7] RESTATEMENT (SECOND) OF CONTRACTS § 212, cmt. d (1981).

written contract unless the resolution depends on disputed parol evidence.[8] Parol evidence may be disputed in two ways, as the Restatement (Second) of Contracts [Restatement (Second)] indicates:

> A question of interpretation of an integrated agreement is to be determined by the trier of fact if it depends on the credibility of extrinsic evidence or on a choice among reasonable inferences to be drawn from extrinsic evidence. Otherwise, a question of interpretation of an integrated agreement is to be determined as a question of law.[9]

This passage means, in effect, that the resolution of ambiguity is *presumptively* a question of fact *only* when a party offers credible extrinsic evidence and it is disputed reasonably.[10] A judge should resolve an ambiguity as a matter of law in at least five situations in which the presumption may be overcome. First, neither party offers relevant extrinsic evidence. Second, one party offers relevant extrinsic evidence, and a reasonable jury could credit it. Third, both parties offer extrinsic evidence, but a reasonable jury could credit only one party's evidence. Fourth, both parties offer relevant extrinsic evidence, but there is no conflict in the evidence. Fifth, both parties offer credible extrinsic evidence, but a jury could draw only one reasonable inference from it as to the contract's meaning. At least in these five situations, moreover, an appellate court will review a trial court's decision *de novo*.[11] A number of jurisdictions, in addition, allocate even more decision-making authority to the court by requiring a judge to draw any needed inferences from extrinsic evidence.[12] And, in a few jurisdictions, any ambiguity whatever must be resolved against the drafter, leaving no role for the jury at all.[13]

---

[8] *E.g.*, Smith v. Prudential Property and Cas. Ins. Co., 10 S.W.3d 846, 850–51 (Ark. 2000); Chuy v. Philadelphia Eagles Football Club, 595 F.2d 1265, 1271 (3d Cir. 1979). *See generally* Joseph M. Perillo, Calamari and Perillo on Contracts § 3.15 (5th ed. 2003). *But see* Gillmor v. Macey, 121 P.3d 57, 71 (Utah App. 2005 (resolution of ambiguity a question for the court, with deference to the finder of fact).

[9] Restatement (Second) of Contracts § 212(2) (1981). *See, e.g.*, McCollough v. Regions Bank, 905 So.2d 405, 411 (Ala. 2006); *State of New York*, 486 N.E.2d at 829; Parsons v. Bristol Development Co., 402 P.2d 839, 842–43 (Cal. 1965).

[10] Nadherny v. Roseland Property Company, Inc., 390 F.3d 44, 49 (1st Cir. 2004); Compagnie Financiere de CIC et de L' Union Europeenne v. Merrill, Lynch, Inc., 232 F.3d 153, 160 (2d Cir. 2000).

[11] *Parsons*, 402 P.2d at 842–43.

[12] ASP Properties Group v. Fard, Inc., 32 Cal.Rptr. 3d 343, 349 (Cal.App. 2005); *see* Klebe v. Mitre Group Health Care Plan, 894 F.Supp. 898, 905–06 (D.Md. 1995).

[13] *See* § 5.1.

A number of courts, however, hold that resolving an ambiguity normally presents a question of fact for the jury.[14] Such a statement differs from the approach of the Restatement (Second) in that the jury's role is not limited to finding extrinsic facts and drawing inferences from those facts: The jury also resolves ambiguities appearing within the four corners of the document. This statement, too, should not be understood to mean that a jury *always* resolves ambiguities.[15] At the least, the court should apply the canons of construction to the whole document before deciding whether a relevant ambiguity remains.[16] It is unrealistic and unreasonable to ask a jury to parse a complicated document and apply the canons, which are guides to interpretation rather than factual considerations. In any event, the normal procedural rules can turn questions of fact into questions of law, as when it is appropriate to dismiss a case on the pleadings, to grant summary judgment on the issue, or to grant a directed verdict or a judgment NOV.[17]

The law may be different in the insurance context. Some courts hold that the task of resolving an ambiguity in an insurance policy is entirely for the court.[18] This may be because these jurisdictions have a default rule requiring the court to decide in favor of the insured, making it unnecessary to resolve the ambiguity interpretively.[19] In such a case, there is no question of meaning or intent, nor are findings of fact based on extrinsic evidence needed. The rule for resolving ambiguities in favor of the insured is a default rule; it is not aimed at discerning the meaning of the parties'agreement.[20] There are other situations in which a court will resolve an ambiguity because there will be no jury, as when a party waives a jury trial and in suits in equity.

The rules allocating decision-making authority to judges and juries do not determine which kinds of extrinsic evidence will move a case to the jury. "Extrinsic evidence" is an ambiguous concept. Yet such a

---

[14] *See, e.g.*, Insurance Adjustment Bureau, Inc. v. Allstate Ins. Co., 905 A.2d 462, 481 (Pa. 2006); Bourne v. Walt Disney Co., 68 F.3d 621, 628–31 (2d Cir. 1995); Millwood Mouldings, Inc. v. Wilson, 338 S.E.2d 60, 61 (Ga.App. 1985).

[15] Bristol-Myers Squibb Co. v. Ikon Office Solutions, Inc., 295 F.3d 680, 684 (7th Cir. 2002).

[16] Extermitech, Inc. v. Glasscock, Inc., 951 So.2d 689, 694 (Ala. 2006).

[17] *Compagnie Financiere de CIC*, 232 F.3d at 159.

[18] *E.g.*, State Farm Mut. Auto. Ins. Co. v. Villicana, 692 N.E.2d 1196, 1199 (Ill. 1998); Honeymead Prods. Co. v. Aetna Cas. & Sur. Co., 146 N.W.2d 522, 529 (Minn. 1966). *But see* Hartford Acc. & Indem. Co. v. Weslowski, 305 N.E.2d 907, 909 (N.Y. 1973) (adopting Restatement (Second) rule for all contracts).

[19] Sawyer v. Farm Bureau Mut. Ins. Co., 619 N.W.2d 644, 648 (S.D. 2000).

[20] *See* § 5.4.1.

determination can be at the center of the task of resolving ambiguity. Disputed extrinsic evidence may concern any of the following elements, as appropriate in the specific jurisdiction or court—the circumstances in which the contract was made, trade usage or custom, practical construction, prior oral or written agreements, contemporaneous oral agreements, the course of negotiations preceding formation, statements of intention made during negotiations, a party's testimony in court about its own past intention, and any course of dealing. In the context of resolving an ambiguity, the parol evidence rule does not preclude the admission of such evidence. In any event, at this stage, the extrinsic evidence will be offered for the purpose of ascertaining the meaning of an ambiguous contract's terms, not for the purpose of establishing the contract's terms.[21] Nor does the four corners rule apply because the court has already decided that there is an ambiguity. Deciding which elements are appropriate considerations—when deciding whether the jury should resolve an ambiguity—is the function of a theory of contract interpretation.

§ 5.1.2. Literalism, Judge, and Jury

Literalism is not the way of the courts in this context either. Because an ambiguous term has no literal meaning, literalism has nothing to say about resolving an ambiguity. Hence, logically, literalism requires that the court dismiss the case when the parties reasonably dispute the meaning of a term or the contract. The fact-finder would play no role at all.

The goals of contract interpretation support a role for the fact-finder. The dispute settlement function of law counsels for providing a legal means for resolving relevant and contested ambiguities in contract language. Many interpretive disputes arise under ambiguous contracts, the huge number of reported cases shows. The number of disputes would probably be much larger under literalism because it works, if at all, in very few cases. Leaving the losses where they lie, moreover, probably would undermine predictability and fail to protect expectations and reliance stemming from the more reasonable branch of an ambiguity.

It might be thought that literalism is involved when a literal meaning is one branch of an ambiguity. The other branch may be a meaning that is dependent on context. Literalism might suggest that the court always

---

21 *See* §§ 3.1.1; 3.3.3.

should resolve the ambiguity in favor of the literal meaning. But this misunderstands literalism. It holds that a literal meaning is the only meaning, an unambiguous meaning. Moreover, literalism is not the prevailing law. The court will resolve an ambiguity against a proposed literal meaning if such a meaning leads to unreasonable, senseless, or absurd results,[22] or when the context clearly indicates that the parties intended a different meaning.[23] In these situations, the case need not go to the jury because the non-literal meaning is the only reasonable meaning.

As one court put it in a government contract case,

> [e]xaggerating to explain our point, we find the Government's [literal] interpretation a little like that of, say, a park keeper who tells people that the sign "No Animals in the Park" applies literally and comprehensively, not only to pets, but also to toy animals, insects, and even chicken sandwiches.[24]

Some context always is crucial to meaning.[25]

§ 5.1.3. Objectivism, Judge, and Jury

Under objectivism, the conventions of language use in the context in which the parties made their contract constitute the meaning of a contract's terms. Consequently, a court or jury may consider a limited context when resolving an ambiguity, not including the parties' course of dealing, the contract's negotiating history, the parties' testimony about their past intentions in court, or other elements bearing only on their subjective intentions. The interpreter, of course, should have before him or her the whole contract document. It would be silly to consider the parol context without the text. The interpreter, whether judge or jury, aims to use the objective context to give an apt meaning to the text in line with the parties' manifested intentions, understood as a reasonable person familiar with the objective circumstances would understand them.[26] In some cases, a party need not prove an ordinary usage by extrinsic evidence because a court may take judicial notice of it.[27] The range of admissible parol contextual

---

[22] Beanstalk Group, Inc. v. AM General Corp., 283 F.3d 856, 862 (7th Cir. 2002).
[23] Bank of the West v. Superior Court, 833 P.2d 545, 552 (Cal. 1992).
[24] United States v. Data Translation, Inc., 984 F.2d 1256, 1261 (1st Cir. 1992).
[25] *See* § 2.1.3.
[26] *E.g.*, Wulf v. Quantum Chem. Corp., 26 F.3d 1368, 1366–67 (6th Cir. 1994).
[27] Restatement (Second) of Contracts § 212, cmt. d (1981).

evidence includes the objective circumstances under which the contract was formed and the parties' practical construction, if any.

§ 5.1.4. *Subjectivism, Judge, and Jury*

Under subjectivism, by contrast, the parties' shared mental intentions, or one party's mental intention if the other party knew or should have known of that intention, constitute the meaning of the contract's language.[28] Consequently, the range of admissible extrinsic evidence expands to include all evidence bearing on what the parties had in mind when they made their contract. Under subjectivism, too, the judge or jury aims to give meaning to the text, not to find independent mental intentions.[29] Subjective meaning does not depend on what a reasonable person would understand from the words according to the relevant conventions of language use. Nonetheless, in all but a very few jurisdictions, the language must be reasonably susceptible to the parties' meaning.[30]

In addition, the subjectivist interpreter may consider the course of negotiations preceding formation, statements of intention made during negotiations, and a party's testimony in court about its own past intentions. All of these elements involve questions of fact. There will be no genuine issue of material fact, or no reasonable jury could come to any conclusion but one, when the contract language turns out to be reasonably susceptible to only one party's meaning. Then, the question of meaning again is a question of law.

§ 5.1.5. *Jury Instructions*

In general, courts do not give helpful instructions to the jury. Some appellate courts, for example, hold that a trial court need not instruct the jury on the locus of the ambiguity in the contract document.[31] Yet the jury's job is to resolve exactly that ambiguity. Furthermore, many courts merely recite some of the rules of contract interpretation or factors to be taken

---

28 *Id.* at § 201.

29 Fort Lyon Canal Co. v. High Plains A & M, LLC, 167 P.3d 726, 728–29 (Colo. 2007); Restatement (Second) of Contracts § 212, cmt. d (1981).

30 Pacific Gas & Elec. Co. v. G.W. Thomas Drayage & Rigging Co., 69 Cal.Rptr. 561, 564 (Cal. 1968).

31 Bohler-Uddeholm America, Inc. v. Ellwood Group, Inc., 247 F.3d 79, 102 (3d Cir. 2001).

into account without making any effort to cull them for those that are relevant in the case or to explain what they mean.[32] Consequently, the research conducted for this study did not reveal anything that is helpful to a good understanding of how juries are instructed.

§ 5.2. Judicial Resolution of Ambiguity

Recall that the elements recognized by the objective and subjective theories overlap. Both, for example, look at the whole contract and the objective circumstances in order to infer the parties' intention. The objective theory aims at what a reasonable person would understand the parties' manifestations of intention to mean, under the objective circumstances. The interpreter attributes this understanding to the parties as their objective intention. The subjective theory, by contrast, treats the contract document as evidence of what was in the parties' minds: This view assumes that the parties "attached" a meaning or meanings to the contract's language and thereby constituted its meaning(s).[33] The meaning a court or jury will give to the contract document need not be the same under the two theories, though often it will be. Certainly counsel may prove different sets of elements under each theory.

Today, the subjective theory prevails when an interpreter turns to resolving an ambiguity, even in jurisdictions that determine whether there is an ambiguity under the the four corners rule.[34] Moreover, because a jury normally is instructed to find the parties' intention, and the concept of objective intention is more unusual and difficult to grasp, it seems likely that juries generally aim at what was in the parties' minds. To counter this, legal authorities that follow the objective theory supervise the jury by excluding evidence bearing only on the parties' subjective intentions.[35]

There follows a series of illustrations of how judges have resolved ambiguities by using many of the elements of and guides to contract interpretation. Note that a single element rarely determines the result in a case. Rather, each element has weight. It is up to the interpreter to weigh

---

[32] *E.g.*, Propet USA, Inc. v. Shugart, 2007 WL 4376201, *7 (W.D.Wash. 2007).

[33] Restatement (Second) of Contracts § 201 (1981). *See Wick*, 54 N.W.2d at 808–09 (Minn. 1952).

[34] *E.g.*, *Baldevon*, 871 F.Supp. at 98–99.

[35] *E.g.*, Cal. Civ. Code § 1644.

the contending elements as evidenced in the particular case.[36] Note also that ambiguities are not always resolved. The evidence may be inadequate to determine the parties' intention, objective or subjective, non-arbitrarily. In such cases, a court may find that there is no agreement on the point in controversy, even though such a finding results in dismissing the claim for lack of a contract.[37] Or, it may imply a term or apply a default rule, as discussed below.[38]

§ 5.2.1. Ordinary Meanings

Judges often instruct juries to resolve an ambiguity by considering, among other things, the ordinary meanings of the words in the contract—according to general or local usage.[39] The generally subjectivist Restatement (Second) supports this objectivist practice, with two exceptions:

> Unless a different intention is manifested,
> (a) where language has a generally prevailing meaning, it is interpreted in accordance with that meaning;
> (b) technical terms and words of art are given their technical meaning when used in a transaction within their technical field.[40]

The first exception is that the parties' may attach an extraordinary meaning to a term when they manifest an intention that their contract be so interpreted. This exception will come into play, for example, if the contract includes a definition of the contested term, which definition expresses an extraordinary meaning.[41] The second exception is that the parties may use technical terms or terms of art.[42] These are terms with extraordinary meanings usually rooted in trade usages or customs. An interpreter may give the words their extraordinary meanings unless the parties

---

36 *See* § 6.2.1.
37 Restatement (Second) of Contracts § 201(3) (1981). *See* § 5.3.3
38 *See* § 5.3.1.
39 *E.g.*, Pub. Serv. Co. of Okla. v. Home Builders Ass'n of Realtors, Inc., 554 P.2d 1181, 1185 n.9 (Okla. 1976) (citing 15 O.S. 1971 § 160).
40 Restatement (Second) of Contracts § 202(3) (1981). *See* City of Bismarck v. Mariner Const., Inc., 714 N.W.2d 484, 490–91 (N.D. 2006).
41 *See* Dualite Sales & Serv., Inc. v. Moran Foods, Inc., 190 Fed. Appx, 294, 290 (6th Cir. 2006).
42 *See* §§ 2.2.5; 5.2.7.

used them in a non-technical sense.[43] To be sure, the provision quoted above is not the only rule or standard of interpretation in the Restatement (Second).[44] Therefore, it should be regarded as giving ordinary meanings substantial weight rather than conclusive effect.

Some—but surprisingly few—courts rely on dictionaries to determine the meaning of a contract's words.[45] Dictionaries often are not helpful in resolving ambiguities. The resolution of contractual ambiguity turns on the parties' manifested intentions, understood in light of their context of use, not the dictionary.[46] Moreover, most words have two or more dictionary meanings and many serve as two or more parts of speech. Even term ambiguities, therefore, cannot be resolved with recourse to the dictionary alone. Further, many contractual ambiguities are not term ambiguities. Sentence ambiguities, structural ambiguities, and vagueness, in particular, cannot be resolved by looking in a dictionary. In addition, no case has been found that limits an interpreter to choosing among an ambiguous word's dictionary meanings. Instead, an interpreter must consider the term's contractual context, whether it be broad or narrow in the relevant jurisdiction. Finally, many courts will subordinate the ordinary meaning(s) of terms to the contract's purpose.[47]

The context may show that the contract language expresses an extraordinary meaning even when the parties have not defined the ambiguous term, and it is not a technical term or word of art.[48] For example, in *Rice v. United States*,[49] a provider of services contracted to clean certain Navy mess facilities in return for a fixed price. The contract provided:

> In the event that there is an increase or decrease in the total number of meals served per month that varies from the estimated monthly total specified in Schedule A . . . by more than 25%, either party may *request* an adjustment of the contract price.[50]

---

[43] Flying J Inc. v. Comdata Network, Inc. 405 F.3d 821, 833–34 (10th Cir. 2005); RESTATEMENT (SECOND) OF CONTRACTS § 202, cmt. f (1981).

[44] *See id.* §§ 202, 203.

[45] *See, e.g.*, Amfac, Inc. v. Waikiki Beachcomber Inv. Co., 839 P.2d 10, 24–25 (Haw. 1992); Southern Farm Bureau Cas. Ins. Co. v. Williams, 543 S.W.2d 467, 469 (Ark. 1976).

[46] *See Bank of the West*, 833 P.2d at 552; *Amfac*, 839 P.2d at 24.

[47] *E.g.*, Teig v. Suffolk Oral Surgery Assocs., 769 N.Y.S.2d 599, 600 (App.Div. 2003).

[48] *E.g.*, Sunex Intern. Inc. v. Travelers Indem. Co. of Ill., 185 F.Supp.2d 614, 621 (D.S.C. 2001); Bennett v. Soo Line Ry., 35 F.3d 334, 336 (8th Cir. 1994); *Bank of the West*, 833 P.2d at 552.

[49] 428 F.2d 1311 (Ct.Cl. 1970).

[50] *Id.* at 1313 (emphasis added).

There followed a formula for calculating such an adjustment. In the event, the number of meals served decreased by more than 25 percent. Without seeking the provider's agreement, the government deducted from the provider's payments a sum computed in accordance with the contract's formula. The provider brought an action for that sum.

The provider argued, in part, that the clause quoted above was permissive or discretionary, not automatic and unilateral. The word *request*, it urged, necessarily implies that the non-requesting party may grant or deny the thing requested as a matter of discretion. The government argued that the contract language gave it a right to an adjustment automatically upon any decrease in meals of more than 25 percent. It urged that *request* meant "demand." Therefore, it argued, the contract did not give the provider any discretion to grant or refuse a request. The language was ambiguous.

The US Court of Claims held for the government by resolving the ambiguity in *request* on the basis of its contractual context. With respect to its ordinary meaning, the court conceded that:

> [t]he word "request" does generally connote asking or soliciting, in response to which assent or permission may or may not be given, as a matter of discretion.[51]

However, "[f]or the interpretation of such a word as 'request,' the context and intention are more meaningful than the dictionary definition."[52] In several contexts, it pointed out, requests are demands. Thus, stockholders may "request" corporate action, grounded on by-laws or articles of incorporation; claimants "request" legal remedies; and testators make "requests" to their executors and trustees.[53] All of these requests are mandatory, though politely stated.

In *Rice*, the court considered several contextual features fixed by the clause as a whole. The contract language stated a clear condition upon the happening of which a request could be made—an increase or decrease in the number of meals served by 25 percent. Furthermore, upon a request, the amount of the increase or decrease in the payment was clearly fixed by the contract's formula. Had the parties intended that they must negotiate a price adjustment, moreover, the clause would have been drafted

---

51 *Id.* at 1314.

52 *Id. See Bank of the West*, 833 P.2d at 552.

53 Rice v. United States, 428 F.2d 1311, 1314 (Ct.Cl. 1970).

differently (as by omitting the formula). Due to these features of the immediate context, the court held that *request* was to be understood as demand, founded on right, for purposes of that case.[54]

§ 5.2.2. *The Whole Contract*

The Pillsbury Co., Inc. v. Wells Dairy, Inc.,[55] an Iowa trial court case in which the author served as an expert consultant, illustrates a court's resolution of a sentence ambiguity from within the four corners of the contract document as a whole. A trade secret owner and distributor of ice cream had concluded a contract with an ice cream manufacturer for the production of Häagen-Dazs® frozen dessert products at the manufacturer's plant. The contract required the manufacturer to produce minimum quantities. During the contract's term, the plant was destroyed when a check valve in a pipeline of the ammonia refrigeration system failed, causing ammonia to spill onto the floor of the plant. An explosion occurred and fires ignited, causing extensive physical damage to the plant. A shutdown resulted, and the manufacturer was unable to produce any Häagen-Dazs at the plant for some time. The distributor brought an action against the manufacturer for breach of contract, seeking lost profits.

The contract contained a *force majeure* clause that said, in part:

> Neither party will be liable for delays or suspension of performance . . . caused by acts of God or governmental authority, strikes, accidents, explosions, floods, fires, or the total loss of manufacturing facilities or any other cause that is beyond the reasonable control of that party ("Force Majeure") so long as that party has used its best efforts to perform despite such Force Majeure.[56]

The manufacturer argued that this clause excused its duty to perform because the failure to perform was caused by an explosion, a fire, and a total loss of manufacturing facilities. The distributor argued to the contrary that the explosion, fire, and loss were not "beyond the reasonable

---

[54] *Id.*

[55] Ruling on Wells Dairy Motion for Summary Judgment against Pillsbury, Iowa District Court for Plymouth County, Law No. LACV029916 & LACV029523, April 17, 2006. [While this book was in press, the Supreme Court of Iowa reversed on questionable grounds. The Pillsbury Co., Inc. v. Wells Dairy, Inc., No. 05/06 7002, slip op. at 19 (Iowa July 11, 2008).]

[56] *Id.* at 1–2.

control" of the manufacturer; therefore, the *force majeure* clause did not ground an excuse. The manufacturer responded that the clause, "that is beyond the reasonable control" of the manufacturer, modified only "any other cause," not the preceding list of specifically enumerated *force majeure* events.[57]

The clause suffers from sentence ambiguity as between these two interpretations. The court held that the manufacturer's argument was correct as a matter of law. (After discovery was complete, neither party relied significantly on extrinsic evidence.) The court gave five arguments to support its holding.

First, the court relied on the rule of the last antecedent.[58] This rule of grammar requires that a limiting clause be interpreted as modifying its immediate antecedent, not remote antecedents. The immediate antecedent to the clause, "that is beyond the reasonable control of" is the phrase, "any other cause." The remote antecedents were on the list of specifically enumerated *force majeure* events. Therefore, the court held, '[t]he rule of the last antecedent requires that the phrase 'that is beyond the reasonable control of" modifies only the immediate antecedent, 'any other cause.'"[59]

Second, the court relied on two converse canons of construction.[60] One provides that a contract should be interpreted in a way that gives all of its provisions some effect.[61] The other says that all of a contract's language should be given effect so as to avoid rendering part of it unnecessary and meaningless.[62] The court found that the distributor's argument created a redundancy because the list of enumerated *force majeure* events included acts of God, strikes, and acts of a governmental authority. Yet these events would be outside either party's control under any circumstances. By contrast, if the clause "that is beyond the reasonable control" modifies only the last antecedent, "any other cause," there would be no redundancy. Therefore, the manufacturer's argument was more persuasive.

---

57 *Id.* at 3.

58 *Id.* at 9 ((citing Winthrop Resources Corp. v. Eaton Hydraulics, Inc., 361 F.3d 465, 470 (8th Cir. 2004)).

59 *Id.* at 9.

60 *Id.* at 9–10.

61 *Id.* ((citing Current Technology Concepts, Inc. v. Irie Enterprises, Inc., 530 N.W.2d 539, 543 (Minn. 1995)).

62 *Id.* at 9 ((citing Casey v. Bhd. of Locomotive Firemen and Enginemen, 268 N.W. 737, 739 (Minn. 1936)).

Third, the court relied on a basic rule of grammar that requires a predicate verb to agree in number with its subject.[63] Under the distributor's argument, there would be no such agreement. If the clause "that is beyond the reasonable control of a party" modifies the specifically enumerated *force majeure* events, the sentence would read, in effect: "[A]cts of God . . . that is beyond the reasonable control of [the manufacturer]; strikes . . . that is beyond the reasonable control of [the manufacturer]; explosions . . . that is beyond the reasonable control of [the manufacturer]," *etc.* By contrast, reading the clause to modify only "any other cause" produces subject-verb agreement—"any other cause that is beyond the reasonable control of a party."

Fourth, the court relied on the rule that ambiguous provisions will be construed against the drafter.[64] This is a default rule, not a rule of interpretation, because it does not bear on the parties' intention but, rather, on which party is at fault for the ambiguity.[65] Nonetheless, though there were some negotiations, the court found that the distributor was the primary drafter.

Fifth, the court relied on another provision of the document as it revealed the parties' intention when they made it.[66] The contract provided that either party could terminate for any cause two years after written notice given after the expiration of its initial term (an eight-year period). It also provided, in the *force majeure* clause following the language quoted above, that the distributor could terminate immediately if the manufacturer was unable to produce for more than sixty consecutive days due to a *force majeure* event. According to the distributor's interpretation, should a fire occur for reasons that were *within* the manufacturer's reasonable control, the distributor could not terminate until the term had expired and two further years (after notice) had elapsed. There would be no *force majeure* event to justify invoking the immediate termination provision. By contrast, the manufacturer's interpretation would allow the distributor to terminate immediately after a sixty-day hiatus because a *force majeure* event would have occurred. The court found that it was "hard pressed to believe that the parties intended [the distributor's] result."[67]

---

[63] *Id.* at 10.

[64] *Id.* at 11 ((citing Hilligoss v. Carroll, Inc., 649 N.W.2d 142, 148 (Minn. 2002)).

[65] *Klapp*, 663 N.W.2d at 456. *See* § 5.3.2.

[66] Ruling on Wells Dairy Motion for Summary Judgment against Pillsbury, *supra* note 55, at 11 ((citing Midway Center Assocs. v. Midway Center, Inc. 237 N.W.2d 76, 78 (Minn. 1975)).

[67] *Id.* at 11.

To avoid that result, "that is beyond the reasonable control of a party" would have to modify only "any other cause," not the specifically enumerated *force majeure* events.

The *force majeure* clause contained an ambiguous, contested sentence. The court resolved the ambiguity on the foregoing mutually reinforcing grounds, indicating the parties' objective intentions based on the contract document as a whole, which sets part of the context of the disputed sentence. The court, consequently, granted the manufacturer's motion for summary judgment.

§ 5.2.3. The Course of Negotiations

A potentially persuasive way of resolving an ambiguity can be with reference to the course of negotiations leading to the contract in question. Few appellate opinions elaborate on how to use this element. We can suppose, however, that deletions to a draft document can reveal the parties' subjective intentions, when they agree to the final text, on a subsequently contested issue. If a word or clause or more was deleted, and the parties agreed on a final text omitting that language, the final text probably does not include whatever the deleted text provided. A deletion followed by the addition of substitute language also can reveal the parties' intention. The addition may broaden or narrow the draft's meaning, so the ambiguity can be resolved accordingly, all else being equal. Solely adding to a draft in itself probably is less significant. The final text contains the added language; there is no point to considering the course of negotiations. An addition takes on significance when the court allows a party to testify as to its intention in making an ambiguous addition, or when the court admits negotiating documents, such as a party's letter, e-mail, or other communication with the other party, explaining its reason for proposing or accepting the addition. Moreover, the give-and-take of negotiations, though not involving deletions or additions to the specific governing language, can ground inferences as to the parties' subjective intentions.

Relying on written evidence of the negotiating history generally is consistent with the subjective theory. Evidence of deletions and additions to a draft document is part of the complete circumstances.[68] Such evidence allows the interpreter to draw inferences about what a party or the parties

[68] Bolling v. Hawthorne Coal & Coke Co., 90 S.E.2d 159, 170 (Va. 1955).

probably had in mind. The same evidence, plus testimonial evidence of the course of negotiations, allows the interpreter to draw inferences about the parties' subjective intentions when agreeing to the changes and when concluding the contract.

In *Stroud v. Stroud*,[69] the divorcing parties to a property settlement agreement disputed the proper interpretation of a clause providing for termination of the wife's right to support payments. The clause said that the payments would cease, among other things, upon the wife's "cohabitation with a person in a situation analogous to marriage."[70] An issue was whether the word *person* in the context of the agreement referred only to males or also to females. The court found that the word was ambiguous based on an "objectively reasonable standard."[71] It resolved the ambiguity by holding that *person* included females.

In doing so, the court did not rely on the ordinary or dictionary meaning of *person*. Instead, it relied on a change that the husband made to a draft. The draft had provided that payments would cease upon the wife's "cohabitation with a *male* in a situation analogous to marriage."[72] The husband testified that he had scratched out "male" and put in "person," and he had submitted the draft to his attorney, who submitted it to the wife's attorney. The wife signed the final text, which said "person." The court relied on this negotiating history, together with the wife's testimony about her practical construction of the agreement, to reach its conclusion.

The give-and-take of negotiations also can ground inferences as to the parties' subjective intentions without focusing on a specific governing term. In *Sound of Music Co. v. Minnesota Mining & Mfg. Co.*,[73] a written contract between a dealer and a provider of background music said that the contract would continue in force for some years, but that it could be terminated sooner under some circumstances. One of the circumstances in which the contract allowed early termination was described in §15.0(D):

> 15.0. *TERMINATION*. This Agreement may be terminated by the parties as follows: . . .
>
> D. Upon [the manufacturer's] exit from the business by sale, divestiture, assignment of assets, or any other manner of exit, or any

[69] 641 S.E.2d 142 (Va.App. 2007).
[70] *Id.* at 145.
[71] *Id.* at 145.
[72] *Id.* at 146 (emphasis added).
[73] 477 F.3d 910 (7th Cir. 2007).

> other material transfer of ownership of the Equipment or Music Service portion of either party's business upon twelve (12) months' advance written notice.[74]

Because it was exiting the background music business, the provider gave more than twelve months' written notice of termination. Upon termination, the dealer brought an action for breach of contract, alleging that the provider could not terminate unilaterally under § 15.0(D). The dealer argued that that section was introduced by language referring to termination by "the parties," in the plural. Further, §§ 15.0(A)–15.0(C) said expressly that "either party" could terminate under the circumstances specified in those sections. Section 15.0(D), by contrast, did not by its terms empower "either party" to terminate. From this, the dealer asked the court to infer that § 15.0(D) required both parties to agree to an early termination should the manufacturer exit from the business. The provider, by contrast, argued that § 15.0(D) allowed it to terminate unilaterally upon the requisite notice.

The court rejected the dealer's claim. The prefatory language in § 15.0, consisting of "the parties," was ambiguous in the court's view because it could mean either party or both parties.[75] The requirement of twelve months' advance notice in § 15.0(D), moreover, would not be necessary if a party could simply decline to agree to a proposed termination.[76] In addition, extrinsic evidence of the negotiations showed that the provider had offered a draft of the contract providing that it could terminate early upon ninety days' advance notice should it leave the background music business. The dealer proposed that the provision be removed entirely or that sixty months' notice be required. The provider would not agree to either counterproposal, but after some back-and-forth negotiations, the parties settled on twelve months of notice.[77] By focusing on the notice period in this way, it would seem that the dealer accepted the provider's right to terminate unilaterally. Consequently, the court resolved the ambiguity in favor of the provider.

An interpreter should take care to consider the course of negotiations in their broader context. Negotiations typically require a "package deal" before a party consents to be bound. An agreement reached on one provision may be superseded by subsequent negotiations on that provision.

---

[74] *Id.* at 915–16.
[75] *Id.* at 916–17.
[76] *Id.*
[77] *Id.*

The parties later may trade off part of such a provision for something else. Provisions in drafts, too, require interpretation. Here, as elsewhere, context can be critical.

Many courts also take into account a party's statement(s) of intention during negotiations, especially when the intention pertains to a change in a draft. This kind of evidence will be considered below.[78]

§ 5.2.4. The Circumstances

The courts always say that an ambiguity in a contract should be resolved in light of the circumstances existing at its formation. Many courts include in the circumstances the negotiations leading to the contract and the parties' statements of intention before and when they concluded the contract.[79] Any court should include objective facts, whether or not judicial notice is appropriate. The circumstances provide important context for the contract. They can be decisive.[80]

The circumstances, other than those involving a party's subjective intention, consist of objective facts. With the following exception, considering the objective circumstances is consistent with both the objective and subjective theories. When the circumstances include things such as the parties' statements of intention before or at that time of concluding the contract, however, those parts of the circumstances are relevant only to the parties' subjective intentions. Hence, courts that follow the objective theory would not allow such statements.

Gillmor v. Macey,[81] discussed in Chapter 4 above,[82] illustrates a simple and straightforward use of the circumstances to help resolve what the court treated as an ambiguity. To repeat for convenience, the case involved a contract granting an easement to the grantor's neighbor. The contract stated:

> [The grantee] agrees that he will not allow use of and will not himself use any three-wheeled motorized All Terrain Vehicles or any

---

[78] *See* § 5.2.6.

[79] *Stroud*, 641 S.E.2d at 146.

[80] *E.g.*, *Amfac*, 839 P.2d at 24–26; Robson v. United Pac. Ins. Co., 391 S.W.2d 855, 860–62 (Mo. 1965).

[81] 121 P.3d 57 (Utah App. 2005).

[82] *See* § 4.3.3.2.

> two-wheeled motorcycles or motorized 'dirt bikes' on the Easement at any time.[83]

Later, the parties disagreed about whether the grantee could use or allow the use of four-wheeled all-terrain vehicles (ATVs) on the easement. Extrinsic evidence showed that both parties were aware of the grantor's intention to limit the use of ATVs and dirt bikes on the easement because they caused noise and dust. The parties, moreover, were not aware that four-wheeled ATVs existed because such vehicles were new to the market when the contract was made.[84] The court held that the grant forbade the use of four-wheeled ATVs on the easement.[85]

The opinion illustrates a strongly subjective approach because the court considered, as part of the circumstances, the parties' awareness of the grantor's mental intention. This intention was not expressed in the contract. Both the objective and subjective theories of interpretation generally require that the contract's terms express the relevant intention, even if only as one branch of an ambiguity.[86] The interpretive task is to resolve an ambiguity in the contract or its terms. The court also considered the parties' lack of awareness that four-wheeled ATVs existed, and the newness of four-wheeled ATVs to the market. These facts, however, do not seem sufficient to justify the court's holding. Without the grantor's intention to prevent noise and dust on the easement, which intention was known to the grantee, the result would be groundless.

The circumstances also can include the law existing when and where the contract was made. The contract might use a distinctively legal term that has a well-settled legal meaning in an appropriately related context and for an appropriately related purpose. Under such circumstances, a court might find that the parties contracted with reference to it. [87] Such a conclusion, of course, may well be false. When on the New York Court of Appeals, Judge Benjamin N. Cardozo wrote:

> The proper legal meaning . . . is not always the meaning of the parties. Surrounding circumstances may stamp upon a contract a popular or looser meaning.[88]

---

[83] *Gillmor*. 121 P.3d at 69.
[84] *Id.* at 71.
[85] *Id.* at 73.
[86] *See* Restatement (Second) of Contracts § 201 (1981) (subjective theory).
[87] *See* Alicia F. v. Department of Educ., 2007 WL 593633, *3 (D.Haw. 2007).
[88] Utica City Nat. Bank v. Gunn, 118 N.E. 607, 608 (N.Y. 1918).

In other words, the parties' intention is paramount. For this reason, Corbin and the Restatement (Second) oppose the use of legal meanings as such, and some courts refuse to use them in contract interpretation.[89]

Bank of the West v. Superior Court[90] illustrates an appropriate use of the law as part of the circumstances in an insurance context, where a comprehensive general liability policy insured against certain legal liabilities. The policy covered "damages" for advertising injury caused by "unfair competition." The question was whether "unfair competition" in the contract included statutory violations, which harm the public, or only common law violations, which harm competitors only. The Supreme Court of California considered the ordinary meaning of *unfair competition*, which included both kinds of violations, according to the dictionary. The term was ambiguous. The court rejected reliance on ordinary meanings, however, calling such an approach "abstract philology."[91] Instead, the court looked to the law. Damages were available for common law unfair competition. But the unfair competition statute did not provide for damages; instead, its only non-punitive remedy allowed restitution of the benefits gained by means of unfair competition. Consequently, the court decided that there was no coverage.[92]

Bank of the West uses the law because the policy's purpose was to insure against legal liabilities. Hence, the parties probably intended "damages" and "unfair competition" to have their legal meanings. Consequently, the objection to using legal meanings—that the parties' intention should prevail—does not apply.

§ 5.2.5. Purpose(s)

The purpose(s) of a contract or a term is often "of paramount importance" when a court resolves an ambiguity.[93] In *Wulf v. Quantum Chemical Corp.*,[94] an employer's (Quantum's) employee stock bonus plan included an account for hourly employees which was to be distributed to the employees when

---

[89] *See* Gallagher v. Lenart, 874 N.E.2d 43, 59–60 (Ill. 2007); Mirpad v. Calif. Ins. Guarantee Assoc., 34 Cal.Rptr. 3d 136, 147 (Cal.App. 2005); *Pub. Serv. of Okla.*, 554 P.2d at 1185 (quoting 15 O.S. 1971 § 160); Restatement (Second) of Contracts § 201, cmt. c and Ill. 3 (1981); 3 Arthur L. Corbin, Corbin on Contracts § 534 (1961).

[90] 833 P.2d 545 (Cal. 1992).

[91] *Id.* at 552.

[92] *Id.*

[93] *Teig*, 769 N.Y.S.2d at 60; *see* Restatement (Second) of Contracts § 202(1) (1981).

[94] 26 F.3d 1368 (6th Cir.1994).

their employment was "terminated."[95] A letter to the employees explaining the plan said: "You receive the value of your account when you leave Quantum."[96] An employer's newsletter said that it wanted to provide "all employees with ownership of the company."[97] Later, the employer sold one of its divisions, and some employees were transferred to the other firm. The employees brought an action for breach of contract when the employer then refused to make a distribution to them.

The employer argued that the employees were not "terminated" upon the sale of the division, as required by the plan document. The employees argued that they had "left Quantum" when they started work for the new owner of the division. The court resolved the ambiguity in *terminated* in part by considering the evident purpose of such a plan. The purpose, it wrote, was motivational—to increase productivity by conferring on the employees part ownership of the company. The plan's purpose would not be served by keeping the employees in the plan after they had gone to work for someone else.[98] Consequently, the court held, the employer-employee relationship was "terminated" when Quantum sold the division and transferred the employees.[99]

Like other elements, purpose can outweigh the ordinary or technical meaning of a term or sentence. For example, in *Reardon v. Kelly Services, Inc.*,[100] an employment contract for a business executive and general counsel provided:

> If your termination by the Company is other than for cause . . . you will be paid a separation allowance representing the difference between your first year's compensation of $256,000 . . . and the compensation payments you will have already received.

There was a corporate restructuring after the employee had worked for six years, and the employee then was terminated (without cause). The employer offered a separation payment equal to nine months' salary with other benefits. In the employee's action for breach of contract, he argued that the plain language of the above-quoted sentence entitled him to a separation payment of about $2.1 million, representing the compensation

---

[95] *Id.* at 1370.
[96] *Id.* at 1377.
[97] *Id.*
[98] *Id.*
[99] *Id. See also* Falkowski v. Imation Corp., 33 Cal.Rptr. 3d 724, 722–23 (Cal.App. 2005).
[100] 210 Fed. Appx. 456 (6th Cir. 2006).

payments he received over the six years of his employment (over $2.4 million) minus his first year's salary ($256,000).[101]

The ordinary meaning of the sentence, apart from its purpose and context, clearly supports the employee's argument. The court, however, found the sentence ambiguous due to conflicting plausible readings of it in isolation and in the context of the contract as a whole.[102] It resolved the ambiguity against the employee. In light of the negotiating history, the purpose of the severance package was, as the employee had written in a letter to the employer during negotiations, "to deal with the potential risk of immediate financial crisis through loss of position."[103] The employee's argument, if accepted, would lead to a payment of much more than he would need for an immediate financial crisis while he looked for another job.[104] Thus, the court did not follow the ordinary meaning of the disputed sentence; instead, it implemented the sentence's purpose.

There is a subtle difference in the use of purpose(s) under the objective and subjective theories. The objective theory considers the *evident or conventional purpose(s)* of the contract or the governing term.[105] This follows from the theory's focus on a reasonable understanding of the document, not what the parties had in mind. The subjective theory considers *the parties' purpose(s)*.[106] The latter focus results from the theory's effort to get at what the parties had in mind as their goal. On the subjective approach, purpose and intention are hard to distinguish. Perhaps this is why many courts follow the objective theory here.

§ 5.2.6. Statements of the Parties' Intention or Understanding

The principal goal of contract interpretation is to ascertain the parties' intention. Whichever kind of intention the courts pursue at other steps in the interpretive process, when resolving an ambiguity most will allow a party to testify about its past subjective intention. They may testify about statements of intention during negotiations or when the contract was

---

101 *Id.* at 457.
102 *Id.* at 462.
103 *Id.* at 462–63.
104 *Id.*
105 *Falkowski*, 33 Cal.Rptr 3d at 732; *Klapp*, 663 N.W.2d at 454; *Teig*, 769 N.Y.S.2d at 60.
106 *See Reardon*, 210 Fed.Appx. at 462; Paul W. Abbott, Inc. v. Axel Newman Heating and Plumbing Co., Inc., 166 N.W.2d 323, 324–25 (Minn. 1969).

formed.[107] A party or its attorney may testify directly about its own past intentions or understandings.[108] However, a party may not testify about its own intentions when they were not disclosed to the other party.[109] The evidence as a whole must show a mutual intention.[110]

In *Allstate Ins. Co. v. Watson*,[111] for instance, a lease for real property provided that the tenant would be responsible "for all damages . . . intentional or non-intentional."[112] The issue was whether the tenant was strictly liable for damage to the property. Strict liability, of course, does not require intentional action and so is "non-intentional." A literal interpretation of the lease provision consequently would lead to the conclusion that the tenant was strictly liable for damage to the property. The court, however, refused to adopt the literal meaning. Taking a subjective approach, it relied on the testimony of the tenant and the person who drafted the contract on behalf of the landlord. Both stated in affidavits that it was not their intention to hold the tenant strictly liable but, instead, to require some degree of fault. Therefore, the court held, *non-intentional* within the meaning of the lease was not so broad as to make the tenant strictly liable.[113]

Allowing a party to testify about its own intention, or to report a statement of intention it made in the course of negotiations, carries a risk that the testimony will be self-serving and misleading. A party may perjure itself. More likely, a party may convince itself, consciously or unconsciously, of the truth of its testimony. In the latter case at the least, it may be difficult to ferret out the truth through cross-examination. Fact-finders may be misled.

§ 5.2.7. Trade Usages and Customs

The UCC makes trade usages, if any, integral to all agreements governed thereby.[114] It defines a trade usage as "any practice or method of dealing

[107] Mark V, Inc. v. Mellekas, 845 P.2d 1213, 1236 (N.M. 1993); Kern Oil and Refining Co. v. Tenneco Oil Co., 792 F.2d 1380, 1384 (9th Cir. 1986).

[108] Lobo Painting, Inc. v. Lamb Const. Co., 231 S.W.3d 256, 258–60 (Mo.App. 2007); *Flying J*, 405 F.3d at 835; Garcia v. Truck Ins. Exchange, 682 P.2d 1100, 1104 (Cal. 1984).

[109] Nadherny v. Roseland Property Co., Inc., 390 F.3d 44, 51 (1st Cir. 2004).

[110] *Baladevon*, 871 F.Supp. at 98; Lonnqvist v. Lammi, 134 N.E. 255, 266–67 (Mass. 1920).

[111] 195 S.W.3d 609 (Tenn. 2006).

[112] *Id.* at 611–12.

[113] *Id.* at 612.

[114] UCC § 1-201(b)(3) (2001); Capitol Converting Equip., Inc. v. Lep Transp., Inc., 750 F.Supp. 862, 866 (N.D. Ill. 1990).

having such regularity of observance in a place, vocation, or trade as to justify an expectation that it will be observed with respect to the transaction in issue."[115] Other authorities require—much more stringently—that a usage or custom be known to both parties or be of long-standing, well-established, notorious, and invariable such that both parties should have known of it.[116] Remarkably, at least one court has

> regarded the established practices and usages within a particular trade or industry as a *more* reliable indicator of the true intentions of the parties than the sometimes imperfect and often incomplete language of the written contract.[117]

By all other authorities, this is wrong.

Reliance on a trade usage requires that the party advocating the usage prove that a relevant usage existed at the time when and place where the contract was concluded[118] and that the usage binds both contract parties because each knew or should have known of it.[119] Unless the parties otherwise agree, a trade usage under the UCC "is relevant in ascertaining the meaning of the parties' agreement, may give particular meaning to specific terms of the agreement, and may supplement or qualify the terms of the agreement."[120] This means that a trade usage may be used to resolve an ambiguity in an express term. It also may add a term to the express agreement (by implication), and it may qualify a term. A few courts hold that *qualifying* a term allows a trade usage to contradict an express term to some extent, but not to negate it altogether.[121] Under Article 2 of the UCC, though a trade usage always may explain or supplement even an integrated agreement, it apparently may not qualify the terms in an integrated

---

115 UCC § 1-303(c) (2001).

116 *E.g.*, SR Intern. Business Ins. Co., Ltd. v. World Trade Center Prop., LLC, 467 F.3d 107, 134 (2d Cir. 2006).

117 Urbana Farmers Union Elevator Co. v. Schock, 351 N.W.2d 88, 92 (N.D. 1984) (emphasis added) (citing Nanakuli Paving & Rock Co. v. Shell Oil Co., 664 F.2d 772 (9th Cir. 1981)).

118 Mullinnex LLC v. HKB Royalty Trust, 126 P.3d 909, 918–22 (Wyo. 2006).

119 *Id.*; *SR Intern. Business Ins.*, 467 F.3d at 134; Farnsworth, *supra* note 1, at § 7.13.

120 UCC § 1-303(d) (2001).

121 *E.g.*, *Nanakuli*, 664 F.2d at 805; Restatement (Second) of Contracts § 221 (1981). *But see* Hazen First State Bank v. Speight, 888 F.2d 574, 577–78 (8th Cir. 1989) (evidence of trade usage inadmissible because it contradicted an express term); Tannenbaum v. Zelle, 552 F.2d 402, 414 (2d Cir. 1977) (because industry custom did not contradict express terms, evidence of custom was admissible); *Pub. Serv. Co. of Okla.*, 554 P.2d at 1185–86 (evidence of usages and customs admissible only when express contract is ambiguous).

agreement or subtract a term in any agreement.[122] Outside of the UCC, there is no known precedent allowing a trade usage or custom to qualify an agreement.

In general, the jurisdictions are split on whether the contract's text must be ambiguous before admitting evidence of a trade usage or custom.[123] Article 2, however, does not require a finding of ambiguity before admitting evidence of a trade usage in cases governed thereby.[124] The Restatement (Second) is to the same effect.[125]

Judges allow evidence of trade usages to resolve ambiguities, whether patent or latent. The fact that a trade usage or custom reveals an ambiguity does not necessarily mean that the meaning which the trade usage reveals will or should prevail. The trade usage or custom reveals a presumptively reasonable meaning and must be weighed along with other relevant elements of interpretation in order to implement the parties' agreement.[126] Thus, the UCC treats a trade usage as "a factor in reaching the commercial meaning of the agreement that the parties have made."[127] It may be overridden or outweighed by the express terms, a course of dealing, or a course of performance.[128] The parties, of course, need not conform their contract's meaning to a trade usage or custom; they can agree otherwise. Trade usages and customs also are relevant in commercial contracts not governed by the UCC, especially insurance contracts.[129]

The court determines whether proffered evidence qualifies as evidence of a trade usage.[130] The fact-finder decides whether the evidence establishes a usage, its scope, whether it binds both parties, and what weight to give it.[131] If, however, a party proves that a trade usage is "embodied in a trade code or similar record, the interpretation of the record is a question

---

122 UCC § 2-202 (2001).

123 *Compare* Sunbeam Corp. v. Liberty Mut. Ins. Co., 781 A.2d 1189, 1193 (Pa. 2001) *with* Somerset Sav. Bank v. Chicago Title Ins. Co., 649 N.E.2d 1123, 1127–28 (Mass. 1995).

124 UCC § 2-202, com. 1(c) (2001).

125 Restatement (Second) of Contracts § 220, com. d (1981).

126 *Id.* at § 203(b).

127 UCC § 1-303, cmt. 3 (2001).

128 *Id.* at § 1-303(e); Joseph H. Levie, *Trade Usage and Custom Under the Common Law and the Uniform Commercial Code*, 40 N.Y.U. L. Rev. 1101, 1112 (1965).

129 *E.g., Sunbeam*, 781 A.2d at 1193-95; Restatement (Second) of Contracts § 220 (1981).

130 American Mach. and Tool Co. v. Strite-Anderson Mfg. Co., 353 N.W.2d 592, 597 (Minn. App. 1984).

131 UCC § 1-303(c) (2001).

of law."[132] This last point reflects the view that a court is more qualified than a jury to ascertain the meaning of a written document.

Trade usages and customs are objective elements. They exist as a matter of fact grounded in the general practices of firms or persons at the time when and place where the contract was concluded. Presumably, the parties intended to follow an applicable trade usage unless they departed from it by their agreement (interpreted in light of all elements and guides).[133] Evidence of a trade usage is admissible whether the jurisdiction follows an objective or subjective theory for resolving ambiguities.

§ 5.2.8. Course of Dealing

The parties' course of dealing, when there is one, also can be an important element of contract interpretation. The Restatement (Second) follows the UCC in its definition:

> A course of dealing is a sequence of previous conduct between the parties to an agreement which is fairly to be regarded as establishing a common basis of understanding for interpreting their expressions and other conduct.[134]

One instance of dealing will not do because a "sequence" is required.[135] When a course of dealing exists, it is integral to a commercial agreement and part of its context, like a trade usage or custom.[136] It differs from a trade usage or custom, however, because it concerns what the parties to the contract in question have done in previous transactions, not what firms or persons generally do in similar circumstances. It differs from a practical construction (course of performance) because it does not concern what the parties have done under the contract in question, subsequent to its formation. When in conflict, a course of dealing weighs more heavily than a trade usage. A practical construction weighs more than a course of dealing.[137] The express terms normally have the greatest weight;[138] parties can, of course, change their course of dealing. Most courts hold

---

[132] *Id.*

[133] UCC § 303(e) (2001).

[134] Restatement (Second) of Contracts § 223(1) (1981); UCC § 1-303(b) (2001).

[135] Kern Oil & Refining Co. v. Tenneco Oil Co., 792 F.2d 1380, 1385 (9th Cir. 1985).

[136] UCC § 1-201(b)(3) (2001).

[137] *Id.* at § 1-303(e); Restatement (Second) of Contracts § 203(b) (1981).

[138] UCC § 1-303(e) (2001); Restatement (Second) of Contracts § 203(b) (1981).

that a course of dealing must reveal what the parties intended by the language they used, not an intention independent of the contract's express terms.[139] However, the Restatement (Second) would allow a course of dealing to "supplement or qualify" the agreement unless the parties otherwise agreed.

A striking use of a course of dealing will be found in *American Federation of State, County, and Municipal Employees Local 2957 v. City of Benton.*[140] A union contract, concluded with an employer in 2002, provided:

> The Employer [the City of Benton] shall continue to provide health, accidental death and dismemberment, disability, life and retirement insurance. Employee and employee dependent's health insurance coverage is set forth in Appendix B.[141]

Appendix B provided that "[t]he City of Benton shall provide insurance coverage for each employee while employed with the City of Benton."[142] A dispute arose when the city terminated the health insurance it had been providing for retired employees. The union brought an action against the City for breach of contract, arguing that the quoted clause in Appendix B did not apply because health insurance was part of "retirement insurance." The city relied on the clause from Appendix B.

The court decided that the contract was ambiguous and considered the parties' course of dealing. The course of dealing revealed that the city had paid retiree health insurance for many years. The city changed this policy in 1989 by a resolution to withhold retiree health insurance. But it did not apply the change to union-represented retired employees. In part for this reason, the court held that the city's reliance on Appendix B was misplaced. The retired, union-represented employees were entitled to health insurance as part of "retirement insurance."[143] The court's holding is remarkable because Appendix B, by a clear, express term, limited the provision of health insurance to employees "while employed" with the City of Benton. The appendix was part of the contract, attached and incorporated by reference. The course of dealing prior to 2002 was more specific than and inconsistent with this express provision. The court, however,

---

139 Intern. Ins. Co. v. RSR Corp., 426 F.3d 281, 295 (5th Cir. 2005); Hollis v. Garwall, 695 P.2d 836, 843 (Wash. 1999).

140 2007 WL 496760 (E.D. Ark. 2007).

141 *Id.* at *1.

142 *Id.* at *3.

143 *Id.*

for better or worse, gave greater weight to the course of dealing than to the express terms.

Recourse to a course of dealing, as normally defined, implements a subjective theory of contract interpretation. By requiring prior "conduct" by the parties, course of dealing relies on an objective factor. However, as the Restatement (Second) and the UCC define it, that conduct must be "fairly to be regarded as establishing a common basis of understanding for interpreting [the parties'] expressions and other conduct."[144] A "common basis of understanding" is subjective. In this respect, course of dealing is part of the law's generally subjective approach to the resolution of ambiguities.

§ 5.2.9. Practical Construction (Course of Performance)

When resolving an ambiguity, evidence of the parties' practical construction, also called a "course of performance," is very strong evidence of their intention when making the contract.[145] The Restatement (Second) explains a narrow view of a course of performance, as follows:

> Where an agreement involves repeated occasions for performance by either party with knowledge of the nature of the performance and opportunity for objection to it by the other, any course of performance accepted or acquiesced in without objection is given great weight in the interpretation of the agreement.[146]

The UCC is to the same effect, except that a course of performance is only "relevant to interpretation," though it has greater weight than a course of dealing or usage of trade.[147] Unlike a course of dealing, which concerns the parties' dealings before concluding the contract in question, or a trade usage, which concerns what similar firms or persons generally do in similar circumstances, a course of performance concerns what the parties to the contract in question repeatedly do after formation and in its performance. A broader view will be discussed in this section below.

To illustrate, in *Robson v. United Pacific Insurance Co.*,[148] a construction subcontract called for a subcontractor to crush some dolomite rock.

---

[144] Restatement (Second) of Contracts § 223(1) (1981); U.C.C. § 1-303(b) (2001).
[145] Restatement (Second) of Contracts § 202, cmt. g (1981).
[146] *Id.* at § 202(4).
[147] U.C.C. § 1-303(a) & (d) (2001); U.C.C. § 2-208 (2001).
[148] 391 S.W.2d 855 (Mo. 1965).

A dispute arose when the prime contractor's surety refused to pay for crushed rock that the subcontractor had not crushed to the size specified in the prime contract. The subcontract was ambiguous as to who was responsible for meeting the specification. The court looked to the parties' performances under the contract to resolve the ambiguity. The subcontractor had crushed much rock to a size greater than the specifications called for. The prime contractor's agent had directed the crushing to those sizes, and he had accepted the rock as the subcontractor had crushed it. This pattern continued for some time, during which the prime contractor repeatedly visited the site, knew what was happening, and did not object. The court held:

> There is a recognized rule to the effect that, where the parties to a contract have agreed upon the acts which will be accepted as full performance of a contract, the courts will generally follow that agreement.[149]

However, notwithstanding the Restatement (Second) and the UCC, some courts go beyond the parties' conduct in performance of the contract in question to include other conduct under the rubric of practical construction. A party, for example, may act, prior to the interpretive dispute arising, inconsistently with the interpretive position it later advances. The courts will rely on such conduct as an indicator of what that party's intention was when making the contract.

This broad view was employed in *Coliseum Towers Associates v. County of Nassau.*[150] The issue centered on who had contracted to pay the real estate taxes on certain leased property. The lease was ambiguous on the point. After the contract was concluded, however, the lessee paid the taxes for seven years without protest. This conduct is consistent with the narrow view because it was in performance of the lessee's contractual obligation. The court, however, did not stop there. It considered that the lessee had challenged the taxes assessed against the property and, in a separate proceeding, had challenged the property's assessed valuation. This conduct shows that, before the dispute arose, the lessee believed that it was obligated to pay the taxes. But this conduct was not in performance of its contractual obligations. The court did not report that the lessor

---

149 *Id.* at 862.

150 769 N.Y.S.2d 293 (App.Div. 2003). *See also* Sawyer v. Farm Bureau Mut. Ins. Co., 619 N.W.2d 644, 649 (S.D. 2000); *Klebe*, 894 F.Supp. at 905–06.

knew of this conduct. And, it follows, the evidence did not show that the lessor accepted or acquiesced in it. Hence, the court considered facts that would not be relevant under the narrow view of a practical construction.

The broader view is the better one. In *Coliseum Towers*, the lessee's conduct in contesting the taxes and the assessment clearly show that, prior to the dispute, the lessee believed it was responsible for the taxes. It would not be in the lessor's interest to have believed otherwise. The reasonable inference is that the parties subjectively intended for the lessee to pay the taxes. Moreover, evidence of this conduct is objective evidence. It is not part of the circumstances when the contract was made, but it does show objectively how the lessee interpreted the lease—not only what was in the parties' minds. A party's conduct before a dispute arises, whether or not in performance of the contract, should be considered when relevant to the resolution of an ambiguity.

§ 5.2.10. Statutes and Judicial Precedents

Statutes and judicial precedents may give a meaning to a word that also is used ambiguously in a contract. It is tempting to take the word out of its context in the contract and give it the meaning it was given in the statute or precedent. Such a practice generally should be avoided.[151] It is too often inconsistent with the first rule for resolving ambiguities—that the interpreter should give an ambiguous contract a meaning that is in accordance with the parties' intention. Taking into account the entire contractual context in which the words were used serves to particularize the inquiry so as to do this. The meaning of a word or term in another context may have nothing to do with the parties' intention in the present context.[152]

The Restatement (Second) gives the following illustration:

> A agrees to sell beer to B at a specified price per barrel. At the time of the agreement both parties and others in their trade use as standard barrels wooden barrels which originally hold 31 gallons and

---

[151] *See* Flintkote Co. v. General Acc. Assur. Co., 410 F.Supp.2d 875, 887 (N.D. Cal. 2006); Somerset Area School Dist. v. Somerset Area Educ. Ass'n., 907 A.2d 1178, 1182 n.6 (Pa. Cmwlth. 2006); World Trade Center Props., L.L.C. v. Hartford Fire Ins. Co., 345 F.3d 154, 186–89 (2d Cir. 2003); RESTATEMENT (SECOND) OF CONTRACTS § 212, cmt. a (1981).

[152] *See* § 2.2.6.

hold less as they continue in use. A statute defines a barrel as 31½ gallons. The statute does not prevent interpretation of the agreement as referring to the barrels in use.[153]

The same thing should be true when a word in a non-standardized contract in question is ambiguous and also was used in a different contract that was the subject of a different litigation. The meaning a court gave to the word in that contractual context should not control its meaning in another contractual context.[154]

This criticism of the use of statutes and judicial precedents to define words out of context should be distinguished from two other uses. First, in *Falkowski v. Imation Corp.*,[155] an ambiguous contract provided for a stock option plan. The court interpreted its provisions in light of the plan's evident purpose—the attraction and retention of desirable employees. It confirmed that this was the purpose with reference to judicial precedents ascribing this purpose to other stock option plans.[156] Such a use is different because it concerns purpose and a matter that is appropriate for judicial notice. It is not definitional. Second, terms in standardized agreements, to be discussed in the next section, sometimes are given standard meanings based on statutes or judicial precedents.[157]

§ 5.2.11. Standardized Agreements

Standardized agreements, including many insurance contracts, are very useful in a number of ways.[158] To maintain their usefulness, the courts sometimes resolve ambiguities in the standard terms of such agreements in a standardized way, based on trade association explanations of standard industry forms, statutes, or legal precedents.[159] This practice protects the

---

153 Restatement (Second) of Contracts § 201, cmt. c, Ill. 3 (1981). *See also id.*, cmt. c, Ill. 1.

154 *But see* In re Estate of Uzelac, 114 P.3d 1164, 1168–69 (Utah 2005) (following precedent to resolve an ambiguity).

155 33 Cal.Rptr.3d 724 (Cal.App. 2005).

156 Langer v. Iowa Beef Packers, Inc., 420 F.2d 365, 368 (8th Cir. 1970).

157 Brinderson Corp. v. Hampton Roads Sanitation Dist., 825 F.2d 41, 44 (4th Cir. 1987).

158 Todd D. Rakoff, *Contracts of Adhesion: An Essay in Reconstruction*, 96 Harv. L. Rev. 1173, 1222–23 (1983).

159 *Flintkote*, 410 F.Supp.2d at 487; *cf.* West American Ins. Co. v. Prewitt, 401 F.Supp.2d 781, 785, (E.D.Ky. 2005) (accepting relevance of certain judicial precedents but distinguishing them from the case at bar); Stephenson v. Oneok Resources Co., 99 P.3d 717, 722–23 (Okla.App. 2004) (rejecting proposed jury instruction requiring standardized interpretation based on industry forms).

interest of the standard form's maker because an accumulation of consistent precedents, and the use of boilerplate terms tracking the language of the contracts that were authoritatively interpreted before, enhances the predictability and efficiency of the contract. Further, boilerplate clauses in financial contracts, such as indentures and debentures, may be interpreted uniformly to maintain their fungibility in capital markets; trading in such contracts would be hampered if their value varied depending on the proper interpretation of their terms.[160] However, some courts do not resolve ambiguities in a standardized way unless there is a usage of trade.[161] And many courts particularize the resolution of ambiguity by favoring separately negotiated or added terms over inconsistent printed terms.[162]

Adhesion contracts are a special kind of standardized contract. An adhesion contract is one between parties of unequal bargaining power, whereby the stronger party presents the contract to the weaker party on a take-it-or-leave-it basis, and the weaker party has little choice but to agree to the standard form.[163] Adhesion contracts generally are enforceable unless they are unconscionable or otherwise invalid.[164] In principle, an adhesion contract is interpreted in the same way as is any other contract.[165] However, due to the inequality of bargaining power and the unilateral drafting, courts are more likely to resolve ambiguities against the drafter of an adhesion contract.[166]

§ 5.2.12. Reasonableness, Lawfulness, and Fairness

When resolving an ambiguity, the courts do not often consider, or instruct a jury to consider, what is reasonable, lawful, or fair.[167] The Restatement

---

[160] Sharon Steel Corp., v. Chase Manhattan Bank, 691 F.2d 1039, 1048 (2d Cir. 1982).

[161] *See* Parks Real Estate Purchasing Group v. St. Paul Fire and Marine Ins. Co., 472 F.3d 33, 42 (2d Cir. 2006).

[162] *E.g.*, Bristol-Meyers-Squib Co v. Ikon Office Solutions, Inc., 295 F.3d 680, 685 (7th Cir. 2002); Eureka Inv. Corp., N.V. v. Chicago Title Ins. Co., 530 F.Supp. 1110, 1118 (D.D.C. 1982): RESTATEMENT (SECOND) OF CONTRACTS § 203(d) (1981).

[163] *See generally* Rakoff, *supra* note 158.

[164] Broemmer v. Abortion Services of Phoenix, Ltd., 840 P.2d 1013, 1016 (Ariz. 1992).

[165] Rory v. Continental Ins. Co., 703 N.W.2d 23, 41 (Mich. 2005).

[166] Chicago & North Western Transp. Co. v. Emmet Fertilizer & Grain Co., 852 F.2d 358, 360 (8th Cir. 1988).

[167] Shelby County State Bank v. Van Diest Supply Co., 303 F.3d 832, 838 (7th Cir. (2002) (stating the principle but finding both parties' interpretations reasonable); Mgmt. Sys. Assocs., Inc. v. McDonnell Douglas Corp., 762 F.2d 1161, 1172 (4th Cir. 1985).

(Second), however, approves of considering reasonableness and lawfulness. It provides that

> an interpretation which gives a reasonable, lawful, and effective meaning to all the terms is preferred to an interpretation which leaves a part unreasonable, unlawful, or of no effect.[168]

Probably for reasons considered below,[169] the Restatement (Second) does not approve of taking into account the fairness of the parties' exchange when interpreting. Note that the provision quoted also incorporates the mere surplusage rule, which holds that every provision of a contract should be given some effect if possible, as the parties would have intended; none should be idle.[170] The provision does not allow an interpretation to end-run this rule by giving a meaning to a term when that meaning would be unreasonable or unlawful.

§ 5.2.12.1. Reasonableness

Any question of reasonableness in interpretation should be decided when determining whether there is an ambiguity, which determination logically and procedurally must be made before an interpreter resolves an ambiguity. When deciding the question of ambiguity, the court decides whether the contract's language is reasonably susceptible to both conflicting meanings advanced by the parties.[171] An unreasonable meaning consequently should be excluded at that stage, normally leaving only one eligible meaning and an unambiguous contract in the contested respect, as a matter of law.[172] Summary judgment or a directed verdict then is appropriate.

Nonetheless, some courts have considered the reasonableness of a proffered meaning when purporting to resolve an ambiguity.[173] In *Crestview Bowl, Inc. v. Womer Const. Co., Inc.*,[174] a ten-year lease required the tenant to make monthly rental payments and to pay any increased property taxes. The lease was extended for ten years and again for another

---

168 Restatement (Second) of Contracts § 203(a) (1981).

169 *See* § 5.2.12.3.

170 Abraham v. Rockwell Intern. Corp., 326 F.3d 1242, 1244 (Fed.Cir. 2003) ((applying § 203(a)).

171 *See* § 4.3.3.1.

172 *See Baladevon*, 871 F.Supp. at 98–99.

173 *E.g.*, Aron v. Gillman, 128 N.E.2d 284, 288–89 (N.Y. 1955).

174 592 P.2d 74 (Kan. 1979).

ten years with increased rent, but without mentioning who would pay any increased property taxes. The court found the lease to be ambiguous and held that the tenant was obligated to pay the increased taxes:

> It is unreasonable to conclude that the payment of any tax increases terminated at the end of the base lease. The net effect of such a holding could result in the landlord receiving less actual compensation each year any extension of the lease is in effect. In our times of rapidly escalating real estate taxes it is unrealistic that the landlord would bind itself to absorbing all such tax increases from 1971 to 1991, while shifting the burden of the additional taxes to the tenant only for the years 1967 to 1971.[175]

Therefore, the court concluded, the base lease's requirement that the tenant pay any tax increases was a part of each ten-year extension.[176] The opposite conclusion would lead to extreme unreasonableness or absurdity in light of the circumstances. If a court is to pursue reasonableness when resolving an ambiguity, it should exclude only an extreme or absurd meaning. Freedom of contract allows the parties to conclude odd contracts that may appear to be unreasonable to others.

§ 5.2.12.2. Lawfulness

Lawfulness is a similar matter because an unlawful meaning is not a reasonable meaning. Consequently, if one party advances a meaning that would require unlawful conduct in performance of the contract, that meaning should be excluded when determining whether the contract is relevantly ambiguous. (If this can be done without gutting the contract, it might not be declared unenforceable on public policy grounds.[177]) Put otherwise, a meaning requiring unlawful conduct should be excluded as a matter of law.

Lawfulness should be distinguished from the interpretive use, to resolve ambiguity, of statutes and legal precedents that give meaning to the same words as those which the parties used in the contract in question. Such a use of statutes and precedents was considered above.[178]

---

175 *Id.* at 79.

176 *Id.*

177 *See* RESTATEMENT (SECOND) OF CONTRACTS § 178 & cmts. (1981).

178 *See* §§ 2.2.6; 5.2.10.

§ 5.2.12.3. Fairness

Fairness also is a questionable consideration when resolving an ambiguity. The principles of contractual freedom—freedom of contract and freedom from contract—require an interpreter to interpret *the parties' agreement*. As it is commonly put, courts do not make contracts for the parties. Resolving an ambiguity by excluding a perceived unfair meaning may make a contract for the parties just as does finding an agreement when the parties did not reach one, or failing to find an agreement when the parties did reach one. When a jury is called on the resolve an ambiguity, however, perceptions of fairness are likely to play a large role as a practical matter.

Insofar as contract law considers fairness, it generally is when applying invalidating doctrines of unconscionability, mistake, duress, fraud, and the like. These doctrines apply when determining whether an agreement is a valid and enforceable contract, before the interpretive questions considered here arise. Legitimate fairness considerations, therefore, are spent before reaching the question of ambiguity or that of resolving ambiguity. One could assume, to the contrary, that the parties intended to reach a fair agreement and interpret it to implement such an intention. More likely, however, they pursued their respective interests more or less aggressively. Judicial review of contract terms for fairness would exceed the scope of review of the parties' agreement provided by the above-referenced doctrines. Those doctrines require extreme unfairness, in part because valuations should be left to the market and because the courts are poorly positioned and unqualified to make evaluations of the fairness of an exchange. It would undercut that law and be unduly interventionist to go beyond those doctrines when interpreting.

An exception to the above occurs when a contract is ambiguous and one meaning-branch of the ambiguity is unconscionable, for example. The court then should resolve the ambiguity as a matter of law by excluding the unconscionable branch. Thus, "a court may so limit application of any unconscionable term as to avoid any unconscionable result."[179]

---

179 UCC § 2-302 (2001); Restatement (Second) of Contracts § 208 (1981); *see* C & J Fertilizer, Inc. v. Allied Mutual Ins. Co., 227 N.W.2d 169, 1769–81 (Iowa 1975).

§ 5.3. Non-Existent or Ambiguous Contexts

In some few cases, interpretive resources will run out of guidance without providing an adequate basis for resolving an ambiguity in accordance with the parties' agreement. There may be an absence of evidence supporting reliance on any of the contextual elements, as when neither party introduces extrinsic evidence so there is no extrinsic context to an ambiguous document. The evidence may support the use of elements that conflict so seriously that the context is as ambiguous as the contract language. In the latter case, the interpreter can "weigh" the elements supporting each branch of the ambiguity and come to a judgment. Such a case is well suited for fact-finder decision because there are conflicting reasonable inferences that can be drawn from the evidence. But maybe the weights of the elements on each side are equal, or there is, in any event, no substantial evidence to support a verdict either way. Non-interpretive standards—standards that do not aim at ascertaining the parties' intention as manifested—then are needed in order to resolve the dispute. Two kinds of non-interpretive standards then can come into play—default rules and findings that the contract or a term thereof has failed.

§ 5.3.1. Default Rules

A *default rule* is a rule that the law imports into a contract when the parties have not "otherwise agreed."[180] It fills a gap in the contract. The UCC contains a great many default rules. Section 1-302 provides with respect to the entire statute:

> (a) Except as otherwise provided in subsection (b) or elsewhere in [the Uniform Commercial Code], the effect of provisions of [the Uniform Commercial Code] may be varied by agreement.
> (b) The obligations of good faith, diligence, reasonableness, and care prescribed by [the Uniform Commercial Code] may not be disclaimed by agreement. The parties, by agreement, may determine the standards by which the performance of those obligations is to be measured if those standards are not manifestly unreasonable.[181]

---

180 Ian Ayres & Robert Gertner, *Filling Gaps in Incomplete Contracts: An Economic Theory of Default Rules*, 99 Yale L.J. 87, 87 (1989).
181 UCC § 1-302 (2001).

In addition, many substantive provisions specifically apply "unless otherwise agreed."[182] A default rule should be distinguished from a mandatory rule, *i.e.*, a rule that cannot be varied by agreement, such as the duty of good faith in the performance and enforcement of a contract.[183]

Before invoking a default rule, the decision maker must determine whether there is a gap in the contract. There is no gap if the disputed part of the contract is unambiguous or if the relevant ambiguity can be resolved using the elements of contract interpretation. There is a gap if the interpretive resources run out of guidance without settling the dispute non-arbitrarily. The decision maker then should invoke an applicable default rule, if there is one.

§ 5.3.2. Interpretation Against the Drafter

In some cases, interpretive resources run out of guidance, and there is no applicable substantive default rule. A decision maker then may invoke a commonly used procedural default rule, *contra proferentem* (interpretation against the drafter), if there is a single or predominant drafter.[184] Like a substantive default rule, *contra proferentem* applies only when the parties have not otherwise agreed. It therefore should be applied only when the interpreter cannot ascertain the parties' intention after using all available interpretive elements and guides.[185] Unlike a substantive default rule, however, this rule does not have any content. It is not like a rule providing, "[u]nless otherwise agreed . . . the place for delivery of goods is the seller's place of business or if he has none his residence."[186] *Contra proferentem* should not be used to block application of a substantive default rule. It does not implement the parties' agreement or give meaning to contract language,[187] so it does not constitute an "agreement otherwise."

Contra proferentem is based mainly on two rationales.[188] First, it poses an incentive for drafters to draft more clearly and completely than they

---

182 *E.g.*, *id.* at §§ 2-206; 2-307; 2-308.
183 *Id.* at § 1-304.
184 *See Coliseum Towers*, 769 N.Y.S.2d at 296–97; Boston Ins. Co. v. Fawcett, 258 N.E.2d 771, 776 (Mass. 1970).
185 *Klapp*, 663 N.W.2d at 469–74.
186 *Id.*
187 *Id.* at 473–74; In re Marriage of Best, 859 N.E.2d 173, 186 (Ill.App. 2006) ((*reversed on other grounds*, In re Marriage of Best, 2008 WL 733225 (Ill. 2008)).
188 *See* Restatement (Second) of Contracts § 206, cmt. a (1981); *see* AIU Ins. Co. v. FMC Corp., 799 P.2d 1253, 1265 (Cal. 1990).

otherwise would, hopefully obviating the need to find or resolve an ambiguity if a dispute ensues. Second, when there is only one drafter, that person can be expected to draft a contract that favors itself or its client. The contract may be a standard form and a contract of adhesion that is downright unfair to the non-drafting party, especially if that party is an insured, a consumer, or an employee with little bargaining power. The contract also may be one that is tailored to one transaction and that is drafted by a more sophisticated and stronger party, but that is not open to negotiation. In such cases, *contra proferentem* may be assumed to correct for an imbalance in the fairness of the exchange, though this is not necessarily so.[189] These rationales indicate that *contra proferentem* does not aim at ascertaining the parties' intention and therefore interpreting a contract's provisions.

A clear majority of courts regards *contra proferentem* as a rule to be applied by the fact-finder as a tiebreaker or last resort.[190] For example, a jury may be instructed to interpret the contract using all relevant elements of contract interpretation, and to apply *contra proferentem* only if those elements do not resolve the ambiguity. Such a use of the rule is unobjectionable. But the interpretive elements first should be exhausted.

§ 5.3.3. No Agreement

There are cases in which the context is non-existent or ambiguous, and neither a default rule nor *contra proferentem* applies. Because the courts are committed to the proposition that they do not make contracts for the parties, they then have little alternative but to declare the contract or a term thereof a failure. If the ambiguous term can be severed because it is not essential to the contract, the contract will be enforceable otherwise.[191] If severing an ambiguous term is not justified, however, the entire contract may fail. Thus, in the famous case of *Raffles v. Wichelhaus*,[192] a buyer agreed to buy goods to be shipped on a ship called the *Peerless*. There turned out to be two ships named the *Peerless*, sailing at different times. On which one must the seller ship the goods? There was no way to resolve

189 Ruttenberg v. U.S. Life Ins. Co. in City of New York, 413 F.3d 652, 666 (7th Cir. 2005).
190 *Id.* at 665–66; *Klapp*, 663 N.W.2d at 472–74; Gardiner, Kamya & Assoc., P.C. v. Jackson, 467 F.3d 1348, 1352–53 (Fed.Cir. 2006).
191 Eckles v. Sharman, 548 F.2d 905 (10th Cir. 1977).
192 159 Eng. Rep. 375 (Exch. 1864).

the ambiguity. The court held that there was no contract.[193] An alternative holding would be that neither the buyer nor the seller could enforce the contract because neither could carry its burden of proving that the ambiguity should be resolved one way or the other.[194]

§ 5.4. Special Kinds of Contracts

§ 5.4.1. *Insurance Contracts*

The courts often say that insurance contracts are to be interpreted in the same way that other kinds of contracts are interpreted.[195] *Contra proferentem*, however, frequently is applied against the insurer.[196] More often than with other kinds of contracts, it seems, courts apply this rule as soon as they decide that the relevant contract language is ambiguous, without attempting to resolve the ambiguity by using all of the interpretative elements, as appropriate.[197] These courts do not treat the rule as a matter of last resort. But some courts treat it as a last resort here, too.[198]

There nonetheless are important rules that courts apply only to insurance contracts. First, in some jurisdictions, interpretation of insurance contracts is a matter of law, appropriate for summary judgment and reviewed on appeal *de novo*.[199] Second, exclusions and exceptions from coverage generally are construed against the insurer.[200] This exception, unlike *contra proferentem*, does not depend on a finding that the insurance company drafted the exclusion. It is based, instead, on a substantive decision not to negate a clear coverage provision with an ambiguous exclusion. Third, exceptions to exclusions may be interpreted broadly.[201] Fourth, courts are more likely to rely on the ordinary and popular sense

---

193 *Id.* at 376. *See also* Oswald v. Allen, 417 F.2d 43 (2d Cir. 1969); Restatement (Second) of Contracts § 201(3) (1981).

194 Frigaliment Importing Co. v. B.N.S. Int'l Sales Corp., 190 F.Supp. 116, 121 (S.D.N.Y. 1960).

195 *E.g.*, *Bank of the West*, 833 P.2d at 551–52.

196 Kenneth S. Abraham, *A Theory of Insurance Policy Interpretation*, 95 Mich. L. Rev. 531, 531 (1996).

197 *E.g.*, Kaplan v. Northwestern Mut. Life Ins. Co., 65 P.3d 16, 23 (Wash.App. 2003).

198 *E.g.*, State Farm Life Ins. Co. v. Beaston, 907 S.W.2d 430, 433 (Tex. 1995).

199 *National Sun Indus.*, 596 N.W.2d at 46; *Powerine Oil Co.*, 118 P.3d at 597.

200 Auto-Owners-Ins. Co. v. Churchman, 489 N.W.2d 431, 433–34 (Mich. 1992). *Contra* Harrison v. MFA Mutual Ins. Co., 607 S.W.2d 137, 142 (Mo. 1980).

201 E.M.M.I., Inc. v. Zurich American Ins. Co., 9 Cal.Rptr.3d 701, 706 (Cal. 2004).

of insurance contract language than they are in regard to other kinds of contracts.[202]

The rules for interpreting insurance contracts should be distinguished from the strong version of the doctrine of reasonable expectations. This doctrine allows a court to find that an insured is covered by a policy even though the language of the policy is unambiguously to the contrary.[203] For example, in *C & J Fertilizer, Inc. v. Allied Mutual. Insurance Co.*,[204] the insurer promised, in policies entitled "Broad Form Storekeepers Policy" and "Mercantile Burglary and Robbery Policy,"

> [t]o pay for loss by burglary or by robbery of a watchman, while the premises are not open for business, of merchandise, furniture, fixtures and equipment within the premises.[205]

The policies, however, also defined *burglary* in fine print as

> the felonious abstraction of insured property (1) from within the premises by a person making felonious entry therein by actual force and violence, of which force and violence there are *visible marks* made by tools, explosives, electricity or chemicals upon, or physical damage to, *the exterior of the premises* at the place of such entry.[206]

Another provision excluded inside jobs.[207] In the event, a theft of chemicals from a storage room inside the insured premises occurred on a Sunday. The trial court found that there were no "visible marks made by tools explosives, electricity or chemicals upon, or physical damage to, the exterior of the premises" at the place of entry.[208] There was, however, abundant evidence that the burglary was an outside job, including visible marks on the storage room door indicating that the thief did not have a key. The Supreme Court of Iowa held that the doctrine of reasonable expectations applied to establish coverage.[209] The definition of burglary, though not ambiguous, did not stand in the way. A reasonable insured

[202] Bay Cities Paving & Grading, Inc., v. Lawyers' Mut. Ins. Co., 855 P.2d 1263, 1270–71 (Cal. 1993).
[203] Abraham, *supra* note 196.
[204] 227 N.W.2d 169 (Iowa 1975).
[205] *Id.* at 176.
[206] *Id.* at 171 (emphasis added).
[207] *Id.* at 177.
[208] *Id.* at 172.
[209] *Id.* at 177.

under a burglary policy would not expect a fine-print definition to limit coverage by defining *burglary* to require a specific kind of proof.

There is, however, a weak doctrine of reasonable expectations. In California, for example, a court should resolve an ambiguity in policy language according to "the sense in which the promisor believed, at the time of making it, that the promisee understood [the policy]."[210] Consequently, as applied to a promise of coverage, this rule does not protect the subjective beliefs of an insurer but, rather, the "objectively reasonable expectations of the insured."[211] This standard is an interpretive one. It is used to give an ordinary meaning to insurance policy coverage provisions, if possible, prior to applying the rule of *contra proferentem* if it is not possible.[212]

§ 5.4.2. Others

Several other kinds of contract are subject to special interpretive and default rules. Only a few are mentioned here. Contracts with a government generally are construed against the government, if the ambiguity is not obvious on the contract's face, because the government usually is the drafter and has greater bargaining power.[213] This includes plea agreements in criminal cases.[214] Option contracts are construed against the optionee.[215] And the scope of an ambiguous agreement to arbitrate disputes is construed in favor of arbitration.[216]

---

[210] *Bank of the West*, 833 P.2d at 552.

[211] *Id.*

[212] *Id.*

[213] United States v. Seckinger, 90 S.Ct. 880, 884–85 (1970); Sunshine Const. & Eng'r., Inc. v. United States, 64 Fed.Cl. 346, 358 (Fed.Cl. 2005).

[214] *E.g.*, United States v. Ready, 82 F.3d 551, 558–59 (2d Cir. 1996).

[215] McArthur v. Rosenbaum Co., 180 F.2d 617, 619–20 (3d Cir.1950).

[216] Mitsubishi Motors Corp. v. Soler Chrysler Plymouth, Inc., 473 U.S. 615, 626 (1985).

CHAPTER 6

Objective Contextual Interpretation

Chapters 2 to 5 largely describe, analyze, and evaluate judicial practice as a practical matter. This chapter takes a different tack. It asks what elements interpreters *should* take into account when interpreting a contract—a normative question. We will address, among other things, the key question that we reserved in the preceding chapters: How much context is needed to reach appropriate results from each of the three tasks in contract interpretation? The answers depend on the goals set forth in Chapter 1 and other reasons, such as the necessity of context to ascertain the meaning(s) of language. The answers may vary depending on whether an interpreter is identifying the terms to be interpreted, determining whether the contract is ambiguous in a contested respect, or resolving any ambiguity that appears. Here, as elsewhere in the law, we should favor the relatively best of the available alternatives; we should not measure a proposal against an ideal that is not implementable at reasonable cost by contract parties and their lawyers before litigation commences, and by judges and juries in courts of law.

In brief, the balance of the goals and other reasons supports a normative thesis that answers the key question at the three steps as follows. First, we should retain the parol evidence rule. To determine whether the rule applies, a court should answer the question of integration by taking into account the allegation of a parol agreement and the writing's intrinsic contextual elements—the whole contract document and its evident purpose(s)—but not extrinsic contextual elements. A merger clause should not be conclusive in all cases, but it should have considerable weight. Second, a court should decide the question of ambiguity by considering the governing contract term in the context of the whole document, the rules of grammar, canons of construction, the document's evident purpose(s), the objective circumstances in which the contract was formed, and any practical construction. The court may take into account, in order to reveal any latent ambiguity, the extrinsic factors (circumstances and practical construction) on the basis of the parties' allegations, contentions, arguments, and affidavits or proffers of evidence rather than by admitting evidence. Third, if the contract is ambiguous, a finder of fact should resolve the ambiguity by weighing the same elements the court considered when deciding the question of ambiguity, after considering evidence of the objective circumstances and any practical construction. Together, these conclusions constitute what we shall call "objective contextual interpretation."

A qualification is that considerations of public policy (including illegality), unconscionability, and other similar infirmities, should be taken into account in the following way: If giving effect to one party's meaning-branch of a contested ambiguity would violate public policy, render the contract unconscionable, or otherwise make it infirm, that meaning-branch should be excluded as a matter of law, leaving the contract unambiguous with the other party's meaning, if it is reasonable as an interpretation. With this qualification, objective contextual interpretation does not allow the parties' agreement to be overidden. Invalidating doctrines should be applied as appropriate when deciding whether an agreement is an enforceable contract. Once we have applied them and decided to enforce a contract, however, we should do what we decided to do. The force of invalidating doctrines is spent at a previous stage of the analysis. The parties' expression of their agreement then becomes the central authoritative guide to their conduct in performance of the contract.[1]

§ 6.1. The Three Tasks in Contract Interpretation

The objective contextual approach to contract interpretation aims to avoid the pitfalls of literalism, on the one hand, and subjectivism, on the other.

---

[1] *E.g.*, Rory v. Continental Ins. Co. 703 N.W.2d 23, 30–31 (Mich. 2005).

Literalism allows too little (indeed, no) context, while subjectivism allows too much. The theoretical and practical reasons for following a middle path follow with respect to the three tasks in contract interpretation.

§ 6.1.1. *Identifying Contract Terms*

As discussed in Chapter 3, an interpreter first must identify the subject matter for interpretation—the terms of the contract. The terms, upon ascertaining their meaning, will determine the parties' contractual rights, duties, and powers. There are no special problems here when a contract is not in writing. When a contract is in writing, however, identifying the terms is the domain of the parol evidence rule. This rule seeks to implement the parties' intention to adopt a writing as the final, or the final and complete, expression of their agreement—that is, as an integration of part or all of their agreement. When there is an integration, parol agreements do not ground contractual rights, duties, or powers. Instead, the writing alone does so.

§ 6.1.1.1. The Question of Integration

Objective contextual interpretation retains a parol evidence rule. If the parties have made an integrated written contract, it should serve as their central authoritative guide to conduct in contract performance. (It is not the *sole* guide because a court may imply additional, consistent terms under appropriate circumstances.) By hypothesis, people most often use the locution *the contract* to refer to a written document, whatever it may permit or require. They do not use this locution to refer, as the Restatement (Second) of Contracts [Restatement (Second)] puts it when defining *contract* as

> a promise or a set of promises for the breach of which the law gives a remedy, or the performance of which the law in some way recognizes as a duty.[2]

As is well-known, the Restatement (Second) definition is useless because it begs the question. Moreover, contract parties and others should not have to consult parol agreements and the entirety of contract law to determine

---

[2] Restatement (Second) of Contracts § 1 (1981).

their contractual rights, duties, and powers, before or after litigation commences. Doing so would require them to find and review the negotiating history, to ask the negotiators what they said or intended, and to research all relevant circumstances under which the contract was made. By dispensing with any such requirements, a parol evidence rule can facilitate contract performance outside the courthouse as well as the settlement of disputes both outside and inside the courthouse.

The favored parol evidence rule is not different from the traditional rule. It is a substantive rule of law. It provides that (1) when an enforceable, written contract is the final and complete expression of the parties' agreement, prior oral and written agreements and contemporaneous oral agreements concerning the same subject as the writing do not establish contract terms when the parol agreement contradicts or adds to the terms of the written contract; (2) in addition, when an enforceable, written contract is the final, but not the complete, expression of the parties' agreement, a parol agreement may add to, but may not contradict, the written terms.[3] Application of the rule turns on whether the contract is integrated—completely integrated in part (1) of the rule, and partially integrated in part (2). We may understand the parties' intention to integrate or not, however, as reflected in the presence or absence of a merger clause alone; the whole written document alone; the whole written document in light of the objective circumstances when it was made; or all elements relevant to finding what was in the parties' minds, including all extrinsic evidence relevant to their intention to integrate their agreement. The best alternative is to understand the parties' intention on the question of integration from the contract document and intrinsic contextual elements. These elements include—the whole contract document and the document's evident purpose(s)—but not extrinsic contextual elements.

Objective contextual interpretation thus employs a four corners rule in conjunction with the parol evidence rule. It does not employ a strong version because it does not hold that a contract can "speak for itself," as would be the case if a merger clause were considered dispositive. A court should ask, in light of the alleged parol agreement and the intrinsic contextual elements identified above, whether it reasonably appears from a writing that the parties intended it to be the final, or the final and complete,

[3] *See, e.g.*, *id.* at § 213; RESTATEMENT (FIRST) OF CONTRACTS § 237 (1932); 2 E. ALLAN FARNSWORTH, FARNSWORTH ON CONTRACTS § 7.3 (3d ed. 2004).

expression of their agreement.[4] If it so appears, the court should hold that the document is partially or completely integrated, as the case may be. A court then should apply the applicable prong of the parol evidence rule.

Merger clauses should be presumptive evidence that the writing is integrated, as provided in the specific clause, as interpreted. The documentary context in which a merger clause sits—the whole document and the other intrinsic elements—may indicate otherwise. For example, this limited context can overcome the presumption, as when the document contains a boilerplate merger clause but is labeled "draft," is unsigned, contains blanks to be filled in, or is too brief to answer many obvious questions that can arise in the contract's performance.

The court should decide the question of integration before deciding the question of ambiguity. Both of these questions should be answered as a matter of law on an appropriate pretrial motion, such as summary judgment, or when a party objects to the admission of evidence of a parol agreement at trial. Because the court should consider only the document and its intrinsic context, the question of integration should not go to a jury. The concepts of an integration, an intention to integrate, and a parol agreement are too difficult for a jury to understand and use. A jury may be more likely to decide whether a parol agreement really was made than whether, if made, it was superseded by the writing. That would be an unfortunate (though common) confusion.

This alternative differs from literalism because it does not look solely to the presence or absence of a merger clause to determine a written contract's state of integration. It differs from subjectivism because it limits the relevant context rather sharply and draws different inferences from it. It goes against the emerging, subjectivist, judicial approach, which considers all relevant evidence in a search for a shared subjective intention to integrate or not.

---

4 The Restatement (Second) employs the same test, only as a presumption that can be overcome by any relevant evidence. RESTATEMENT (SECOND) OF CONTRACTS § 209(3) (1981) ("[w]here the parties reduce an agreement to a writing which in view of its completeness and specificity *reasonably appears* to be a complete agreement, it is taken to be an integrated agreement unless it is established by other evidence that the writing did not constitute a final expression") (emphasis added); *id.*, § 210, cmt. b ("[a] document in the form of a written contract, signed by both parties and *apparently complete* on its face, may be decisive of the issue [of complete integration] in the absence of credible contrary evidence") (emphasis added).

§ 6.1.1.2. Supporting Normative and Other Reasons

The four goals of contract interpretation support objective contextual interpretation's parol evidence rule. The rule, coupled with a four corners rule, would do a good job of implementing the parties' agreement consistently with the contractual freedoms. In the great run of interpretation cases, there probably is no difference between the parties' subjective intentions to integrate (or not) and their manifestations of intention to integrate (or not), in the written document. At least, there is little such difference in the reported judicial opinions reviewed for this study. Nonetheless, there is a theoretical possibility that subjective and objective intentions will come apart in a few cases. In these cases, a parol agreement might not be given effect though both parties intended that it would be effective, or a parol agreement might be given effect though the parties intended that it would be superseded, in either case violating a contractual freedom. A practical approach to contract interpretation should not be held hostage to a theoretical possibility. Moreover, any concern for this possibility may be outweighed by the rule's service to other goals.

One objection to the parol evidence rule is that it embraces a kind of formalism by relying on the objective appearance of a contract document rather than particularizing the inquiry to evidence of the specific parties' mental states.[5] Formalism has been something of a dirty word in academic legal discourse. There are, however, several versions of formalism, not all of which are objectionable. Here, the relevant version of formalism holds only that contract parties should be held to the intention evident from their manifestations of intention, even when such an intention is at odds with what they had in mind. They are required to conform to the law's forms when they conclude an agreement. If they do not conform, they might suffer a harm to their contractual freedoms. Thus, the parol evidence and four corners rules put a burden on the parties to express their intention in the contract document when it reasonably appears to be integrated.

The justification for this version of formalism in the parol evidence rule is twofold. First, it may be justified due to the weight of the other goals of contract interpretation because the favored parol evidence rule best fosters the security of transactions, fairly holds parties responsible

---

[5] *See* Melvin A. Eisenberg, *The Responsive Model of Contract Law*, 36 STAN. L. REV. 1107, 1111 (1984).

for their expressions of intention, settles disputes non-arbitrarily in accordance with Rule of Law values, and achieves administrability. This justification, insofar as it applies, will appear from the discussion below. Second, this kind of formalism may be justified by the absence of a practical alternative in subjectivism, which also can err by imposing on the parties in violation of the contractual freedoms. This justification also will appear in the discussion below.

The favored parol evidence rule, with a four corners rule, furthers the goal of protecting and enhancing the security of transactions. This goal encompasses the sub-goals of protecting reasonable expectations arising from, and reasonable reliance on, promises, and of holding parties to their manifestations of intention when fair. In this context, it is the written contract—not a parol agreement—that parties and others should be able to rely on. As indicated in Chapter 1, contracts serve a number of functions that they did not serve when they were mainly between individuals or individuals and small, local merchants. To repeat for convenience, contracts today generally are between commercial entities, often large ones, or between commercial entities and individuals. Many are international and with parties whose legal traditions are strongly tied to the written agreement. Adhesion contracts, which often allow for no bargaining over pre-printed, standardized terms (such as merger clauses), are common. There are reasons for these developments.

Professor Todd D. Rakoff suggested in a discussion of adhesion contracts that modern firms are internally segmented.[6] Form contracts promote efficiency and reliance within a segmented and complex organization for two main reasons he identified:

> First, the standardization of terms . . . facilitates coordination among departments. The costs of communicating special understandings rise rapidly when one department makes the sale, another delivers the goods, a third handles collections, and a fourth fields complaints. Standard terms make it possible to process transactions as a matter of routine; standard forms, with standard blank spaces, make it possible to locate rapidly whatever deal has been struck on the few customized items. Second, standardization makes possible the efficient use of expensive managerial and legal talent.

---

[6] Todd D. Rakoff, *Contracts of Adhesion: An Essay in Reconstruction*, 96 Harv. L. Rev. 1173, 1222–23 (1983).

> Standard forms facilitate the diffusion to underlings of management's decisions regarding the risks the organization is prepared to bear, or make it unnecessary to explain these matters to subordinates at all.[7]

In addition, form contracts promote a similar kind of efficiency and reliance between allied firms on one side of a contract when parts of the process are subcontracted or outsourced, especially if outsourced to several firms, some of them overseas.

Objective contextual interpretation's approach to the question of integration operates similarly to foster reasonable expectations and reliance on written contracts within and between firms on one side of a contract. None of the functions of standardization would work as well if the various departments in party firms or allied firms could not rely on written contracts without investigating the parties' subjective intentions to integrate or not. They should not have to interview the negotiators or review the course of negotiations. The goals of securing transactions, protecting reasonable expectations and reliance, and holding parties responsible, support confining the contract terms to those in a written document when it reasonably appears to be integrated (plus implied terms).

Moreover, as indicated above, people and firms other than the parties form reasonable expectations from, and reasonably rely on written contracts on the basis of the writing alone. They generally do not investigate the parties' subjective intentions, the course of negotiations, or the extrinsic circumstances when the contract was made, on the question of integration. They treat a contract that reasonably appears to be integrated as the dominant determinant of the parties' rights, duties, and powers. Again, such third parties may include third-party beneficiaries, some assignees, auditors, investors, lenders, executors, and trustees in bankruptcy. Their expectations and reliance may be reasonable due to the costs to a third party of investigating the parties' subjective intentions, if such investigations are feasible without rights to discovery like those in litigation, and even if then. Protecting reasonable expectations and reasonable reliance are central goals of contract law. These goals justify imposing an objective result even in the theoretical case in which the parties' subjective intentions are otherwise, and even when the relying third parties do not have rights. Consequently, it may be justified to follow the parties' intention as constituted by their manifestation of intention, understood reasonably, on the question of integration.

---

[7] *Id.*

In addition, it is generally fair to hold the parties to have intended to integrate an agreement if the writing reasonably appears to be integrated, even when their subjective intentions were otherwise. In a few cases, so holding the parties will fail to enforce a parol agreement when they intended it to survive the writing. Fairness justifies the harm to contractual freedoms here. If the document does not represent the parties' subjective intentions on the question of integration, only they will know it. The burden to speak up can be placed most fairly on the parties because they can prevent a misunderstanding by one of them, courts, subparts of their firms, and/or third parties. It is easy to add or delete a merger clause, or to disclaim an integration by writing "draft" on a negotiating document.

Further, settling disputes non-arbitrarily, on the basis of Rule of Law values, supports a parol evidence rule. One Rule of Law value favors consistency in the law, in part to enhance the predictability of outcomes in and out of litigation. Predictability fosters settlement because neither party would want to incur the costs of litigation only to reach a result that was known in advance. And consistency is necessary to equal treatment under the law. Here, we should insist that the law of contract interpretation accord with the law of contract formation. The law of contract formation is objective, even under the Restatement (Second), which provides:

> An offer is the manifestation of willingness to enter into a bargain, so made as to justify another person in understanding that his assent to that bargain is invited and will conclude it.[8]

Similarly,

> An acceptance of an offer is a manifestation of assent to the terms thereof made by the offeree in a manner invited or required by the offer.[9]

The parties thus make contracts on the basis of their manifestations of assent (or manifestations of intention), not hidden intentions even when shared. Formation rules are consistent with the favored parol evidence rule because the rule gives effect to the parties' manifestations on the question of integration—the written document—not hidden intentions.

Finally, the favored parol evidence and four corners rules are more administrable than a subjective alternative. This is where the emphasis

---

[8] RESTATEMENT (SECOND) OF CONTRACTS § 24 (1981).

[9] *Id.* at § 50.

should be on whether objective contextual interpretation is more implementable than the subjective alternative. It seems likely that it is more implementable because it is objective. The following section, moreover, argues that the subjective alternative has its problems in this respect, too.

§ 6.1.1.3. Skepticism about Subjectivism

Even putting aside the notorious problems of proving subjective intentions, the main alternative to the favored parol evidence and four corners rules is untenable. The alternative is subjectivism, which would decide the question of integration on the basis of all relevant evidence, aiming at the parties' joint subjective intentions to integrate or not. Both Restatements take this approach.[10] Yet, it should be rejected in favor of objective contextual interpretation, for the following reasons.

If the contract is between an individual and a large business, or between two businesses, it may not even make sense to speak of the parties' subjective intentions to integrate or not. Subjective intentions exist only in someone's mind. But commercial entities do not have minds; rather, their officers and employees do. A subjectivist on the question of integration, consequently, must answer five questions: Which of the officers and employees count—those who authorize negotiations, negotiate the deal, approve the deal, or sign the written document? If a team does these things, how can we cumulate the intentions of the team members, since they may differ on a point in controversy, to find a corporate intention? What mental states count as the individuals' subjective intentions—hopes, expectations, predictions, beliefs, a sense of fairness, or some other mental state? Did the parties have shared intentions about the document's state of integration at all? These may be difficult questions that have no clear and reliable answers. We can obviate the need to answer them by objectifying our search for the parties' intention to focus on the reasonable appearance of the writing. It is final and binding, after all, only if an authorized representative signed or otherwise assented to it.

Two individuals, of course, also may conclude a written contract. A similar but less severe problem plagues the idea of two individuals' subjective intentions to integrate. A party may be of two minds on the question. It may hope and think, but not expect or believe, that the written document

---

[10] *Id.* at §§ 209, cmt. c, 210, cmt. b; Restatement (First) of Contracts § 228, cmt. a (1932).

is an integration. Other permutations of complex mental states easily can be imagined. Which mental states or combinations of mental states count as a person's subjective intention? There will, moreover, always be at least two parties to a contract. How can we join the perhaps different and complex mental states of two persons into a univocal subjective party intention to integrate or not?

Moreover, subjectivism assumes that more context, even though it always is fragmentary, will get us closer to the parties' mental intentions. But this may not be true, especially not on the esoteric question of integration. There is no known empirical basis for thinking it is true. We can, however, reasonably suppose that the fragments of subjective context that make it into court may not be representative of the complete context. Even the complete context would require a potentially misleading inference to a mental state. Consequently, any belief that more context will get us closer is not a substantial objection to using the parol evidence and four corners rules here.

Finally, subjectivism probably confuses a jury unacceptably. If there is extrinsic evidence relevant to the question of integration, and it is disputed, a fact-finder must find the facts. It seems likely that the same extrinsic evidence often will be relevant to the existence of a parol agreement, the question of ambiguity, and the question of meaning. There is reason to believe that a jury will confuse the three questions; even law students have considerable difficulty with the distinctions when they first encounter them. The result could be arbitrary jury verdicts. A judge could hold an evidentiary hearing and then decide the question of integration, but the inefficiencies of doing so are, at the least, a drawback.

For these reasons, subjectivism, too, can result in refusing to enforce a parol agreement even though the parties wanted it enforced, or in enforcing a parol agreement even though the parties meant to supersede it, violating their contractual freedoms. There is no basis for believing that subjectivism would err in this way less often than objectivism. Consequently, the theoretical harm to the contractual freedoms posed by objective contextual interpretation is not a reason to disfavor the objective approach.

§ 6.1.2. The Question of Ambiguity

As discussed in Chapter 4, after identifying the subject matter for interpretation—the contract's terms—prevailing law provides that a court must decide whether a term or the contract is ambiguous in a contested respect.

If there is no such ambiguity, the contract is given its unambiguous (plain) meaning as a matter of law. Following Professor E. Allan Farnsworth, we have suggested four ways in which a term or a contract may be ambiguous—term ambiguity, sentence ambiguity, structural ambiguity, and vagueness.[11] We should retain the requirement that judges answer the question of ambiguity, despite the contrary opinions of leading contracts scholars and other leading authorities, (notably Professors Arthur L. Corbin and Farnsworth, the Restatement (Second), Article 2 of the Uniform Commercial Code (UCC), and a small handful of cases.[12])

§ 6.1.2.1. Retaining the Question of Ambiguity

The law of civil procedure thrusts the question of ambiguity into contract law. As then-Judge Stephen G. Breyer wrote:

> In our opinion, an argument between parties about the meaning of a contract is typically an argument about a "material fact," namely, the factual meaning of the contract. But, sometimes this type of argument raises "no genuine issue." The words of a contract may be so clear themselves that reasonable people could not differ over their meaning. Then, the judge must decide the issue himself, just as he decides any factual issue in respect to which reasonable people cannot differ. [citation omitted.] Courts, noting that the judge, not the jury, decides such a threshold matter, have sometimes referred to this initial question of language ambiguity as a question of "law," which we see as another way of saying that there is no "genuine" factual issue left for a jury to decide.[13]

Those who would dispense with the question of ambiguity have not addressed the crucial procedural setting.

To elaborate, having identified a contract's terms, a court must decide upon motion—to dismiss, for summary judgment; to exclude evidence; or for a directed verdict—whether a term or the contract is ambiguous in

---

[11] *See* §§ 1.2.2; 4.4.

[12] *See* §§ 4.3.3.2; 4.5. *But see* Pacific Gas & Elec. Co. v. G.W. Thomas Drayage & Rigging Co., 69 Cal.Rptr. 561, 545 n.8 (Cal. 1968) (subjectivist view retaining the question of ambiguity).

[13] Boston Five Cents Sav. Bank v. Sec'y of Dep't of Housing and Urban Aff., 768 F.2d 5, 8 (1st Cir. 1985).

the contested respect. If there is no such ambiguity, there is nothing for a fact-finder to decide. If there is only one reasonable meaning as between the meanings advanced by the parties, there can be no genuine issue on the interpretive point. And no reasonable fact-finder could come to any conclusion but one.[14] Ascertaining meaning, then, properly is regarded as a question of law to be resolved by the court (and is in all jurisdictions). If a term is ambiguous, or if the question of ambiguity turns on disputed extrinsic evidence of the objective circumstances when the contract was formed, or a practical construction, the case should go to trial.[15]

Moreover, retaining the question of ambiguity makes sense in terms of contract law. As Farnsworth argued, we must decide questions of meaning when language fails.[16] It fails when there is term ambiguity, sentence ambiguity, structural ambiguity, or vagueness, in a term or the whole contract, as the case may be. But language does not always fail in these or other ways. It especially does not fail in a contested respect in all law cases because some context always is available. On a motion for summary judgment, for example, the court can have before it the whole document, the alleged facts of the parties' dispute, and the parties' contradictory contentions, arguments, affadavits, and proffers of evidence regarding the meaning of the contract and the contextual factors. When the relevant language does not fail in this light, it is unambiguous and contested unreasonably. A court then should hold that the term or contract has its unambiguous meaning as a matter of law. (This suggestion endorses the primary plain meaning rule, but not the four corners rule.)

Strong subjectivism would dispense with the question of ambiguity but not for good reasons. If the parties find themselves in a disagreement over the meaning of their contract, subjectivism looks to the meanings that each party "attached" to the terms of the contract and, in case of a misunderstanding, to each party's knowledge or reason to know of the meaning attached by the other. Thus, in a complicated but fundamental provision on "Whose Meaning Prevails," the Restatement (Second) provides:

> (1) Where the parties have attached the same meaning to a promise or agreement or a term thereof, it is interpreted in accordance with that meaning.

---

[14] Restatement (Second) of Contracts § 212(2) (1981).

[15] *See* F.R.C.P. 49(a).

[16] E. Allan Farnsworth, *"Meaning" in the Law of Contracts*, 76 Yale L.J. 939, 952–57 (1967).

> (2) Where the parties have attached different meanings to a promise or agreement or a term thereof, it is interpreted in accordance with the meaning attached by one of them if at the time the agreement was made
>
> (a) that party did not know of any different meaning attached by the other, and the other knew the meaning attached by the first party; or
>
> (b) that party had no reason to know of any different meaning attached by the other party, and the other had reason to know the meaning attached by the first party.
>
> (3) Except as stated in this Section, neither party is bound by the meaning attached by the other, even though the result may be a failure of mutual assent.[17]

Subsection (1) states the pure subjective theory of agreement: If both parties had the same meaning in mind, the term or the contract has that meaning. Subsection (2) switches from a theory of agreement to a theory of who was at fault for a misunderstanding. The only eligible meaning is one that one party had in mind while the other party was at fault for the misunderstanding. Subsection (3) entails that no meaning, including the most reasonable meaning, binds either party unless it was attached by both of them or one of them when the other was at fault.

Strong subjectivism dispenses with the question of ambiguity for three main reasons. First, Corbin, Article 2 of the UCC, and the Restatement (Second) all hold that all language is general and ambiguous, so a court never should find that contract language is unambiguous.[18] Dispensing with the question of ambiguity, however, does not follow from the ambiguity of all language in the abstract, which it is. Lawyers and judges never ascertain the meaning of contract language in the abstract. They choose only between the meanings advanced by the parties in a dispute.[19] They do not adopt anything like a full dictionary definition, which would be general and acontextual. Further, judicial treatment of the question of ambiguity can arise in the context of the whole document and the alleged facts of the dispute, as well as the parties' allegations, contentions, arguments, affidavits, and proffers of evidence. Much context thus is

---

[17] Restatement (Second) of Contracts § 201 (1981).

[18] 3 Arthur L. Corbin, Corbin on Contracts §§ 535, 542 (1961); U.C.C. § 202, cmt. 1(c) (2001); Restatement (Second) of Contracts § 202, cmt. a (1981).

[19] *See* § 4.1.

available to the judge. Ironically, Corbin ignored this rather rich context when he argued from the abstraction of language to dispensing with the question of ambiguity.[20] Because a judge has this context available, Corbin's philosophical point is beside the point. Considering context in this way will reveal both intrinsic and extrinsic ambiguities, and it is sufficient to identify unreasonable meanings non-arbitrarily. For these reasons, Corbin's argument fails.

Second, subjectivism holds that the meaning in a person's mind when that person speaks or hears, reads or writes, a word—her *understanding*—constitutes the meaning of that word for him or her.[21] Accordingly, Corbin defined *interpretation* as follows:

> The interpretation of a written contract is the process of determining the thoughts that the users of the words therein intended to convey to each other.[22]

Similarly, the Restatement (Second) explains:

> The objective of interpretation in the general law of contracts is to carry out the understanding of the parties rather than to impose obligations on them contrary to their understanding: "the courts do not make a contract for the parties."[23]

If a language-user's understanding of an expression's meaning thus constitutes the expression's meaning for her, there is little possibility of finding language unambiguous. Meaning depends on what the user had in mind, not on the language as used in its context according to the relevant conventions of language. The Restatement (Second) allows there to be a misunderstanding between users but, if users give conflicting meanings to a word, the matter is settled on the basis of fault, not interpretation.[24]

Corbin and the Restatement (Second) are wrong. In effect, they endorse Humpty Dumpty's theory of meaning in *Through the Looking Glass*: "When *I* use a word, Humpty said, in a rather scornful tone, it

---

[20] Corbin, *supra* note 18, at § 542.
[21] *See id.* at § 535 (emphasis added).
[22] Arthur L. Corbin, *The Interpretation of Words and the Parol Evidence Rule*, 50 Cornell L. Q. 161, 170–71 (1965).
[23] Restatement (Second) of Contracts § 201, cmt. c (1981).
[24] *Id.* at § 201(2).

means just what I choose it to mean—neither more nor less."[25] Humpty's view, of course, is a humorous *reductio ad absurdum* that drove Alice bonkers. The views of Corbin and the Restatement (Second), however, are even worse. They also mirror Dumpty Humpty's: "When I *hear* a word, it means just what I choose it to mean." Between Humpty Dumpty and Dumpty Humpty, there can be no communication except by coincidence. Yet we do communicate regularly as a matter of fact. The reason is that language is conventional, never private, and always within a context of use. We participate in language communities that constitute the meanings of their language uses socially.[26] So, we can be mistaken about the meaning of what we say or hear, read or write—a possibility Corbin and the Restatement (Second) do not allow. Accordingly, language has meaning by convention, in a context of use, even when neither party had the meaning in mind.

Third, Corbin insisted that we should never give a contract a meaning that neither party subjectively intended.[27] The issue arises in the theoretical case in which the parties did not have the same meaning in mind, and neither party was at fault for the misunderstanding. If the conventional meaning is unambiguous and later is advanced by a party to a dispute, objective conventional interpretation would require a judge to find that the contract has the conventional meaning as a matter of law. The best example is the hypothetical case of the private code, in which the parties secretly agree that *buy* shall mean sell.[28] When one of the parties says *buy*, a subjectivist will take the word to mean sell, while an objectivist will insist that *buy* means buy. As a practical matter, if a relevant dispute were to arise, one party will claim that there was a secret agreement, while the other will deny it. Though the language is relevantly unambiguous, the subjectivist will insist that a fact-finder should decide who is telling the truth. This makes it too easy for the party claiming a secret agreement to get to a jury. Because the claimed private code was a secret, there will be no evidence of it other than the parties' conflicting testimony. The case will turn on credibility alone. But the basis for judgments solely on credibility

---

[25] LEWIS CARROLL, THROUGH THE LOOKING GLASS, *in* ALICE'S ADVENTURES IN WONDERLAND AND THROUGH THE LOOKING GLASS 237 (Puffin Books ed., 3d ed. 1997) (first published in 1871).

[26] *See generally* LUDWIG WITTGENSTEIN, PHILOSOPHICAL INVESTIGATIONS (G.E.M. Anscombe transl. 1958).

[27] CORBIN, *supra* note 18, at § 539.

[28] RESTATEMENT (SECOND) OF CONTRACTS § 212, cmt. b., illus. 4 (1981).

is notoriously unreliable, and the outcome is unpredictable. It is likely to be one party's word against the other's regarding their thoughts. Moreover, the case of the private code is something of an academic plaything. No known precedent raises the issue. Such an outlying case, theoretically illuminating though it may be, should not drive a practical approach to the law of contract interpretation.

What elements should a court consider when deciding whether a term or a contract is ambiguous in a contested respect? The prevailing view is encompassed in the four corners rule. However, it is suggested, for reasons given in the next section, a court should consider the whole document, the document's evident purpose(s), proffers concerning the objective circumstances when the contract was made, trade usages, and proffers concerning any practical construction. This collection of elements is the objective context. It excludes the course of negotiations, a party's statements of intention made in the course of negotiations, a party's testimony as to its own past intentions, any course of dealing, and any other indices solely of subjective intention.

A possible objection to objective contextual interpretation here could be that it will miss extrinsic ambiguities in the contract language. This would not be desirable because it would be an obvious error. The objection, however, would be mistaken. Under this proposal, a judge would take into account the objective context, which will be available on summary judgment through the parties' allegations, affidavits, contentions, arguments, and proffers. Once counsel explains an extrinsic ambiguity and presents the context in these ways (or even hypothetically), the judge will have an ample basis to find that the contract is extrinsically ambiguous, if it is under the conventions of the language use in the parties' context. (If the parties use different languages but the same words, the words are relevantly ambiguous.)

§ 6.1.2.2. Normative and Other Reasons

Objective contextual interpretation rejects the four corners rule in favor of the objective context on the question of ambiguity. Here, the balance of competing goals and other reasons tips in favor of more context than on the question of integration. The question of ambiguity is a question of meaning. An interpreter can ascertain an apt meaning of language in light of the objective context.

By contrast with deciding whether a written contract is integrated, deciding whether a term or a contract is ambiguous involves ascertaining the meaning(s) of language. The question of integration is solely the question whether the parties intended a written agreement to be final, or final and complete. The question of ambiguity, by contrast, involves the interpreter in ascertaining the meaning of contract language by identifying its referent or referents in the imaginary world of the contract, described in Chapter 1.[29] For example, by entering a simple contract for the sale of goods, the parties imagine a possible world in which the buyer has the seller's goods, and the seller has the buyer's money. The term describing the goods refers to that which the buyer has in the world of the contract. Similarly, the price term refers to the amount of the buyer's money that the seller has in that world. The contract commits the buyer and the seller to make the imaginary world into the real world by keeping their commitments to make the exchange.

We may think that we ascertain the meaning of language only when we identify one and only one referent—when we find the language unambiguous or resolve an ambiguity. We ascertain meaning also, however, when we find that language is ambiguous. In fact, in contract interpretation, we then are finding two meanings, both of which the language reasonably and relevantly will bear.

Significant context always is necessary to ascertain reasonable and relevant meaning(s). Consider: A person says to another, "Report improvements." What is an improvement? We cannot say. Now add some context (here, objective circumstances): The speaker was a doctor and the listener was a patient. *Improvements* now refers to the condition of the patient's health. What kind of condition? Add that the patient had visited the doctor with a cut on her hand. *Improvements* now refers more specifically to a healing of the skin on her hand. If the patient had visited the doctor with a pain in the abdomen, *improvements* would refer to the easing of that pain. Assume now that the speaker was the county tax assessor. *Improvements* probably refers to the condition of real property. If the speaker was a teacher, *improvements* would refer to something else altogether. And so on. The example is not atypical. As the dictionary indicates, most words have several meanings in the abstract (acontextually). With a context, we may know easily which meaning is apt. Consequently, language can be unambiguous as used in a context, but normally not otherwise.

[29] *See* § 1.1.1.

It is wrong to say that a contract ever "speaks for itself" on a question of meaning, as the supreme courts of Illinois and Pennsylvania have said.[30]

The necessity of context for ascertaining meaning(s) is the strongest argument against the four corners rule here. Objective contextual interpretation provides the objective context, including the dictionary, the whole document, the objective circumstances at formation, any trade usages, the document's evident purpose(s), any practical construction, and other objective elements. Though not as extensive a context as subjectivism's, the objective context is more than sufficient to ascertain non-arbitrary meaning(s).

In any event, harm to the contractual freedoms would be outweighed by the other goals. Parties and others who rely on conventionally unambiguous meanings, in particular, normally should have their expectations and reliance protected. Even when the parties shared a contrary intention when the contract was made, subparts of firms and subcontractors, as well as some other third parties, generally do not have access to the negotiating records and should not have to interview the negotiators. Only if litigation ensues and rights to discovery come into play, if then, does it become feasible to look for subjective intentions as to the meaning(s) of language when the intentions are the other party's and different from conventional meaning(s). The parties and others, however, should be able to avoid disputes by following their contracts and to settle their disputes reasonably in accordance with their contracts, without resorting to litigation. By objectifying the question of ambiguity, and taking unambiguous contracts from the fact-finder, objective contextual interpretation enhances predictability and hence promotes performance and settlement. (Strong subjectivism, by contrast, sends potentially every interpretive dispute to the finder of fact because it tends to dispense with the question of ambiguity.) Again, parties can be held to their manifested intentions fairly because they are in a good position to manifest intentions that mirror their subjective intentions, if there might be a difference.

§ 6.1.3. Resolving Ambiguity

Once the court has decided that a contract is relevantly ambiguous, the contract document and extrinsic evidence of the objective context should

---

[30] Air Safety, Inc. v. Teachers Realty Corp., 706 N.E.2d 882, 884 (Ill. 1999); Steuart v. McChesney, 444 A.2d 659, 661 (Pa. 1982).

be admissible. The case will move to the fact-finder, often the jury. If there is no disputed extrinsic evidence or controversy over the inferences to be drawn from it, however, the ambiguity should be resolved by the court.

The fact-finder should consider the same elements that the court considered when deciding the question of ambiguity, including the whole document, the contract's purpose(s), the objective circumstances when the contract was formed, any trade usages, and any practical construction. The admissible evidence should not include evidence of the course of the parties' negotiations, statements of intention during their negotiations, a parties' testimony about its own past intention, the parties' course of dealing, and any other evidence that is relevant solely to the parties' subjective intentions. If there is a jury, the instruction should identify the relevant ambiguity in the contract document and the parties' contentions with respect to that ambiguity. It should tell the jury to choose between the contentions in order to give the document the meaning that the parties intended. By admitting evidence only of the parties' objective intentions, the result should be a verdict based on a finding of the parties' objective intentions as manifested. When a judge serves as a fact-finder, of course, he or she should apply the same law.

By contrast, existing law generally requires the court to decide the question of ambiguity based on what is within the four corners of the document. The jury is allowed to resolve an ambiguity based on all relevant evidence and is allowed to find the parties' subjective intentions. This shift at different procedural stages from a strong objective theory to a fully subjective theory is puzzling. Why should some contract parties be limited to an unambiguous meaning that appears from within the document's four corners, while other contract parties are entitled to a resolution of an ambiguity based on all relevant evidence, including evidence of subjective intentions? There lurks beneath this disjoint treatment a potential impairment of Rule of Law values, which require equal treatment before the law. Consider two cases. In both, the parties' objective intention contradicts their mutual subjective intentions. In the first, a party wins on the question of ambiguity based on the four corners rule, *i.e.*, the contract is held to be unambiguous. The parties' objective intention governs. In the second, the contract is held to be ambiguous and the case goes to the jury, and the parties' subjective intentions govern. We get contradictory outcomes due to the difference in theories and elements, not any difference in the parties' objective or subjective intentions, respectively. By using one theory for both decisions, by contrast, the same party intention would govern.

Objective contextual interpretation favors an objective theory for now-familiar reasons. To review, any harm to the contractual freedoms would seem to occur in an unusual case and, therefore, to be unimportant for a practical theory. Any such harm is outweighed by the other goals. Parties and others who rely on the conventional meaning of a contract or a term normally should have their expectations and reliance protected. Even though the parties shared a contrary intention when the contract was made, subparts of firms and subcontractors, as well as some other third parties, generally do not have access to the negotiating records and should not have to interview the other party's negotiators. The negotiators may be unavailable in any event; for instance, they may have left the employ of a party. Only if litigation ensues and rights to discovery come into play, if then, does it become feasible to look for subjective intentions when they are different from the relevant conventional meaning(s). The parties and others, however, should be able avoid disputes by performing their contracts, and to settle their disputes reasonably in accordance with their contracts, without resorting to litigation. By objectifying the resolution of ambiguity, objective contextual interpretation enhances predictability and hence promotes performance and settlements. Parties can be held to their manifested intentions fairly because they are in a position to manifest intentions that mirror their subjective intentions.

Subjectivism is at least as problematic here as it is on the question of ambiguity. To review, subjectivism's underlying theory of meaning is untenable. It supposes that what was in the mind of a speaker or hearer, a reader or writer, constitutes the meaning of the language he or she used. Subjectivism thus reduces true interpretive disputes, in the first instance, to a ridiculous battle between Humpty Dumpty and Dumpty Humpty.[31] And we surely can be mistaken about the meaning of language we speak or hear. The reason is that a language community's conventions of language use constitute the meanings of language used in a context.

Further, when what was in the parties' minds differs, subjectivism turns to a fault principle to decide which of the parties' attached meanings shall govern. Thus, Section 201(2) of the Restatement (Second), quoted above,[32] gives a party the meaning it attaches to contract language if the other party knew or had reason to know of that meaning, and the

---

31 *See* § 6.1.2.1.

32 *See id.* (text accompanying note 17).

first party did not know or have reason to know of the meaning attached by the other party. Such a fault principle, however, seriously undermines predictability and the contract's function as an authoritative guide to the parties' conduct both inside and outside of the courthouse. To find out its contractual rights, duties, and powers under the fault principle, a first party must worry itself about what meaning the second party attached to the contract term, what the second party knew about the meaning the first party attached to the contract term, and what the second party had reason to know about the meaning the first party attached to the term. This seems to be well nigh impossible without rights to discovery in litigation, if then. Consequently, parties will be hampered, prior to litigation, in performing as required and in settling disputes.

Moreover, because strong subjectivism dispenses with the question of ambiguity, it sends potentially all interpretive disputes to the fact-finder. Jury verdicts generally are notoriously unpredictable. In a case involving a contract interpretation dispute, unpredictability probably is even more severe. Many contracts are long, complicated documents requiring great sophistication to parse them well. It is hard to imagine a jury succeeding in finding the parties' intentions in these cases. Such unpredictability, again, hampers the parties outside the courthouse, before litigation commences. Subjectivism, in a phrase, is too litigation-oriented. And it does not work well in litigation, either.

§ 6.2. Pluralism, Economic Analysis, and Conventionalism

This section considers three untidy questions that we should address as we reach the end of this study. First, what is the justification for objective contextual interpretation's pluralist nature? Second, why does objective contextual interpretation reject economic analyses of contract interpretation? Third, what is the underlying basis for objective contextual interpretation's theory of meaning?

§ 6.2.1. Pluralist and Monist Theories

Objective contextual interpretation is a pluralistic theory in three major respects. First, it holds that interpretation is contextual, such that contract interpretation, fiction interpretation, musical interpretation, and other kinds of interpretation may be different.[33] Second, and more specifically, its justification depends on a balance of several goals and other reasons. Third, it identifies the elements that should be considered when performing each task in contract interpretation, and it requires that, when several are relevant and have conflicting implications, they should be weighed to reach a judgment. The objective contextual approach, however, refrains from supplying a meta-rule for assigning weights in the scales of justice. Consequently, different interpreters may disagree reasonably in a hard case. This approach, like the prevailing law, allows the interpreter discretion.

Some leading contracts theorists insist on a need for those who would balance to provide a single and determinate metric or meta-norm for assigning weights to norms. When criticizing Professor Melvin A. Eisenberg's pluralistic approach to various contract issues, Professors Alan Schwartz and Robert E. Scott wrote:

> The problem that pluralist theories without meta-norms pose are nicely illustrated in Melvin Eisenberg's effort, which purports to solve the . . . problem by proposing overlapping sets of norms. Eisenberg recognizes that his theory lacks a metric that would tell the lawmaker just how to give the proper "weight and role" to each social proposition or value when conflicts occur. Since courts or legislatures are likely to be involved when the relevant social propositions or values arguably favor more than one type of litigant or interest group, pluralist theories such as Eisenberg's tend to be least helpful when they are most needed.[34]

If we had a single determinate meta-norm for assigning weights to norms, we would transform contract theory and, by extension, contract law generally, into a monistic field. That is, contract law would have only one justification—that of the metric—which would ramify through the law. For example, we could pursue the goal of making contract law economically efficient and shun any other purpose whatsoever. Respected scholars

---

[33] *See generally* Kent Greenawalt, *A Pluralist Approach to Interpretation: Wills and Contracts*, 42 San Diego L. Rev. 533 (2005).

[34] Alan Schwartz & Robert E. Scott, *Contract Theory and the Limits of Contract Law*, 113 Yale L.J. 541, 543–44 n.2 (2003) (footnotes omitted). *See* Melvin A. Eisenberg, *The Bargain Principle and its Limits*, 95 Harv. L. Rev. 741 (1982); Melvin A. Eisenberg, *The Theory of Contracts*, *in* The Theory of Contract Law: New Essays 206 (Peter Benson, ed. 2001).

who do normative economic analyses of contract law, such as Schwartz and Scott, pursue such monism.[35] Their criticism in effect insists that Eisenberg should transform his pluralism into monism if his theory is to compete well with an efficiency theory.

Monism might be appealing because it promises elegance in contract theory; if successful, it would provide consistent, complete, and determinate norms to govern all contract disputes. Monism, however, has serious drawbacks. Schwartz and Scott, in an article largely devoted to contract interpretation, can pursue their monism only by restricting the domain of contract law to a subset of all contract disputes as conventionally understood—firms selling to firms. They exclude firms selling to individuals, individuals selling to firms, and individuals selling to individuals.[36] They assign disputes involving firms selling to individuals to the domains of consumer protection law, real property law, and securities law. They assign disputes between individuals and firms to the domain of employment law. And they assign disputes between individuals and individuals to the domains of family law and real property law.[37] Schwartz and Scott's efficiency theory of interpretation is not intended to apply to the excluded disputes.

The problem here is that decidedly contractual disputes arise between firms selling to individuals, individuals selling to firms, and individuals selling to individuals—disputes involving offers, acceptances, mistakes, unconscionability, material breaches, *etc.* If these kinds of disputes are to be treated differently depending on the identities of the parties as firms or individuals, there will be unequal treatment across domains in relation to common contract issues. If these disputes are to be treated the same, and the same as disputes between firms and firms, however, there is no point to carving up contract law's traditional domain. The change proposed by Schwartz and Scott would involve an unwise radical restriction of contract law's domain: In effect, it seems, they would shrink the domain to fit the theory in order to achieve theoretical elegance or something similar.

Pluralism in contract law can be somewhat messy, as is democracy. Pluralistic contract law, however, can have the decided advantages of governing all contract disputes with the same rules (subject to minor variations

[35] Schwartz & Scott, *supra* note 34, at 544. *See also* STEPHEN A. SMITH, CONTRACT THEORY (2004); Randy E. Barnett, *A Consent Theory of Contract*, 86 COLUM. L. REV. 269 (1986).

[36] *See* Schwartz & Scott, *supra* note 34, at 544.

[37] *Id.*

when justified) and can produce equal treatment under the law. Most important, a pluralistic contract law respects all relevant normative and other considerations. The contractual freedoms, the security of transactions, non-arbitrary dispute settlement under the Rule of Law, and administrability, all are important considerations. None should be sacrificed due to the theoretical desiderata of monism. One could add economic efficiency to the mix and delete inconsistent goals. Efficiency then would have less than conclusive weight due to the great importance of Rule of Law values and administrability. If we include these values, economic efficiency turns out to be part of a pluralist theory; efficiency presumably would be outweighed by Rule of Law and administrability considerations in some circumstances. And there is no meta-norm here either. There is no justification, however, for excluding *any* legally relevant normative consideration, and especially not to do so to achieve theoretical elegance. So we are led to pluralism.

In addition, no meta-norm could capture the ebb and flow of weight as we vary the facts of a case hypothetically. As we wrote elsewhere in relation to a simple negligence case:

> [A]ssume that a motor vehicle left the road and damaged a storefront. In a tort action, the fact that the operator had an epileptic seizure at the moment looms large, all else being equal, as a reason to find that the motorist was not negligent. The fact of the seizure seems less weighty, as an exculpatory reason, when it turns out that the motorist did not take anti-seizure medication that day. Not having taken anti-seizure medication, in turn, is crucial if the motorist had a history of epilepsy and was under a doctor's orders to take the medication regularly. It shrinks in significance, however, if the motorist had not had a bout of epilepsy for many years. In the same context, the mere fact that an epileptic was operating a motor vehicle probably is insignificant, but gains salience if the motorist's medical history includes many epileptic seizures even while properly medicated.[38]

Weight here is not a property of a norm. Rather, legal norms make facts relevant as concrete legal reasons, as the negligence standard makes each of the hypothetical facts in this illustration relevant. Weight is a property

[38] Steven J. Burton, Judging in Good Faith 55–56 (1992) ((example drawn from Hammontree v. Jenner, 97 Cal.Rptr. 739 (Cal.App. 1971)).

of a legal reason. The *weight* of a legal reason, however, is a function of the other legal reasons in the case together—not of an additional meta-norm specifying the weight of the negligence standard in general or of all possible concrete legal reasons stemming from it. There are too many variations on the facts in any case for a single and determinate meta-norm to do non-arbitrary justice. Weight thus is internal to the congeries of relevant legal reasons in each case: The weight of one reason depends on the weight of the other reasons.[39] As a result, weighing the reasons often requires discretion to do justice under the law in cases.[40] There is nothing wrong with discretion in adjudication when it is justified by a pluralism of applicable normative and other proper considerations, and a meta-norm for assigning weights is absent.[41]

This endorsement of weighing indicates the response to arguments that

> [f]or any given maxim [of contract interpretation] that would persuade a judge to a certain conclusion a contrary maxim may be found that would persuade him to the opposite (or contradictory) conclusion.[42]

This would be true only if one assumes that each single rule or canon of interpretation is supposed to determine the right result in a case on its own. Any rule or canon that cuts against it then would have a contradictory implication. But the rules and canons of interpretation, like legal rules and principles generally, are not thus determinate. Rather, they have a dimension of weight when applied in a case that avoids the claimed contradiction.[43]

§ 6.2.2. Economic Analysis

We have said almost nothing about the economics of contract interpretation. A number of leading scholars, including Judge Richard A. Posner,

---

[39] *Id.* at 56.

[40] *Id.* at 50–62.

[41] *Id.* at 107–202.

[42] Edwin W. Patterson, *The Interpretation and Construction of Contracts*, 64 Colum L. Rev. 833, 852 (1964). *See also* Duncan Kennedy, *Form and Substance in Private Law Adjudication*, 89 Harv. L. Rev. 1685, *passim* (1976).

[43] *See* Burton, *supra* note 38, at 171–78.

Schwartz, and Scott, have put forth interesting economic analyses.[44] The reason for neglecting them is that the leading analyst's conclusions center strikingly on literalism as the preferred theory of contract interpretation.[45] For example, Schwartz and Scott, as the result of their clever and most sophisticated analysis of firm-to-firm contracts, advocate interpretation of these contracts on the basis of what they call B_{min}. They define B_{min} as the minimum necessary evidentiary base for contract interpretation (a minimum set consisting of four interpretive elements) composed of

> the parties' contract, a narrative concerning whether the parties performed the obligations that the contract appears to require, a standard English language dictionary, and the interpreter's experience and understanding of the world.[46]

Their argument in sum is that, in the absence of agreement on another mode of interpretation, firms would prefer that the courts interpret firm-to-firm contracts on the basis of B_{min} and that courts should do so because doing what firms want would foster efficiency.

Though they appear to think that B_{min} is Willistonian, it is best understood as literalist. (Williston was an objectivist.[47]) The contract document and a dictionary stand out in the passage quoted above. The other elements do not bear casual scrutiny. It is a mistake to include the narrative to which Schwartz and Scott refer. We cannot determine whether a party performed its contract obligations until *after* we have identified and interpreted the contract's terms. The last element also is problematic because it is not an interpretive element, part of an evidentiary base, at all. Different interpreters, moreover, will come to an interpretive problem with different experiences and understandings. Schwartz and Scott see the world through the lens of economics; others see the world through common sense, religion, philosophy, social science, or something else. A key function of the law and the evidence is to leaven these differences by providing an obligation to follow the law and common legal standards, for the sake of predictability and equal treatment. It is hard to believe

---

[44] Richard A. Posner, *The Law and Economics of Contract Interpretation*, 83 Texas L. Rev. 1581 (2005); Schwartz & Scott, *supra* note 34.

[45] *See* Posner, *supra* note 44, at 1606; Schwartz & Scott, *supra* note 34, at 572; Robert E. Scott, *The Case for Formalism in Relational Contract*, 94 Northwestern L. Rev. 847, 848 (2000).

[46] *Id.*

[47] *See* § 1.3.1.

that contracting parties would want the resolution of their disputes to depend on whether the interpreter is an economist, a philosopher, or a common sense lawyer. Schwartz and Scott's last element thus should be excluded. We are left (by the best interpretation of the passage) with literalism—the contract's words and the dictionary.

Much has been said in this book about literalism. We have suggested in sum that it is often arbitrary and, in any event, undesirable. Meaning varies with the context of language use. Hence, without considering a context at least implicitly,[48] literalism too often assigns inapt meanings to contract language, undermining the law's predictability. The dictionary typically gives several meanings and grammatical functions for a word. It generally provides no meta-norm for choosing among those meanings and functions. Dictionaries also give general definitions which may not draw the fine distinctions needed to ascertain the parties' intention. Literalism offers no resources for resolving sentence ambiguities, structural ambiguities, or vagueness, all of which are common in contracts. Indeed, there is no literal meaning if an ambiguity appears. When there is no literal meaning, literalism logically requires that the case be dismissed. It thus abandons the law's dispute settlement function in a great many cases. Truly, literalism is not a viable option. Consequently, the leading economic analyses of contract interpretation miss the mark.

§ 6.2.3. *The Conventions of Language Use*

The meaning of language is not constituted by the dictionary or what was in the parties' minds but, instead, by the conventions of language use in various contexts. Consider Ludwig Wittgenstein's famous and influential criticism of St. Augustine's theory of meaning. According to Wittgenstein, Augustine held that the individual words in a language stand for (correspond to) objects: "Every word has a meaning. This meaning is correlated with the word. It is the object for which the word stands."[49] Literalism implicitly embraces a theory of meaning much like this one. It focuses on individual words. It looks to the dictionary to find the meaning that is correlated with the word. And the meaning is supposed to be an object in the real world.

---

[48] *See* § 2.1.3.

[49] WITTGENSTEIN, *supra* note 26, at § 1.

Though accepting that this view of meaning may be true for some words in some contexts of use, Wittgenstein believed that there was much more to a language. He focused on the multifarious ways in which a language can be used: "[T]he meaning of a word is its use in the language."[50] Thus, in addition to naming objects, our language permits us to exclaim (Oh my!), to predict, to ask questions, to do arithmetic, to make a joke, to say something ironically, to thank, to curse, to greet, to play, to guide conduct, to explain, and to use it in many, many other ways.[51] The same word may have different meanings depending on how it is used and in what context. The word *bar*, for example, might refer to an examination when used by a law student who is asking a professor what courses she should take, to a legal organization when used by a client accusing her lawyer of commingling funds, to sand in a river when used in a warning by a riverboat's captain, and to a prohibition when a bar owner ejects a rowdy customer. How words are being used on an occasion—what they mean—depends on the practice(s) in which they are embedded and the conventions of language use which guide that practice—what Wittgenstein called a "language game." A dictionary might indicate that *bar* has these four meanings (and others), some of which are nouns and others verbs, but it cannot tell us which one is the apt meaning on which occasion. For that, we need the relevant language conventions, which require that we know the context of use.

Promising and *contracting*, moreover, involve distinctive uses of language. The content of a promise does not name an object, as can some nouns in descriptive sentences under some circumstances. Its content refers instead to actions, events, persons, states of affairs, and other things in the imaginary world of a contract.[52] Interpretation gives meaning to the content of a promise when it settles the shape of that world, still in the imagination. Observations of the real world do not come into play until after we have settled the shape of the imaginary world. We then can compare the two and determine whether the imaginary world became the real world and, if not, whether the reason is that a party breached by failing to perform its promise when due, without excuse or justification.

Resort to the conventions of language use within a practice is not unproblematic. Conventions sometimes run out of guidance, leaving a

---

[50] *Id.* at § 43.

[51] *Id.* at §§ 23–27.

[52] *See* § 1.1.1.

dispute unresolved. Wittgenstein described the dynamics of a language as follows:

> Our language can be seen as an ancient city: a maze of little streets and squares, of old and new houses, and of houses with additions from various periods; and this surrounded by a multitude of new boroughs with straight regular streets and uniform houses.[53]

Consequently, the conventions may be fractured in a case, as when one party knew of a trade usage and contracted in that light, while the other did not know and contracted in light of ordinary usage, producing a dispute. The parties then are engaged in different practices, possibly with different conventions of language use, which conventions may produce contradictory results. In the case of a fracture, the conventions might produce ambiguity.

Wittgenstein's conventionalism nonetheless is objective contractual interpretation's theory of meaning. It will not produce difficult disputes in many, many cases. This kind of interpretation identifies and resolves ambiguities on the basis of the contract's objective context. Like Wittgenstein, it rejects the notion that the meaning of language is constituted by what a speaker or hearer, reader or writer, had in mind. Instead, a contract's meaning is constituted by objective factors—the conventions of the practice in which the parties are engaged. An interpreter can use these conventions by considering the objective context to ascertain the meaning of contract language as used in that context. Accordingly, circumstances and purpose are essential. The objective circumstances at formation (including trade usages) provide the context of the use. The contract's evident purpose indicates the relevant use. By contrast, the course of negotiations, a party's statements of intention made in the course of negotiations, a party's testimony as to its own past intentions, and any course of dealing bear on what a party probably had in mind. Suffice it to say here that Wittgenstein's complex arguments against the possibility of a private language strongly dispute the relevance of such subjective elements to the contract's meaning.[54]

When the dynamics of the relevant language make the conventions ambiguous and the meanings contradictory as applied in a case, objective contractual interpretation holds that the contract is ambiguous. It addresses

---

[53] WITTGENSTEIN, *supra* note 26, at § 18.

[54] *See id.* at § 243 *et seq.*; § 6.1.2.1 (discussion of Humpty Dumpty).

the ambiguity in two steps. The first is for a finder of fact to resolve it if possible by weighing the cross-cutting elements that support each of the conflicting meanings, in the manner summarized above.[55] If this fails, the second is to apply a default rule or to declare a failure of mutual assent.[56]

§ 6.3. Summary of Major Points

Objective contextual interpretation rests on many of the major points made in the descriptive and analytical portion of this book (Chapters 2 to 5). To forestall possible misunderstanding, it may be helpful to conclude with a summary and consolidation of the major points.

First, once we have decided to enforce a contract, we should do what we decided to do—enforce *it*. Whether to enforce a contract requires us to apply formation and invalidating doctrines, including doctrines of public policy and unconscionability. We reach the problems of interpretation within the scope of this book only after we have applied these doctrines and found that the agreement passes the tests. Subject to one exception, these doctrines then are spent; we should not reconsider them when interpreting a concededly enforceable contract. The parties' agreement becomes the central authoritative guide to their conduct in contract performance. The exception is that, if a contract or term is ambiguous in the contested respect, and one of the advocated meaning-branches of the ambiguity is against public policy or is unconscionable, a court should exclude that branch. The contract or term then has the other meaning if it is reasonable, and the contract or term is unambiguous as a matter of law.

Second, contract interpretation pursues four main goals—respecting the contractual freedoms, enhancing the security of transactions, settling disputes non-arbitrarily under the Rule of Law, and achieving administrability. A theory of contract interpretation tells us how to perform the three interpretive tasks—identifying the contract's terms, deciding whether they are ambiguous in a contested respect, and resolving any ambiguity—to further the goals. Because it pursues these four goals, objective contextual interpretation is pluralistic as opposed to monistic. It holds than no applicable normative consideration should be excluded for the sake of theoretical elegance or other monistic concerns. Consequently, competing

[55] Burton, *supra* note 38 and accompanying text.

[56] *See* § 5.3.

legal reasons should be balanced in a hard case if the relevant elements have cross-cutting implications.

Third, there are three relevant theories of contract interpretation—literalism, objectivism, and subjectivism. Contracts scholarship heretofore has recognized only two—literalism and subjectivism—on the questions of meaning. Corbin vigorously attacked literalism because it is acontextual. He, followed by Farnsworth, Professors John D. Calamari and Joseph M. Perillo, and (largely) the Restatement (Second), concluded that subjectivism was the better theory because acontextual interpretation is impossible. Corbin's arguments, however, do not touch objective contextual interpretation. The favored approach includes enough context to avoid his criticisms when interpretation involves a question of meaning.

Fourth, identifying the terms of a written contract is the province of the parol evidence rule. It provides in brief that, *when* a written contract is integrated, certain parol agreements are discharged. It is not the same as the four corners rule, which provides in this context that *whether* a written contract is integrated depends on the contract document alone. Further, parol evidence may be excluded when a contract is unambiguous but, again, that is on the basis of the four corners rule. It is not the case—but a source of much confusion—that, whenever a court excludes parol evidence, it is on the basis of the parol evidence rule.

Fifth, the question whether a contract or term is ambiguous depends on whether it is ambiguous in a contested respect, not in the abstract. That is, a court normally must decide whether the contract or a term bears two reasonable meanings, each of which is advanced by a party. A third or fourth meaning is irrelevant to the case at hand. Consequently, abstract arguments suggesting that all language is ambiguous, such as the one advanced by Corbin and others, are irrelevant in the law of contracts.

Sixth, the question of ambiguity is thrust upon contract law by the law of civil procedure. When a contract is unambiguous, there is no material question of fact for a fact-finder to decide. Moreover, while strong subjectivism would send most interpretive questions to the fact-finder, objective contextual interpretation prefers that judges decide the question of ambiguity as a matter of law. Doing so enhances predictability in the law.

Seventh, the plain meaning rule mainly provides that unambiguous contracts or terms shall be given their unambiguous (*i.e.*, plain) meaning as a matter of law. It is a tautology. The important question is whether an interpreter should determine whether a contract is ambiguous by looking at the contract document alone or in the light of contextual elements. Answering this question depends on whether the four corners rule should apply when addressing the question of ambiguity. Objective contextual interpretation rejects the four corners rule here because deciding this question involves ascertaining the reasonable meanings of contract language. Objective contextual interpretation requires, instead, that the court decide the question of ambiguity by considering the contract document in light of its objective context as presented by counsel, without admitting evidence.

Eighth, focusing on the elements of contract interpretation and extruding literalism permits us to distinguish between a contract's objective and subjective contexts. The objective context consists of those elements that bear on the conventional meaning(s) of the parties' manifestations of intention. The subjective context consists of those elements plus other elements from which inferences may be drawn solely about the parties' subjective intentions as to the meaning(s) of their manifestations. Objective contextual interpretation employs the objective context both on the question of ambiguity and when resolving an ambiguity.

Ninth, objective contextual interpretation is highly critical of the currently popular alternative, subjectivism, for several reasons. For one thing, there are well-known hazards in conceiving and proving what a person had in mind in the past. Subjectivism assumes that considering more context will get an interpreter closer to the parties' past subjective intentions; there is no basis for this assumption. And what an individual person had in mind when speaking or hearing, reading or writing language does not constitute the meaning of that language; so subjectivism can produce arbitrary interpretations that do not respect the contractual freedoms. For the foregoing three reasons, subjectivism will err and impair contractual freedom in some cases. Moreover, even if subjectivism would not, contractual freedom is not the sole goal. Enhancing the security of transactions also is a goal and may outweigh the contractual freedoms in some cases. Additionally, by comparison with objective contextual interpretation, subjectivism weakens predictability and equal treatment under the law. Finally, subjectivism applies only to interpretive questions that arise at the performance stage of the contracting process, not to interpretation questions arising at the formation stage, the latter of which are decided objectively by all accounts. Objective contextual interpretation at the performance stage does a better job of achieving congruence between these two kinds of interpretive question.

Tenth, literalism and subjectivism depend on defective underlying theories of meaning. Literalism holds that the dictionary constitutes the meaning of a word in a contract. Subjectivism holds that such meaning is constituted by what a party had in mind when speaking or hearing, reading or writing the word. Objective contextual interpretation rejects both. It favors conventionalism, the view that meaning is constituted by the conventions of language use within the context of use. Objective contextual interpretation's focus on the objective context and purpose flows from this theory of meaning.

INDEX

www.ingramcontent.com/pod-product-compliance
Lightning Source LLC
Chambersburg PA
CBHW022137270226
40388CB00001B/36